HIKING INDIANA

HELP US KEEP THIS GUIDE UP TO DATE

Every effort has been made by the author and editors to make this guide as accurate and useful as possible. However, many things can change after a guide is published—regulations change, facilities come under new management, and so forth.

We would love to hear from you concerning your experiences with this guide and how you feel it could be improved and kept up to date. While we may not be able to respond to all comments and suggestions, we'll take them to heart, and we'll also make certain to share them with the author. Please send your comments and suggestions to 64 S Main St, Essex, CT 06426.

Thanks for your input!

HIKING INDIANA

A GUIDE TO THE STATE'S GREATEST HIKING ADVENTURES

FOURTH EDITION

Phil Bloom

ESSEX, CONNECTICUT

FALCONGUIDES®

An imprint of The Globe Pequot Publishing Group, Inc.
64 South Main Street
Essex, CT 06426
www.globepequot.com

Falcon and FalconGuides are registered trademarks and Make Adventure Your Story is a
trademark of The Globe Pequot Publishing Group, Inc.

Distributed by NATIONAL BOOK NETWORK

British Library Cataloguing in Publication Information available

Library of Congress Cataloging-in-Publication Data available

ISBN 978-1-4930-7543-0 (paper: alk. paper)
ISBN 978-1-4930-7544-7 (electronic)

Printed in India

The author and The Globe Pequot Publishing Group, Inc., assume no liability for accidents
happening to, or injuries sustained by, readers who engage in the activities described in
this book.

CONTENTS

Big Clifty Creek flows over a rocky streambed at Clifty Falls State Park.

THE HIKES

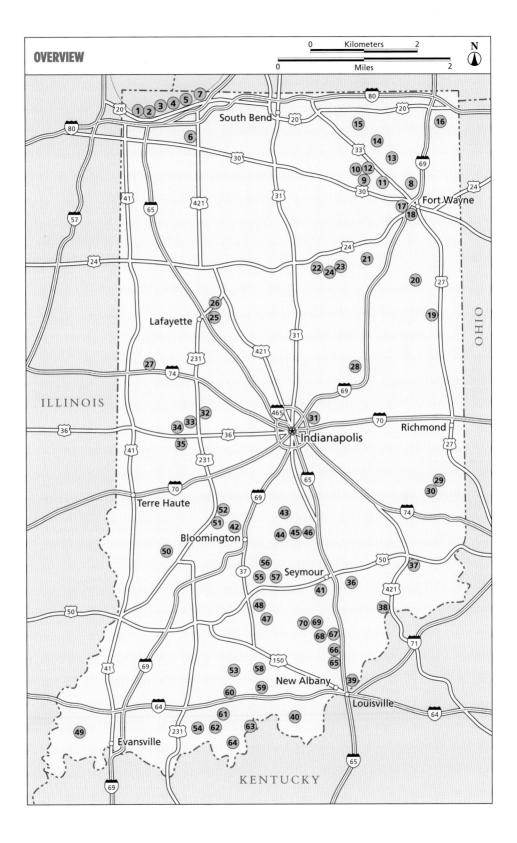

ACKNOWLEDGMENTS

Hiking can be a solitary endeavor. Sometimes it is the best way to enjoy nature. Researching and writing a hiking book, however, requires considerable help, and there are several people to whom I am grateful.

To begin with, my late parents, Mike and JoAnne Bloom, deserve credit for giving me my first taste of the outdoors. I am sure my siblings remember the times Mom and Dad took us for hikes along the banks of the Salamonie River or in some other state park.

Bill McArdle, scoutmaster of Boy Scout Troop 20 at Queen of Angels Grade School, taught me and hundreds of other boys the basic hiking skills that helped make those 20-milers endurable.

Years later I met Judy Esterline and Judy Deimling, hiking buddies who showed me a different way to hike—going slower and with eyes wide open to what was at your feet. They made the woods come alive with their knowledge of wildflowers and native plants.

A special thanks to Kay Ellerhoff, formerly of Falcon Publishing, who helped make the professional connection that allowed those past influences to be transformed into this work.

This project took time—the first edition as well as three updated versions. Thanks to the many editors at FalconGuides and Globe Pequot Publishing who exhibited patience throughout.

Thanks also to family and friends whose interest in how "the book" was progressing contributed regular reminders that I needed to stick with it or let them all down.

It can get lonely out there on the trail, so I particularly enjoyed the time shared with special people. Thanks to my brother-in-law, Dr. John Herber, with whom I spent a splendid day on the Lakeview and Boundary Trails (revamped since as the Bloodroot Trail), the last hike taken in the first-edition marathon.

Thanks to my children, Jacob and Jennifer, a teenager and pre-teen, respectively, when this project began years ago but now both adults. I hope you always remember our time on the trails in the same special way that I remembered those spent with my parents, brothers, and sisters.

To my grandchildren—Benjamin, Claire Marie, Matthew, and Thomas—this fourth edition is as much for you as it is for anyone. I hope you come to think of it as your doorway to nature.

The person who deserves the most praise is Jessie, my wife. Without her this book would not exist. Her encouragement was constant. Her personal sacrifices were many; her love, sustaining. She is the best hiking partner I've ever had.

Jessie, I'll go hiking with you . . . anywhere, anytime. Always.

INTRODUCTION

God crowned her hills with beauty,
Gave her lakes and winding streams,
Then He edged them all with woodlands
As the settings for our dreams.

—From the official state poem,
"Indiana," by Arthur Mapes

This is a hiking guide to Indiana. Why Indiana? Why not?

After all, it was from here that renowned hiker and conservationist John Muir began his exploration of nature and wilderness. Following recovery from a work accident in Indianapolis, Muir walked 1,000 miles from Indiana to the Gulf of Mexico. He later went west to California, founded the Sierra Club, and was instrumental in establishing several national parks.

Scottish-born and educated in Wisconsin, Muir's connections to Indiana are coincidental, but within the state boundaries are the kinds of natural wonders he might have appreciated had he stuck around.

The Hoosier State is far more than steel mills, the Indianapolis 500, 10 of the 12 largest high school basketball gymnasiums in the world, and flat fields of corn and soybeans. Yet Indiana's natural treasures are unknown or underappreciated by many people, including a lot of Hoosiers.

Indiana has richly diverse offerings—from Indiana Dunes National Park on Lake Michigan to four state parks dotting the banks of the Ohio River, from "lake country" in northeast Indiana to the Charles C. Deam Wilderness in Hoosier National Forest.

Indiana's mix of wild places and civilization may be exemplified best by the outline of the state. Except for a dip in the northwest corner where Lake Michigan intrudes, much of the western, northern, and eastern boundaries are as straight as an arrow. The hand of nature carved out the rest, as shown by the twisting course of the Ohio River to the south and the Wabash River along the lower third of the west boundary.

Publicly held land—where most hiking trails are located—accounts for less than 5 percent of Indiana's 36,185 square miles. Large cities dominate the state—Indianapolis with more than 1 million residents; Fort Wayne with nearly 300,000; Gary, South Bend, Evansville, and Terre Haute all with more than 100,000 residents.

The demand for green spaces is being met by the state's Department of Natural Resources (DNR), federal agencies (National Park Service, US Fish & Wildlife Service, and US Forest Service), city and county park departments, and private land trusts.

Since 1995 the DNR has opened four state parks—Falls of the Ohio, Fort Benjamin Harrison, Charlestown, and Prophetstown—and added thousands of additional acres with acquisitions like Goose Pond Fish and Wildlife Area.

The National Park Service operates Indiana Dunes National Park and two other sites—Lincoln National Boyhood Memorial and George Rogers Clark National Historical Park. There are three national wildlife refuges managed by the US Fish & Wildlife Service—Big Oaks, Muscatatuck, and Patoka River. The US Forest Service manages the 204,000-acre Hoosier National Forest.

Two dozen land trusts have protected nearly 170,000 acres in pockets as small as an acre to thousands of acres, like The Nature Conservancy's 7,200-acre Kankakee Sands in northwest Indiana.

The DNR manages twenty-four state parks, eight reservoirs, a couple dozen fish and wildlife areas, and fourteen state forests. Some of the more than 300 state-dedicated nature preserves are owned or managed by the DNR; others are owned by land trusts, city or county park departments, or colleges and universities.

Hiking opportunities exist at nearly every location—from routes of 0.25 mile or less to the 49-mile Knobstone Trail, Indiana's scaled-down version of the Appalachian Trail. Some trails have historic significance, like the Wabash Heritage Trail. Others, like the Knobstone, have geologic significance. Most are just fun to hike.

Yet it's sometimes hard to escape the rush of the modern world, even on a trail. Consider, for example, a spot on the Wabash Heritage Trail. At this point alongside Burnett's Creek, the dirt path converges on a paved county road, a railroad track, and a four-lane interstate passing overhead. There may not be another location in the state where as many modes of transportation intersect.

Best of all, Indiana continues to aggressively expand its trail inventory in concert with increasing public demand for more. Using trail counters at various sites, the DNR tallied a three-fold increase in users from 2017 to 2022. Hiking enthusiasts also have taken to social media with group Facebook pages. Formed in August 2016, Hoosier Hikers/ Backpackers has grown to 14,100 members, and Hike Indiana, formed in December 2016, has more than 50,000 followers.

A few of Indiana's state parks have incentivized trail use by creating challenge hikes, such as the 3 Dune Challenge at Indiana Dunes, Hell's Point Challenge at Pokagon, and Four Falls Challenge at Clifty Falls.

In 1996 the DNR published the Indiana Trails 2000 Initiative, a project intended to promote and enhance hiking opportunities across the state. The report charted 392 trails covering 950 total miles designated specifically for hikers. A decade later, a new state-issued report titled "Hoosiers on the Move" tallied 1,542 miles of footpaths open to the public and set a goal to have a hiking, biking, or equestrian trail within 7.5 miles or 15 minutes of every Indiana resident by the year 2016. It was so successful the targets were revised in 2013 to 5 miles or 10 minutes.

By mid-year 2023 the DNR was reporting just over 2,400 miles of natural surface trails and an overall total of 4,400 miles of motorized and non-motorized trails.

Trail development received a significant boost in 2018 when Gov. Eric Holcomb announced the Next Level Trails program to allocate $180 million in available matching grant money for non-motorized trails. In the first five years, seventy-five projects received funding.

Incorporated in the state's ongoing trails plan is a visionary statewide system that creates a backbone to connect some of Indiana's major trails. Priority projects include extension of the Cardinal Greenway from Marion to Richmond, the National Heritage Road Trail from Richmond to Terre Haute, developing the 88-mile Poka-Bache Trail in northeast Indiana, and linking the state's two longest backcountry hikes—the Knobstone and Tecumseh Trails with the Pioneer Trail—to create a 160-mile backcountry experience.

Some trails have been closed for various reasons, including three that were described in earlier versions of *Hiking Indiana*: Kekionga at Roush Lake, Boy Scout at Mississinewa Lake, and one at Muscatatuck National Wildlife Refuge.

They've been replaced in subsequent editions with new hikes. Paul H. Douglas (Miller Woods) at Indiana Dunes National Park, Continental Divide at Eagle Marsh, Lost Sister at Mississinewa, the combined Turkey and Bird Trails at Muscatatuck, and Veronica's Trail, a wheelchair-accessible path at Loblolly Marsh, were added in the last edition.

New trails in this edition are Beanblossom Bottoms Nature Preserve, Dygert Woods Nature Preserve, Meltzer Woods Nature Preserve, Pisgah Marsh, Prophetstown State Park, and Shrader-Weaver Nature Preserve.

Obviously, the hikes included in this book offer only a sample of all that Indiana has to offer. Additional trails worth considering are the Tecumseh Trail, a 48-miler in south-central Indiana; Wolf Creek Trail, which skirts the west shores of Brookville

Reservoir; Pate Hollow Trail in the Hoosier National Forest; and the Ten O'Clock Line Trail, which runs between Brown County State Park and Yellowwood State Forest.

Befitting Indiana's nickname as the Crossroads of America, the American Discovery Trail has not one but two routes through the state. One draws a diagonal 250-mile course between northwest Indiana and Richmond along the east-central border, while the 366-mile southern route travels over the rolling hills that parallel the Ohio River.

In summary, just about anywhere you go in Indiana, there's a trail to be traveled.

ECOLOGY

Before European settlers arrived in Indiana, the state was a blanket of trees—huge trees. More than 85 percent of Indiana—about 20 million acres—was forested, primarily with hardwood species such as beech, hickory, maple, oak, sycamore, tulip poplar, and walnut. Trees in this dense forest towered 150 to 200 feet high and measured as much as 9 or 10 feet in diameter. Settlers managed to cut down almost all those trees as they cleared the way for farming. The work proceeded at such a pace that Indiana led the nation in lumber production in 1899.

Ironically, much of the rocky soil in southern Indiana proved unsuitable as cropland. As agriculture gave way to industry, many farms were abandoned, paving the way for establishment of the Hoosier National Forest—a patchwork covering almost 200,000 acres in southern Indiana.

What wasn't forest or glacial lakes in pre-settlement Indiana was prairie or wetland, and both suffered the same fate as woodlands.

The Grand Kankakee Marsh in northwest Indiana was to the Midwest what the Everglades are to southern Florida. Somewhere between a half-million and a million acres, it was the largest inland wetland in the country. The marsh was fed by the Kankakee River that wound its way for 240 miles from near South Bend until crossing into Illinois. In turn, its abundant wildlife earned it the nickname "Chicago's food pantry" and drew hunters from across the country as well as Europe.

Destruction of the marsh began shortly after the Civil War, with construction of ditches and channels—a true "draining of the swamp" that transformed Indiana's richest natural resource into farm fields and communities.

As the late John Prine wrote in his song "Paradise": "They wrote it all down to the progress of man."

Despite such runaway efforts to subdue the land, pockets of natural splendor remain due to steadfast efforts to safeguard or restore their integrity.

The fauna of Indiana includes thousands of species, from the smallest insects to white-tailed deer. Aquatic insects, freshwater mussels, Karner blue butterflies, crawfish, salamanders, bluebirds, bald eagles, bobcats, coyotes, wild turkeys, river otters, ruffed grouse, largemouth bass, and catfish are just a few of the species that inhabit the state. But there are other species that no longer exist in Indiana. Among those that have been lost are elk, bison, wolves, and mountain lions. Black bears, which hadn't existed in the wild in Indiana since before the Civil War, have made temporary visits from neighboring states in recent years before retreating.

Examples of rare or endangered flora in Indiana and their locations include Canada blueberry and Forbe's saxifrage at Portland Arch Nature Preserve; yellowwood trees at Brown County State Park and Yellowwood State Forest; Deam's foxglove on the

Smokey Bear offers a
safety reminder.

Knobstone Trail; black cohosh at Harmonie State Park; and eastern hemlock at Turkey Run State Park, Hemlock Bluff Nature Preserve, and Hemlock Cliffs in the Hoosier National Forest.

GEOLOGY

Like giant bulldozers, ancient glaciers shaped the northern two-thirds of Indiana's landscape, which was part of a giant sea in the Paleozoic era, about 250 to 750 million years ago.

The Pleistocene epoch began almost 2 million years ago and ended about 10,000 years ago. The glacial advance scraped southward across Indiana but never reached the Ohio River. Consequently, southern Indiana is distinguished from the rest of the state by hilly terrain with deep ravines, lowland areas, and underground streams that have carved out caves in the limestone bedrock in a landscape known as karst topography.

The most recent glacier—the Wisconsin lobe—moved no more than one-third of the way through the northern part of the state. As it retreated about 10,000 years ago, its meltwaters created rolling hills, rivers and streams, and hundreds of lakes. The deposits of gravel, sand, and soil known as eskers, kames, and moraines are other glacial features of the northern lakes region.

In between the northern lakes and southern hills is a relatively flat expanse known as the Central Till Plain, which draws its name from the mixture of glacial deposits. It is the largest geographic region in the state.

Despite the region's flat appearance, the highest point in the state—1,257 feet above sea level near Richmond in Wayne County—is located here. Don't be fooled though. Dubbed Hoosier Hill, the site, on private property, is barely more than a bump on the landscape.

Two of the most recognizable features of Indiana lie at its borders—a sliver of Lake Michigan in the northwest corner and the Ohio River, which forms the entire southern boundary of the state.

Numerous rivers crisscross the state, but none has greater influence than the Wabash, which appropriately is designated as the official state river. From its headwaters just across the Ohio border, the Wabash cuts across the northern half of Indiana and meanders 475 miles south to join the Ohio River west of Evansville. The Wabash watershed drains two-thirds of the state.

Other major rivers include the St. Joseph and St. Marys, which meet in Fort Wayne to form the Maumee, which flows eastward into Lake Erie; a second St. Joseph River, which dips down from Michigan through South Bend before heading back through Michigan to Lake Michigan; and the White River system, which drains much of central and southern Indiana.

Two minerals have played important roles in Indiana industry—limestone and bituminous coal. Limestone cut from central Indiana was used in the construction of several famous buildings, including the Empire State Building and Rockefeller Center in New York City, the National Cathedral and the Pentagon in Washington, DC, Yankee Stadium, and thirty-five state capitol buildings.

Indiana is among the top-ten coal-producing states in the country, churning out more than 30 million tons annually. According to the Indiana Geological and Water Survey at Indiana University, there are still 57 billion tons of unmined coal in the state.

HUMAN HISTORY

Indiana's name means "Land of Indians," and while there is evidence of inhabitants from 160 BC, the greatest influence of Native American culture came less than 200 years ago.

Nomadic cultures from the Paleo-Indian and Archaic periods may have roamed part of Indiana as far back as 10,000 BC, but more recent impact of Native Americans came during the Early, Middle, and Late Woodland periods, which extended from about 500 BC to AD 1000. The mound-building Adena (Early Woodland) and Hopewell (Middle Woodland) cultures gave way to Late Woodland–era peoples and eventually to the Mississippian culture, which lasted from AD 1000 to 1450.

Native populations probably peaked during the early 1700s. Numerous tribes inhabited the state at that time, the largest being three northern tribes: the Miami, the Potawatomi, and the Delaware. Members of all three tribes were descendants of the Early Woodland peoples. At one time or another, the area was also home to such tribes as the Chickasaw, Huron, Kickapoo, Menominee, Mohican, Piankashaw, Shawnee, and Wea.

French explorer Robert Cavalier was the first known white man to enter Indiana, passing through in 1679 in search of a passage to the Pacific Ocean. French fur traders soon followed, setting up trading posts near present-day Fort Wayne, Lafayette, and Vincennes. The first permanent European settlement was established at Vincennes in 1732.

Competition between the expansion-minded British and French over fur trade with Indians was a factor leading to war between the two countries over rights to American soil. The British won, and France surrendered its claim to Indiana in 1763.

The British began military occupation of Indiana during the Revolutionary War. Fort Sackville at Vincennes became a focal point in the conflict, but George Rogers Clark and his Virginia troops seized it from the British for good in 1779. Eleven years later, Congress established the Indiana Territory, which included not only present-day Indiana but also Illinois, Wisconsin, and parts of Michigan and Minnesota.

As settlers gained greater control of the territory, Indian resistance increased. Tecumseh, a Shawnee leader, was attempting to build a confederacy of fourteen tribes, but those forces dissolved after the Battle of Tippecanoe in 1811 against American soldiers led by Gen. William Henry Harrison, who was later elected US president. Tecumseh, meanwhile, sided with the British in the War of 1812.

When Indiana became the nineteenth state on December 11, 1816, its population was about 64,000.

In 1838 nearly 700 members of the Potawatomi tribe were forced out of the state at gunpoint and marched hundreds of miles to a reservation in Kansas.

Lavish road and canal construction projects drove the state to bankruptcy by 1840, but railroads brought economic improvement prior to the Civil War. However, it wasn't until the 1880s that the discovery of natural gas and development of the automobile paced an industrial boom.

By 1900 the state's population had reached 2.5 million. Today it is 6.8 million.

Following is a listing of other noteworthy dates in Indiana history:

1732: Vincennes becomes Indiana's first permanent settlement.
1800: Congress establishes the Indiana Territory with Vincennes as the capital.
1803: Lewis and Clark form the nucleus of the Corps of Discovery near Clarksville on the Ohio River.
1813: Territorial capital moved to Corydon.
1816: Indiana becomes the nineteenth state.
1816–1830: Abraham Lincoln spends his boyhood and young adult years on an Indiana farm.
1824: Indianapolis is established as state capital.
1841: William Henry Harrison dies after only thirty days in office as US president.
1889: Benjamin Harrison, grandson of William Henry Harrison, is sworn into office as US president.
1906: US Steel builds a factory in Gary.
1909: Gene Stratton-Porter's novel *Girl of the Limberlost* is published.

1911: Ray Harroun wins the first Indianapolis 500 auto race.

1916: The Indiana state park system is established with the dedication of McCormick's Creek State Park.

1934: Infamous gangster John Dillinger escapes from Indiana jail using a wooden gun colored with black shoe polish.

1935: Hoosier National Forest is created.

1966: Indiana Dunes is designated as a national lakeshore.

1982: Congress approves Charles C. Deam Wilderness in the Hoosier National Forest.

1994: Patoka River National Wildlife Refuge is established.

2000: Big Oaks National Wildlife Refuge is established on 50,000 acres of a former military munitions test facility.

2008: Indiana DNR allocates $19 million to trail enhancement projects and doubles ownership of abandoned rail corridor property for future trail projects.

2010: Indiana launches the Healthy Rivers Initiative to conserve 70,000 riverside acres along three waterways: Sugar Creek, Wabash River, and Muscatatuck River.

2012: Then-governor Mitch Daniels announces the Bicentennial Nature Trust, a $20 million investment to expand parks, wetlands, and trails in celebration of Indiana's 200th anniversary of statehood in 2016.

2016: Indiana State Parks throws a year-long hundredth birthday party in conjunction with Indiana's 200th anniversary of statehood.

2017: Fort Wayne passes the 100-mile mark with its greenway trails program.

2018: Gov. Eric Holcomb launches the Next Level Trails program, allocating $180 million for trail acquisition and development.

2019: Congress reclassifies Indiana Dunes National Lakeshore as Indiana Dunes National Park.

2023: State awards $29.5 million to develop 62.3-mile Monon South Trail spanning five southern counties.

2023: Toothwort Woods approved as Indiana's 300th state-dedicated nature preserve.

FUNDAMENTALS

Hiking really is a simple activity, which perhaps explains its popularity. It usually does not require specialized gear, although all sorts of gadgets are available. Hiking does not require special training. Nevertheless, there are some basic guidelines that all hikers should follow.

First, choose the right hike. Figure out what you want to accomplish with a hike. Do you want to discover new places? Explore nature? Simply exercise?

Understand your limitations, and do not overdo it. Figure out how physically fit you are and what you can handle before charging off on longer, more-demanding hikes.

Take a map whenever possible, even if it's only the brochure available at the park gate or nature preserve registration box. For longer hikes, or hikes in remote areas like the Hoosier National Forest, take a compass or a handheld Global Positioning System (GPS) unit, grab a US Geological Survey (USGS) topographic map, and learn how to use it.

Stay on designated trails. Taking shortcuts, especially on switchbacks, contributes to erosion and may disturb or damage sensitive areas.

Pack water, even for short hikes. Water is essential to keeping the body hydrated. A rule of thumb is to drink 16 ounces before embarking on a hike, then pause every half hour for another 4 to 6 ounces. If you must use water from a lake or stream, be sure to purify it first with a filter or iodine tablets or by boiling it.

Avoid crowds by planning your hike for midweek. State parks draw their biggest crowds during the summer months, especially on weekends.

Be aware of stream conditions. Some trails, particularly those through the ravines of southern Indiana, cross streams that can be dangerous during periods of heavy rain. Do not attempt to ford a stream unless you are sure you can make it safely across.

Practice the zero-impact outdoor ethic: Pack it in; pack it out. This is a mandatory policy in the Charles C. Deam Wilderness, but it is a good approach to adopt for all situations. Pack out everything, including gum wrappers, cigarette butts, and twisty ties. Avoid building campfires unless necessary. Leave the place you have visited looking as if you were never there.

Avoid making needless noise. Nothing disturbs the solitude of nature more than hearing boisterous people tromping down the trail.

Most of all, enjoy.

CLOTHING

Seasons and weather conditions usually dictate proper attire on the trail, but so will each hike.

Begin at the bottom by properly outfitting your feet. Most trails can be hiked in tennis or gym shoes, but longer hikes and hikes in rugged terrain require a good pair of hiking boots. And don't forget socks. I prefer to start with a thin pair of socks, over which I wear wool socks. For me this combination helps prevent blisters. Pack an extra pair of socks for longer hikes; changing them along the way can be refreshing.

Pack rain gear. Weather changes can occur rapidly in Indiana, so it is best to be prepared. A light jacket will suffice on short hikes, but a full outfit of waterproof, breathable material is a must for longer trips.

The rest is personal preference, but make sure your clothing is appropriate for the season. Some people wear long pants and long-sleeved shirts even in warm weather; others prefer shorts and T-shirts. Be assured, the latter will be uncomfortable on the hottest of days if the trail leads through heavy brush or areas with mosquitoes or ticks.

In cooler weather, dress in layers. It is easier to remove a layer if you get too hot than it is to add something you do not have.

WEATHER AND SEASONS

Indiana has a varied climate, but it usually can be described as humid in summer and cold in winter. Temperatures in winter can dip well below freezing, and summer days can be unbearably hot and humid.

Conditions can be unpredictable, especially in early summer, when powerful storms can pop up on short notice. Average June temperatures range from a low of 60°F to the mid-80s for central Indiana, with variances to the north and south. Average January temperatures range from the low 20s to the upper 30s. Annual rainfall averages about 38 to 40 inches, with additional precipitation coming from snow that varies from 10 inches in the south to around 40 inches in the north.

Some areas of the state have become synonymous with certain seasons—Brown County State Park for fall foliage; Pokagon State Park for cross-country skiing and a refrigerated toboggan run that carries sledders downhill at speeds reaching 40 miles per hour; and Indiana Dunes State Park for summer fun on the sandy beaches of Lake Michigan.

Spring: If you like wildflowers, consider a hike this time of year. It is easy to find woodlands carpeted with Virginia bluebell, large-flowered trillium, wild columbine, Jack-in-the-pulpit, Dutchman's breeches, or Solomon's seal. Spring also is a good time for watching wildlife, especially migrating birds like Canada geese, ducks, sandhill cranes, and certain songbirds.

Indiana springs are known for erratic weather patterns and are prone to violent storms that can spawn tornadoes. It is a good idea when hiking in spring to pack rain gear and perhaps a sweater or fleece to ward off sudden temperature changes. Some trails may be messy because of spring thaw or even impassable due to rain or flooding.

Summer: June, July, and August can be among the toughest months to hike in Indiana. It's not only a time when weather can be stifling but also a time when trails, campgrounds, and parks are frequently packed with vacationers. Although the weather can reach extremes, it is also more stable in summer than in other seasons, allowing for extended periods of good hiking. Be alert for quickly developing thunderstorms with dangerous lightning. Summer is also the season for bugs—mosquitoes, bees, wasps, hornets, flies, gnats, and ticks.

Fall: If there is a better time of year to hike in Indiana than spring, it is during the fall. Temperatures begin to drop in September and October, especially at night, when it can get quite chilly. Daytime temperatures often are still warm enough for shirtsleeves, even shorts. With schools back in session, trail traffic diminishes, and campsites are more available after the Labor Day weekend. But the real beauty of autumn is the rich display of color presented by the hardwood forests and woodlands across the state. Oak, maple, tulip poplar, hickory, and other trees switch color schemes from uniform green to orange, red, and yellow. Since hunting seasons begin in autumn, it is a good idea to make yourself more visible by wearing one or more pieces of blaze-orange clothing.

Winter: If solitude is your desire, this may be the time to consider a hike, especially in the southern half of the state, where snow is less frequent. Daytime temperatures can be almost mild, and traffic along the trails is at its low point. Even in the deepest woods, it is often easier to see wildlife because the sightlines are so clear with the absence of vegetation. If there is snow on the ground, wildlife tracks can be easily spotted. Trails can be slippery, though.

ANIMALS

Black bears and mountain lions once roamed Indiana, but it's highly unlikely you'll encounter any today despite evidence of their recent return.

The DNR confirmed a single mountain lion in 2010 and again in 2011. It is not known if it was the same mountain lion, but there have been no confirmed sightings since. In 2015 a single black bear wandered into northwest Indiana from Michigan; a year later a different bear swam the Ohio River from Kentucky and spent about a year roaming remote areas of southern Indiana. Additional confirmed bear sightings occurred in 2018, 2021, and 2023.

Deer in "velvet"
INDIANA DEPARTMENT OF NATURAL RESOURCES

State biologists report no evidence of breeding populations of either species for more than a century. They attribute the rare arrivals—and occasional unconfirmed sightings—as evidence that black bear and mountain lion populations are expanding elsewhere, prompting young males to disperse in search of new home ranges.

The largest mammal in the state today is the white-tailed deer, which is abundant in most parts of Indiana. Canada geese are almost as plentiful as deer, especially in the northeastern lakes region and in urban areas. Other common animals are squirrels, rabbits, raccoons, and wild turkeys, as well as foxes, coyotes, and opossums.

Bobcats and badgers are also present.

There are four venomous snake species in Indiana, the copperhead being the most common. It usually is found in southern Indiana, where timber rattlesnakes and cottonmouths (water moccasins) are also found, but rarely enough that both are on the state endangered-species list. The eastern massasauga rattlesnake is found in swampy areas of northern Indiana, but in such small numbers that it is considered endangered by the state.

Snakebites are rare and almost always nonfatal but play it safe by steering clear of snakes. Timber rattlesnakes live in high, rocky terrain and are often found on ledges. A timber rattler will usually, but not always, send a warning by raising and rattling its tail. Copperheads frequent the same habitat as timber rattlers, but they are not as easy to detect. Its copper-red head and brown bands allow the snake to blend into fallen leaves. Copperheads offer no warning before striking, so be careful walking over fallen logs. Cottonmouths have an especially aggressive nature, but this aquatic species is the least common of the state's venomous snakes and are found only in a few isolated areas. The

Copperheads are one of four venomous snake species in Indiana.
INDIANA DEPARTMENT OF NATURAL RESOURCES

best way to avoid venomous snakes and their dangerous bites is to be alert and watch your step.

Indiana has played an active role in restoration efforts involving raptor species like the bald eagle, peregrine falcon, and osprey.

Other restoration success stories are the reintroduction and establishment of river otters and wild turkeys.

BUGS

Hikers in Indiana need to be aware of only a few pesky bugs. The most serious concerns have to do with ticks and stinging insects such as bees, hornets, and wasps.

Ticks often carry diseases that can cause serious problems for humans, such as Rocky Mountain spotted fever and Lyme disease. Several species of ticks have been found in the state, but the most common are American dog tick, lone star tick, and deer tick. Hikers should check themselves for ticks, particularly after a hike in brushy or grassy areas where ticks reside.

Two spiders—the black widow and brown recluse—have bites that can be life-threatening, but such occurrences are not common.

Mosquitoes and gnats are more of a nuisance, especially during warm, wet seasons. They generally can be dealt with by using insect repellent.

HOW TO USE THIS GUIDE

Hiking Indiana is organized largely by geographic regions, beginning in the northwest corner of the state with the Dunelands and working southward to finish with the Knobstone Trail.

If you are familiar with other Falcon guidebooks, you may notice the absence of elevation charts in *Hiking Indiana*. That is because few of the hikes have significant elevation changes, and those that do rarely change more than 250 feet. However, some of these hikes, particularly those in southern Indiana, can provide even the most avid hiker with a pretty good workout.

Once endangered, bald eagles have flourished in Indiana due to an aggressive reintroduction effort begun in 1985.
IDNR/OUTDOOR INDIANA

Map Legend

Municipal

🛡65🛡	Interstate Highway
🛡421🛡	US Highway
🛡327🛡	State Road
🛡727🛡	County/Forest Road
= = = =	Unpaved Road
⊢—⊣	Railroad
· · — · ·	State Boundary
•—•—•	Power Line

Trails

▬ ▬ ▬	Featured Trail
- - - - -	Trail

Water Features

⬭	Lake/Reservoir
	Marsh/Swamp
	Sandbar
⌇	River/Creek
⌇	Intermittent Stream
≋	Waterfall
⌀	Spring

Land Management

⬚	National Wildlife Refuge
▭	National Lakeshore
▣	State/Local Park/ Wildlife Area/Preserve

Symbols

⊟	Bench
⬟	Boat Ramp
‖‖‖‖	Boardwalk/Steps
⌣	Bridge
▲	Campground
✪	Capital
∧	Cave
▬	Dam
•—•	Gate
⬛	Lodging
🅿	Parking
▲	Peak/Elevation
⊞	Picnic Area
▪	Point of Interest/Structure
🕅	Restrooms
🗼	Tower
○	Town
①	Trailhead
⊢—⊣	Tunnel
◪	Viewpoint/Overlook
❷	Visitor/Information Center

DUNELANDS

One word defines the Dunelands of northwest Indiana: conflict. Whether by the natural forces that originally shaped the area or the social forces of modern times, conflict has been at the heart of the Dunelands story.

Lake Michigan—the first of the Great Lakes—was formed by glacier movement more than 14,000 years ago. Left behind when the glacier receded was the residue that makes up the dunes, which in some instances are still being formed today. Mount Baldy at the east end of the Indiana Dunes National Park and Smoking Dune at the West Beaches are "living" dunes—in other words, they continue to grow and move as they are reshaped by the wind that created them.

Mount Baldy creeps inland at the rate of 4 feet or more per year, gobbling up trees in its path. At Smoking Dune, further evidence can be seen where a boardwalk has been rerouted over a section now buried in sand.

As magnificent as the dunes are—including bogs, marshes, ponds, and varied forests—the area remains in conflict because of competing forces. The Indiana Dunes National Park is fragmented by private residences and smokestack industry over its 23-mile stretch. It was proposed as a national park in 1916, but the idea was shelved due to World War I. In late 2017, the 15,000-acre site finally was elevated to national park status.

The shift to national park status boosted annual visitation at Indiana Dunes from 1.7 million to more than 3 million in 2021, prompting the National Park Service to implement an entrance pass requirement for all locations except the Paul H. Douglas Center.

The older Indiana Dunes State Park, which lies almost in the center of the national park, has the same challenge: high visitation. Most of the annual 1 million-plus visitors congregate at the beach or explore the nearby dunes. The area's three tallest dunes—Mount Jackson, Mount Holden, and Mount Tom—are in the state park and are part of the 3 Dune Challenge sponsored by Indiana Dunes Tourism. Completing the challenge earns you a sticker, but it requires a combined 552 feet of sandy elevation change in the span of 1.5 miles.

Although most of the hikes in this section are in proximity to the dunes, some are not. One of those is the Heron Rookery Trail, located about 10 miles southeast of Chesterton but still part of the national park complex.

The dunes have long been an area of discovery. In fact, they are the birthplace of plant ecology—the scientific study of how living things relate to one another and their environment. Henry Cowles, the acknowledged father of this field, was intrigued by the dune environment, first as a graduate student and later as head of the botany department at the University of Chicago in the early 1900s. Cowles was fascinated by the coexistence of plant species usually found in different environments—arctic bearberry and prickly pear cactus, northern jack pine, and dogwood. The more important discovery was the progression of plant life from the beaches to inland areas—sand stabilized by grasses, followed by shrubs, and then trees.

Trails in this section are presented starting near Gary to the west and moving east to Michigan City.

1 PAUL H. DOUGLAS (MILLER WOODS)

WHY GO?
This trail has it all: wetlands, oak savanna, interdunal pannes, towering dunes, and views of Chicago from the beach.

THE RUNDOWN

Location: Near Gary, northwest Indiana
Distance: 3.4 miles out and back
Elevation change: 46 feet
Hiking time: About 2.5 hours
Difficulty: Moderate; loose sand in many spots
Jurisdiction: National Park Service
Fees and permits: No fee for parking at Paul H. Douglas Center; seven-day or annual passes required at all other Indiana Dunes National Park locations
Schedule: Open daily, 6 a.m. to 11 p.m.
Maps: USGS Gary; Indiana Dunes National Park map; Miller Woods Trail map

Special attractions: Globally rare black oak savanna, open sand dunes, sweeping views of Lake Michigan and Chicago
Camping: No camping permitted on-site; 66 drive-in or walk-in sites at Indiana Dunes National Park's Dunewood Campground (17 miles east), open Apr 1 through Oct 31; 134 modern electric campsites at Indiana Dunes State Park (13 miles east)
Trailhead facilities: Parking lot at the Paul H. Douglas Center for Environmental Education; year-round restrooms and water located in the center. Center is staffed by National Park Service rangers.

FINDING THE TRAILHEAD

From the interchange of I-65, I-90, and US 12, take US 12 east for 2 miles to Lake Street. Turn left (north) and continue 0.6 mile to the Paul H. Douglas Center parking lot on the right. Cross the pedestrian overpass to the trailhead.

THE HIKE
Begin at the Paul H. Douglas Center and walk across an overpass to reach the trailhead. Walk north around the eastern edge of the wetland full of wildlife, including beavers. After 50 yards the trail turns left near an auxiliary parking lot and runs west along the north edge of the wetland. At 0.2 mile turn right onto a boardwalk over the wetland. At 0.3 mile turn left (west) for another 0.1 mile before turning right. You will now be on an out-and-back trail to the beach. The trail winds around small interdunal ponds nestled among the rare black oak savanna that covers dunes teeming with wildflowers in spring and summer.

At 1.0 mile cross the footbridge over the remnants of Grand Calumet River, which is now a series of lagoons. The landscape changes into a world of towering sand dunes. The trail winds around and through the dunes all the way to the shore of Lake Michigan.

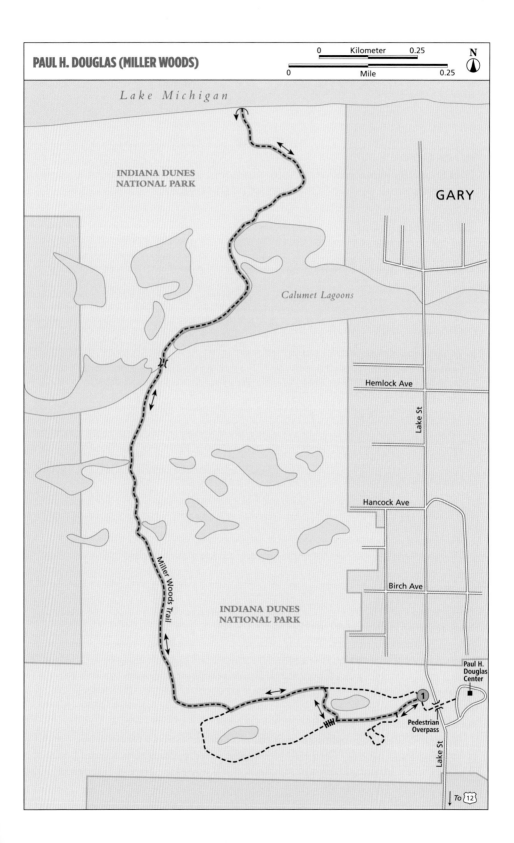

PAUL H. DOUGLAS (MILLER WOODS)

0   Kilometer   0.25

0   Mile   0.25

N

Lake Michigan

INDIANA DUNES
NATIONAL PARK

GARY

Calumet Lagoons

Hemlock Ave

Lake St

Hancock Ave

Birch Ave

Miller Woods Trail

INDIANA DUNES
NATIONAL PARK

Paul H.
Douglas
Center

1

Pedestrian
Overpass

Lake St

To 12

(**Note:** Stay on the trail to protect the fragile ecosystem.) Lake Michigan and Chicago come into view in the distance. At 1.7 miles reach the beach and enjoy the views and sounds of the shoreline. Retrace your steps to the trailhead.

If time permits, walk out onto the boardwalk, grab a seat, and relax for a few minutes before ending the hike. Be sure to stop into the Douglas Center to view the interpretive displays or chat with a park ranger.

MILES AND DIRECTIONS

0.0 Begin at the center building and cross the pedestrian overpass to reach the trailhead.

0.2 Stay straight through the trail junction with a wetland boardwalk.

0.3 Turn right (north) at the trail junction.

1.0 Cross the footbridge over the Grand Calumet River lagoons.

1.7 Reach the shoreline of Lake Michigan. Retrace your steps to the trailhead.

3.4 Arrive back at the trailhead and the Paul H. Douglas Center.

2 LONG LAKE LOOP

WHY GO?

This loop trail skirts a lake and passes over and through dunes, ponds, and woodlands.

THE RUNDOWN

Location: Near Portage, northwest Indiana

Distance: 2.0-mile loop

Elevation change: 85 feet

Hiking time: About 1 hour

Difficulty: Moderate; stairs, loose sand, and some uphill sections

Jurisdiction: National Park Service

Fees and permits: Standard (7-day) or annual entrance pass required; federal lands pass is valid

Schedule: Open 6 a.m. to 9 p.m. year round

Maps: USGS Portage; Indiana Dunes National Park map; West Beach Trail map

Special attractions: Prickly pear cactus, dune-vista views of Long Lake

Camping: No camping permitted on-site; 66 drive-in or walk-in sites at Indiana Dunes National Park's Dunewood Campground (14 miles east), open Apr 1 through Oct 31; 134 modern electric campsites at Indiana Dunes State Park (9 miles east)

Trailhead facilities: Parking lot at the Long Lake Trail trailhead; seasonal bathhouse, year-round restrooms, and potable water located at main park lot

FINDING THE TRAILHEAD

From IN 49, go west 9 miles on US 12 to a four-way stop. Turn right (north) onto County Line Road, cross the railroad tracks, and continue to the West Beach entrance sign. Turn right (east) to enter the park. From the gatehouse, drive east for 0.4 mile to a small parking lot on the right (south) side of the main road. To begin the hike, walk south from the parking lot toward Long Lake.

THE HIKE

Most visitors to this western edge of the Indiana Dunes National Park come for the sandy beaches and a chance to swim in Lake Michigan on hot summer days. They don't know what they are missing—an ecological mix of trees, shrubs, and plant life, some that seem completely out of place in this part of the country. For instance, the early part of the trail is lined with prickly pear cactus, a species most people would associate with the deserts of Utah, Arizona, or New Mexico. But here it is.

The trail begins on the south side of the parking lot toward Long Lake at a green sign noting that this is a Chicago Region Birding Trail Site.

Turn right (northwest) for a flat walk that goes back across the main road. After crossing the road, follow the trail northwest toward the distant tree-covered dune. At the base of the dune, turn left (southwest) at the trail junction and begin the outbound loop that

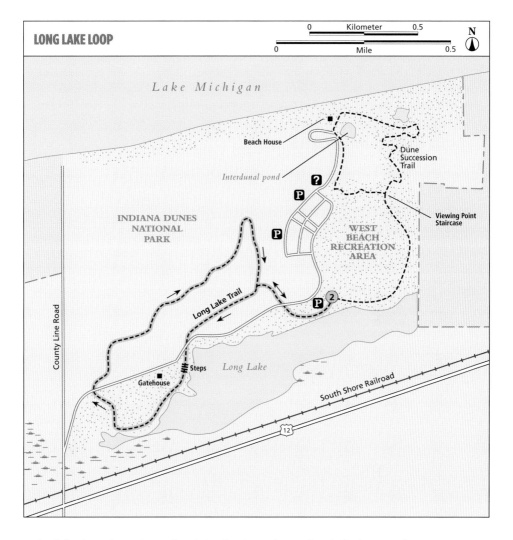

LONG LAKE LOOP

Lake Michigan

Beach House

Interdunal pond

INDIANA DUNES
NATIONAL
PARK

Dune
Succession
Trail

Viewing Point
Staircase

WEST
BEACH
RECREATION
AREA

County Line Road

Long Lake Trail

Steps

Gatehouse

Long Lake

South Shore Railroad

12

0   Kilometer   0.5

0   Mile   0.5

N

leads back to the main road at 0.4 mile. Cross the road and climb a wooden staircase to the top of a dune, where a wooden deck overlooks Long Lake.

Continue southwest off the staircase, crossing a wooden bridge and beginning a downhill stretch that skirts the west edge of a small pond on the right before returning to the main road. Cross the road to reach a maintenance road at 0.9 mile. Turn right (northeast) and walk along the road. You may see signs for the Marquette Trail.

After about 50 yards, the Long Lake Loop passes a park service building and picks up on the opposite side of a paved access road. There are no trail markers here; the easiest way to find the trail is to look for it on the inside elbow of the bend in the road.

The trail goes north through a heavily wooded area adorned with ferns. A wooden staircase leads to a hairpin turn in the trail and around another pond. Continue northeast and uphill as the trail cuts through a valley with high, wooded dunes on both sides to reach the high point of the trail—85 feet higher than the trailhead parking lot—at 1.7

miles. From here you can see the main West Beach parking lot, picnic shelters, and the massive wooden staircase of the Dune Succession Trail to the east.

Walk down the sandy face of the dune to pick up the trail at the base of the hill. Turn right (south) and at 1.9 miles return to the trail junction that begins the outbound leg of the loop. Turn left here and return to the parking lot while taking one more look at the prickly pear cactus.

MILES AND DIRECTIONS

0.0 Begin at the trailhead at the south side of the parking lot.

0.1 Turn left (southwest) at a trail junction.

0.4 Cross the main road and climb a wooden staircase.

0.9 Cross the main road and turn right (northeast) onto a maintenance road.

1.7 Descend from a dune and turn right (southwest).

1.9 Return to the trail junction for the outbound loop; turn left (south).

2.0 Arrive back at the trailhead.

3 DUNE SUCCESSION TRAIL

WHY GO?
This interpretive hike highlights the stages of dune development through plant succession and offers spectacular views of Lake Michigan and the Chicago skyline.

THE RUNDOWN

Location: Near Portage, northwest Indiana

Distance: 1.0-mile loop

Elevation change: 100 feet

Hiking time: About 45 minutes

Difficulty: Strenuous; 270-step staircase and loose sand in sections

Jurisdiction: Indiana Dunes National Park

Fees and permits: Standard (7-day) or annual entrance pass required; federal lands pass is valid

Schedule: Open 6 a.m. to 9 p.m. year round

Maps: USGS Portage; Indiana Dunes National Park map; West Beach Trail map

Special attractions: Interdunal pond, dunes, viewing platform; great views of Lake Michigan and Chicago

Camping: No camping permitted on-site; 66 drive-in or walk-in sites at Indiana Dunes National Park's Dunewood Campground (14 miles east), open Apr 1 through Oct.31; 134 modern electric campsites at Indiana Dunes State Park (9 miles east)

Trailhead facilities: Seasonal bathhouse; year-round restrooms located at parking lot. Potable water available in restrooms

FINDING THE TRAILHEAD
From IN 49, go west 9 miles on US 12 to a four-way stop. Turn right (north) onto County Line Road, cross the railroad tracks, and continue to the West Beach entrance sign. Turn right (east) to enter the park. From the gatehouse, drive east for 0.8 mile to the main parking lot at the end of the road. To begin the hike, walk north from the parking lot toward the bathhouse and Lake Michigan.

THE HIKE
Along the trail you will discover how dunes are formed by elements of nature—water, sand, and vegetation. Part of the hike is on loose sand; the rest is on boardwalks and staircases designed to reduce dune erosion. From the parking lot, follow the paved road for 0.2 mile to the bathhouse, which can be a busy area on hot summer days. Pause for a moment on the wood deck to view the interdunal panne, or pond, created when strong winds blasted through an opening in the dune and scooped out sand to beneath the water table. Plants found here—horned bladderwort and Kalm's lobelia—differ from plants along the nearby dunes.

Staircase on the south side of the dune on the Dune Succession Trail

Walk through the bathhouse to the beach, turn right (east), and walk on the beach for 0.1 mile. Look for the trail markers and head right (south), away from the lake up the dune.

These are newer dunes, perhaps formed in the past 5,000 years. Marram grass is one of the first "dune builders" and is evident along the beach and on the beginning section of the hike. Marram grass stabilizes the sand through an underground network of roots and rhizomes. Another important plant is the cottonwood tree, which appears on the leeward side of the first dune. Although these cottonwoods appear short, they are just the tips of much taller trees buried in the sand. Protected from the wind, the leeward area hosts little bluestem grass, sand cherries, hop trees, and more wildflowers, such as puccoon and sand cress.

At around 0.4 mile there is a stand of jack pines, which provide shelter for arctic bearberry. Both are northern plant species, uncommon this far south, that were carried here by ice age glaciers.

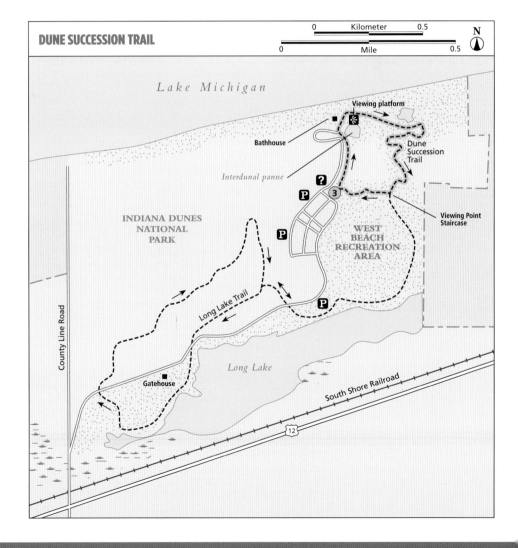

Jump onto a boardwalk at 0.5 mile to continue the hike, which continues through a steep-sided valley. This valley was created by a blowout that occurred when strong winds carved out an opening in the dune. A portion of the old boardwalk has been buried, evidence of how the dune continues to wander under the force of wind. The extensive boardwalk and staircase system leads uphill on a wooded dune featuring black oak, hickory, basswood, dogwood, and sassafras trees. Such trees indicate how protected this area is from the wind and storms coming off Lake Michigan. The staircase system helps reduce erosion as well as make the climb easier. Atop the hill at 0.7 mile is an overlook, followed by a long stairway to the bottom of the dune and a soft, sandy hike back to the parking lot at the 1.0-mile mark.

MILES AND DIRECTIONS

0.0 Begin at the trailhead, walking north from the parking lot.

0.2 Reach the bathhouse.

0.3 Arrive at the viewing platform near the interdunal panne.

0.5 Follow the boardwalk.

0.6 Climb the staircase to the inner dune and tree graveyard.

0.7 Reach the viewing platform atop the highest inner dune.

1.0 Arrive back at the trailhead.

4 COWLES BOG

WHY GO?

The hike loops around a bog, through wooded dunes, past marshes, and along the Lake Michigan shoreline.

THE RUNDOWN

Location: Near Dune Acres, northwest Indiana
Distance: 4.5-mile loop
Elevation change: 100-foot dune climbs near beach
Hiking time: About 3 hours
Difficulty: Easy to moderate; strenuous dune climbs near the beach
Jurisdiction: Indiana Dunes National Park
Fees and permits: Standard (seven-day) or annual entrance pass required; federal lands pass is valid
Schedule: Open daily, 6 a.m. to 11 p.m.

Maps: USGS Dune Acres; Indiana Dunes National Park map; Cowles Bog Trail map
Special attractions: Cowles Bog, Lake Michigan shoreline
Camping: No camping permitted on-site; 66 drive-in or walk-in sites at Indiana Dunes National Park's Dunewood Campground (6 miles east), open Apr 1 to Oct 31; 134 modern electric campsites at Indiana Dunes State Park (1.5 miles east)
Trailhead facilities: Small parking area and a year-round portable toilet at the trailhead; no water available

FINDING THE TRAILHEAD

Drive 2 miles north from Chesterton on IN 49 to US 12 and turn left (west). Drive 1.4 miles and turn right (north) onto Mineral Springs Road. Cross the tracks of the Chicago South Shore Railroad, drive 0.6 mile, and turn right (east) onto a gravel road just short of the town guardhouse for Dune Acres. Drive 0.1 mile on the dirt road to a parking lot; walk back down the dirt road to the Cowles Bog trailhead on the west side of Mineral Springs Road.

THE HIKE

Cowles Bog is a historically significant site. It was here in the early 1900s that Dr. Henry Cowles, a professor at the University of Chicago, did much of his scientific research on plant ecology. The area was designated a National Natural Landmark in 1965. Access to the bog is restricted, but it can be seen from a distance while you are hiking the trail. This trail is well defined with marked intersections, although windblown sand can obscure the inbound marker along the beach.

This is an easy stroll at the start. Walk back along the parking lot entry road before crossing to the west side of Mineral Springs Road to the actual trailhead. The trail begins straight and level, and a boardwalk splits a marshy area on the north side of the bog. Sprays of ferns coupled with duckweed and skunk cabbage provide a rich green backdrop, and wildflowers give the area a sweet aroma. Dune ridges rise and fall along the right side of the trail.

At 0.8 mile you reach a junction with a shortcut trail that goes left (south) around the bog. Turn right (north) instead. Climb a sandy hill and begin a meandering stroll over humps and ridges of the wooded inner dunes dotted with occasional ponds.

At 1.3 miles there is another shortcut. Again, stay right (north). Near the 1.7-mile mark, climb a steep crest of the foredune, which provides a clear view of downtown Chicago to the west. Immediately to the west is a coal-fired power plant, an ironic contrast to the serenity of the Cowles Bog area. Descend the dune to the beach and turn left (west), walking about 0.2 mile before turning inland. The trail marker sometimes is nearly buried by blowing sand and difficult to find. If the marker is not distinguishable, head southeast toward the dune; the path up the dune will become visible.

It is another steep climb on a soft, sandy trail to the top of the dune, which drops off sharply to the right. Walk 30 to 40 yards on a level grade before heading downhill. With each stride it will seem as though you're sliding an extra foot in the loose sand.

Cross several dips and rises over sand hills that form the inner dunes of the property. Keep to the right (south) as you pass both connecting shortcut paths from the outbound trek. Before reaching the second connecting path, you'll pass a small pond at the edge of the Northern Indiana Public Service Company (NIPSCO) power company property that forms the southern boundary of Cowles Bog.

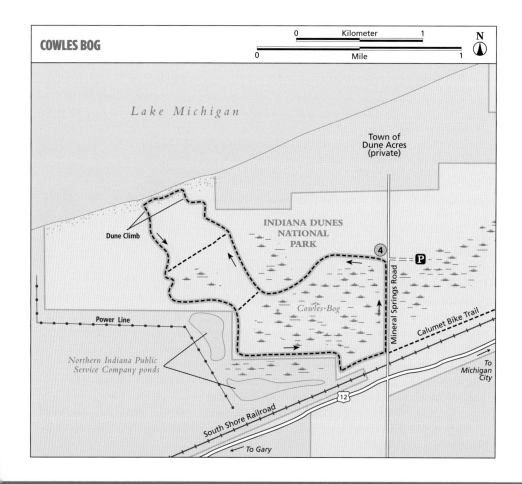

Just past the 3.0-mile mark, reach a service road with the bog on the north side and large NIPSCO ponds on the south. The road is arrow-straight to the east for 0.75 mile, then bends right for 100 yards and connects to a crushed-stone roadway. Walk 0.2 mile to a parking lot that serves as the starting point of the Calumet Bike Trail. Turn left out of the parking lot at 4.0 miles and walk north along Mineral Springs Road to the trailhead. Although the trail concludes along this paved stretch of roadway, you'll get a good look at the bog on both sides.

MILES AND DIRECTIONS

0.0 Begin at the trailhead, on the west side of Mineral Springs Road.

0.1 Pass Cowles Bog.

1.7 Reach the beach at Lake Michigan; turn left.

1.9 At a trail marker that may be buried by sand, turn left.

2.0 Climb the dune.

3.0 Reach the NIPSCO pond.

4.0 Reach the Calumet Bike Trail trailhead and Mineral Springs Road. Turn left out of the parking lot.

4.5 Arrive back at the trailhead.

5 BEACH TRAIL

WHY GO?

A loop trail through woods and along Lake Michigan concludes with a climb through the three tallest dunes in the area.

THE RUNDOWN

Location: Indiana Dunes State Park, near Chesterton
Distance: 7.0-mile loop
Elevation change: About 200 feet from Lake Michigan shore to Mount Tom
Hiking time: About 3 hours
Difficulty: Strenuous
Jurisdiction: Indiana Department of Natural Resources, Division of State Parks
Fees and permits: Park daily entry fee; season passes available
Maps: USGS Dune Acres; Indiana Dunes State Park brochure

Special attractions: Lake Michigan shoreline; the three tallest dunes in the area: Mount Tom, Mount Holden, Mount Jackson
Camping: 134 modern electric campsites plus a youth tent area at Indiana Dunes State Park; 66 drive-in or walk-in sites at Indiana Dunes National Park's Dunewood Campground, open April 1 through Oct. 31
Trailhead facilities: Large parking lot and a nature center at the trailhead; water available at the nature center and other locations throughout the park

FINDING THE TRAILHEAD

From Chesterton, drive 3 miles north on IN 49 to the Indiana Dunes State Park gatehouse. From the gatehouse drive 0.1 mile to a roundabout; take the first right (southeast) and go 0.6 mile to the nature center parking lot. The trailhead for Trails 8 and 10 is clearly marked at the south side of the nature center.

THE HIKE

Established in 1925, Indiana Dunes State Park is one of the oldest parks in the state system. The park features a combination of sand dunes, woods, and marshes nestled within the boundaries of the Indiana Dunes National Park. The dunes are home to a diverse variety of plant species.

The park has a network of seven trails that can be hiked separately or in combination. The best way to get a good feel for the park and the dune environment is a hike that includes all or part of Trails 10 and 8. This hike is best taken in the morning for two reasons: (1) White-tailed deer and other wildlife are more visible just after sunrise, and (2) on hot summer days the sand has not yet been toasted by the sun.

The route can be walked either clockwise or counterclockwise, but I prefer the latter. Hitting the high, sandy dunes right off might discourage you from completing the rest of the hike, which is worth the effort. On the leeward side of the dune, the trail is easy to follow. So is the beach portion, but hikers along the beach must be alert to markers to connect with Trail 8 near the swimming beach. The trails in the park are busiest on weekends and holidays.

Note: Due to the fragile nature of the dune ecosystem, it is important to stay on park trails.

Begin the hike at the nature center. There is a slightly tricky maneuver at the outset when the path from the nature center reaches a crossroads with Trails 8 and 10. Go straight about 10 yards to where the trail splits and take the right (northeast) fork to stay on Trail 10. It is a gentle stroll between heavily wooded older dunes on the left and an extensive marsh on the right. Unlike the much younger dunes toward the lakeshore, these back dunes are an established forest of oak, hickory, sassafras, and maple trees, along with an abundance of ferns and wildflowers.

At 1.3 miles things begin to change. Pass a junction with Trail 2, which comes in from the right. (*Note:* Trail 2 loops south on a boardwalk through a marsh that runs through the heart of the park.) Go straight (east) on Trail 10 and within 0.25 mile reach an area called The Pinery—the last stand of virgin white pine in the area.

Just beyond the 2.0-mile mark, cross a boardwalk and enter Paradise Valley, a flat expanse that swings through a splash of wildflowers and ferns. This is the turning point of the hike as the trail curves to the northwest over a small dune to reach the shore of Lake Michigan. On most days you can see the Chicago skyline to the west from here.

Take note of the zipping sound as your feet sweep through the loose sand. Quartz crystals combine with moisture, pressure, and friction to create "singing sand." Few beaches in the world have this type of sand. If it is too difficult to walk through the loose sand, slip down to the shoreline, where pounding waves pack the sand tighter.

While hiking the lakeshore, be alert for tall signposts on the sandy ridges that identify the Big Blowout/Tree Graveyard, the Furnessville Blowout, and the Beach House Blowout. Blowouts occur when strong winds carve out large chunks of established dunes, sometimes exposing graveyards of dead trees previously buried in the sand.

Plants are plentiful along the shoreline side of the dunes—Kalm's St. John's wort, spiderwort, marram grass, and little bluestem are common. Also watch for places where swallows have built nests in the compacted sand.

Nearing the supervised beach at the west end of the park at 5.5 miles, look for the signpost for Trail 8. Wild lupine, a host plant for the federally endangered Karner blue butterfly, grows along Trail 8. So does low-bush blueberry, which offers a tasty treat in July.

At the Trail 8 signpost, take a left turn to begin climbing Mount Tom. It will not be easy, so pause atop Mount Tom for a couple reasons: to catch your breath and to take in the view. Mount Tom provides great opportunities to see such rare birds as summer tanagers, black-throated green warblers, and black-and-white warblers.

A wooden staircase descends Mount Tom to the left (east) as the trail crosses a saddle to Mount Holden (184 feet above Lake Michigan). The trail turns south as it descends from Mount Holden before beginning a more gradual climb of Mount Jackson. Go down the wide, sandy swath off the southwest side of Mount Jackson. Pick up the trail and follow its lengthy downhill path to a crossroads where Trail 8 meets up again with Trail 10. Turn right (west) and walk 100 yards to return to the nature center parking lot.

Note: Indiana Dunes Tourism, in conjunction with Dunes State Park, promotes the 3 Dune Challenge. Walk or run the challenge to earn a free sticker or the chance to buy a T-shirt or sweatshirt to prove you did it. Visit www.indianadunes.com/3dc/ for details.

Tree graveyard along the Lake Michigan shoreline at Indiana Dunes State Park

MILES AND DIRECTIONS

0.0 Begin at the trailhead at the south side of the nature center.

0.1 At the junction with Trail 8 and 10, go right (northeast) on Trail 10.

1.3 Reach the junction with Trail 2; stay straight.

3.0 At the beach, go left.

5.5 Reach the junction with Trail 8; go left.

6.9 Arrive at the crossroads of Trails 8 and 10. Go right to return to the nature center parking lot.

7.0 Arrive back at the parking lot and trailhead.

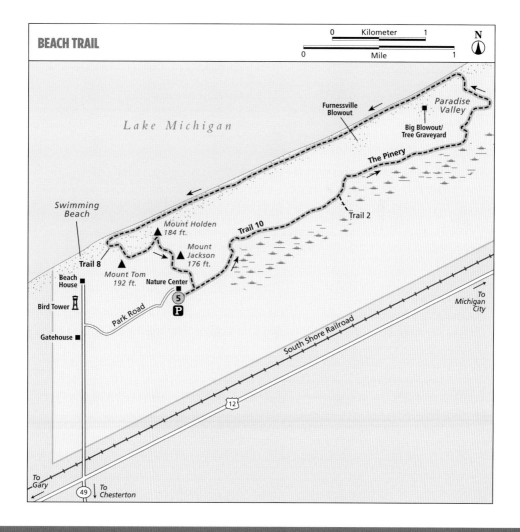

6 HERON ROOKERY TRAIL

WHY GO?

This linear trail along the Little Calumet River features some of the best spring wildflowers in the region.

THE RUNDOWN

Location: Michigan City, northwest Indiana
Distance: 3.2 miles out and back
Elevation change: Minimal
Hiking time: 1.5 to 2 hours
Difficulty: Easy; can be muddy and slippery
Jurisdiction: Indiana Dunes National Park
Fees and permits: Standard (7-day) or annual entrance pass required; federal lands pass is valid
Schedule: Open daily, 6 a.m. to 11 p.m.
Maps: USGS Michigan City West and Westville; Indiana Dunes National Park map; Heron Rookery Trail map

Special attraction: Spring wildflowers
Camping: No camping permitted on-site; 66 drive-in or walk-in sites at Indiana Dunes National Park's Dunewood Campground (6 miles northwest), open Apr 1 through Oct 31; 134 modern electric campsites at Indiana Dunes State Park (9 miles west)
East trailhead facilities: Ample parking; no restrooms or water
West trailhead facilities: Limited parking; no restrooms or water

FINDING THE EAST TRAILHEAD

Go 2 miles west on US 20 from its intersection with US 421 on the south side of Michigan City. Turn left (south) onto LaPorte/Porter County Line Road and go 2 miles to Porter CR 1500 North. Turn right (west) and drive 1 mile to Porter CR 600 East. Turn left (south) and go 1.6 miles to the Heron Rookery Trail east parking lot, located on the right.

THE HIKE

From the northwest corner of the east parking lot, walk about 15 yards and take the left fork in the trail. The right (north) fork leads to a spot on the south bank of the Little Calumet River overlooking a former great blue heron nesting site, or rookery. The rookery once featured more than one hundred nests. After sixty years of nesting here, the herons have moved to new nesting grounds, but these woods remain alive with dozens of other birds, including kingfishers, woodpeckers, and a wide variety of migrating and nesting warblers.

The trail is a peaceful walk along the Little Calumet, a small but vital river for both Native Americans and early European settlers. The trail is narrow, and on wet days this can be a sloppy, slippery hike. Footing can be tricky at places where the river has washed out the bank.

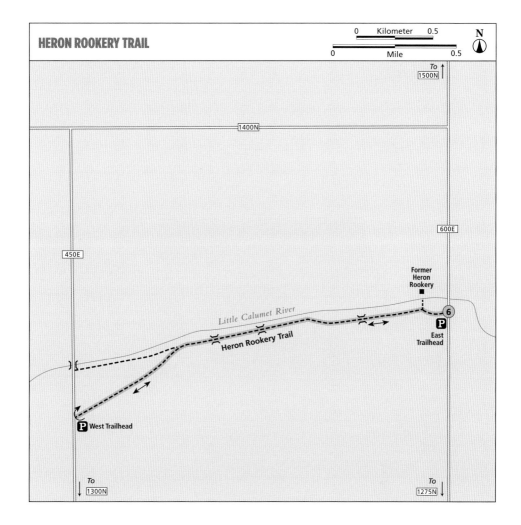

0   Kilometer   0.5

N

0   Mile   0.5

To
1500N

1400N

600E

450E

Former
Heron
Rookery

Little Calumet River

6

Heron Rookery Trail

P

East
Trailhead

P West Trailhead

To
1300N

To
1275N

In the spring (especially in May), before the trees leaf out, the woodlands along this trail are blanketed with one of the most extensive displays of spring wildflowers in the national park. Trilliums, spring beauties, and Dutchman's breeches are just a few of the flowers you'll see along this trail.

Three small footbridges along the trail cross feeder streams at 0.4, 0.8, and 0.9 mile. After the third bridge, the trail widens a bit. The trail splits at 1.3 miles, with the left fork leading to the west parking lot and the right fork hugging the riverbank to the bridge on Porter CR 450 East. If you choose the right fork, turn left (south) at the paved county road and go about 0.1 mile to the west parking lot.

Retrace your steps to return to the main lot at the east end.

MILES AND DIRECTIONS

0.0 Begin at the trailhead at the northwest corner of the parking lot. Bear left at the fork.

0.4 Cross the first small footbridge.

0.8 Cross the trail's second footbridge.

0.9 Cross a third footbridge.

1.3 Reach the junction with the trail to the west-end parking lot. Bear left.

1.6 Arrive at the west-end parking lot. Retrace your steps.

3.2 Arrive back at the trailhead.

Parking lot sign at the Heron Rookery Trail, part of Indiana Dunes National Park

7 MOUNT BALDY BEACH TRAIL

WHY GO?
A ground-level view of a "living" sand dune on the shores of Lake Michigan.

THE RUNDOWN

Location: On western edge of Michigan City, northwest Indiana
Distance: 0.8 mile out and back
Elevation change: Minimal
Hiking time: About 30 minutes
Difficulty: Moderate
Jurisdiction: Indiana Dunes National Park
Fees and permits: Standard (7-day) or annual entrance pass required; federal lands pass is valid
Schedule: Summit Trail is open only for ranger-led hikes. For a schedule, call the Paul H. Douglas visitor center at (219) 395-1824.

Maps: USGS Michigan City West; Dunes National Park brochure
Special attraction: Sunset on Lake Michigan with the Chicago skyline as a backdrop
Camping: No camping permitted on-site; 66 drive-in or walk-in sites at Indiana Dunes National Park's Dunewood Campground (4 miles southwest), open Apr 1 through Oct 31; 134 modern electric campsites at Indiana Dunes State Park (9 miles southwest).
Trailhead facilities: Restrooms and picnic tables; water available in the restrooms

FINDING THE TRAILHEAD
From the intersection of US 12 and Michigan Boulevard in downtown Michigan City, go 2 miles west on US 12 to the Mount Baldy entrance of the Indiana Dunes National Park. Turn right off US 12 and follow the entry road 0.1 mile to the parking lot. The trailhead is off the southwest corner of the parking lot at the wooden staircase adjacent to the entrance road.

THE HIKE
Mount Baldy is a fascinating sand dune that is being pushed inland about 4 feet or more per year by the wind off Lake Michigan. It's called a "living" dune because of the ongoing movement and reshaping.

Unfortunately, climbing up Mount Baldy is now restricted due to two factors.

One is a shortage of fragile dune grass atop Mount Baldy (enabling the wind to move sand more easily) caused by too many visitors climbing the dune and the "starving" of the dune caused by the Michigan City Harbor break wall. Erosion robs more sand than the natural water current can supply because the break wall captures sand. To offset the imbalance, the US Army Corps of Engineers has fed the beach by bringing in tens of thousands of cubic yards of sand four times since 1974.

Second is a public safety concern after a near tragedy in 2013 when a boy fell more than 10 feet into a hole in the dune and was buried by the collapsing sand. Luckily, the boy was rescued and made a full recovery. Geologists have identified dozens of these "holes"—voids where buried trees decomposed over many decades—present on Mount Baldy.

The combination of erosion and public safety led park officials to restrict access to Mount Baldy except for ranger-led tours. Call the Paul H. Douglas visitor center at (219) 395-1824 for dates and times of daytime and sunset tours. If you can get on a ranger-guided hike to the summit, you will get a breathtaking view of Lake Michigan's seemingly endless blue waters.

The closure has allowed park staff to plant dune grasses to stabilize Mount Baldy. It appears to be working.

Although the dune itself is off-limits, the beach trail that skirts it is open to the public year-round.

The trailhead begins at a three-tiered wooden staircase southwest of the parking lot and adjacent to the entry road.

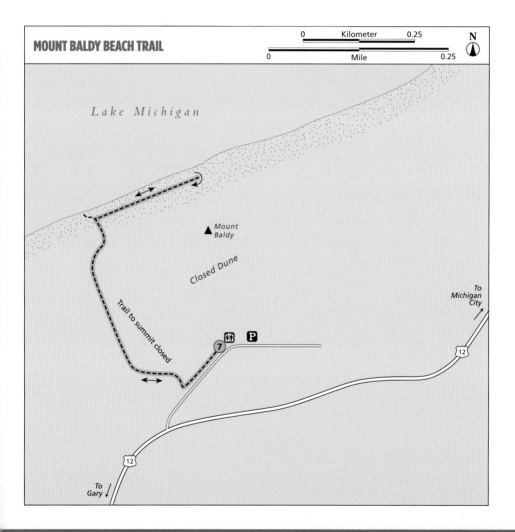

From the top of the staircase, turn right (north) to hike through a forested area to the Lake Michigan beach at 0.4 mile. Stroll the beach and check out the size of Mount Baldy before retracing your steps to the parking lot.

MILES AND DIRECTIONS

0.0 Begin at the trailhead at the base of the stairs.

0.1 Go straight (north) on the trail to the beach.

0.4 Reach the beach.

0.8 Arrive back at the parking lot and trailhead.

GLACIAL LAKES

People who move to northeast Indiana frequently are confused when they hear locals talk about going to "the lake" on summer weekends. The newcomers get the impression there is one giant lake nearby or that they are closer to one of the Great Lakes than first imagined. True, Lake Michigan and Lake Erie are only a few hours away from most of northeastern Indiana. In reality, what the locals call "the lake" is a generic reference to any body of water where they, a relative, or a close friend has a cottage.

There are more than one hundred natural lakes in Steuben County; a few hundred more form a beltway connecting LaGrange, Noble, and Kosciusko Counties. Some are small ponds only a few acres in size. Others represent the largest natural lakes in the state, including 3,000-acre Lake Wawasee in Kosciusko County; 1,900-acre Lake Maxinkuckee in Marshall County; and 1,000-acre Lake James in Steuben County.

Regardless of size, nearly all the lakes that grace this area of the state were created by glaciers that last passed through Indiana about 10,000 years ago. But the ten largest lakes pooled together pale in comparison to long-lost Beaver Lake, which was situated in northwest Indiana. At 28,500 acres, this shallow lake was the largest in the state until drainage of the nearby Kankakee River eventually dried it up.

When ancient glaciers bulldozed across the state, they pushed along tons of debris in the form of rocks, mud, and sand. As the glaciers retreated, blocks of ice were left behind in the pockets and depressions. As the ice blocks melted, lakes were formed. A common type of lake in northeast Indiana is the kettle lake—a deep hole with steeply contoured shorelines. A prime example is Lake Lonidaw at Pokagon State Park. The lake is only a few acres in size, but it is more than 40 feet deep.

Lake Lonidaw is protected as part of a state nature preserve, but nearly every other lake in northern Indiana is highly developed—ringed by summer cottages, year-round homes, trailer courts, campgrounds, marinas, or golf courses. The "lake" season typically runs from Memorial Day weekend through Labor Day weekend, a time during which the nearby small towns experience population explosions with the influx of vacationers.

Nevertheless, it is possible to find pockets of nature that provide an escape from the hubbub. Olin Lake and Crooked Lake Nature Preserves are two such sites. Olin Lake is the largest undeveloped lake in the state; at more than 100 feet deep, Crooked Lake is one of the deepest. Hikers can reach the scenic shorelines of both lakes, as well as other glacial lakes, by hiking along the trails listed in this section. Trails are presented clockwise from the Eagle Trail in Bicentennial Woods near Fort Wayne toward Angola.

8 BICENTENNIAL WOODS

WHY GO?

A short loop wanders along a wooded trail by a quiet creek, with a side trek to a secluded marsh.

THE RUNDOWN

Location: North of Fort Wayne
Distance: 1.4-mile lollipop loop; optional loops totaling 1.0 mile
Elevation change: Minimal
Hiking time: About 1 hour
Difficulty: Moderate
Jurisdiction: ACRES Land Trust
Fees and permits: No fees or permits required

Maps: USGS Huntertown
Special attractions: Several gigantic oak, maple, and sycamore trees, some estimated to be 200 to 250 years old
Camping: No camping permitted
Trailhead facilities: Small parking lot at the trailhead; no potable water or restrooms

FINDING THE TRAILHEAD

Go north from Fort Wayne for 8 miles on IN 3 from the I-69 interchange to Shoaff Road; turn right (east). Go another 1.5 miles to the Bicentennial Woods parking lot, passing West and Kell Roads. The parking lot is on the right (south) side of the road.

THE HIKE

Although this hike is not exactly in "lake country," it is close enough. Impacted by ancient glaciers, the area is certainly worthwhile. As the city of Fort Wayne approached its 200th anniversary in 1994, a regional land preservation group—ACRES Land Trust—looked for an appropriate property to commemorate the historic occasion. The group selected this 80-acre tract because the gigantic trees growing here are representative of what much of the area looked like before it was settled.

Only a few trees were ever removed from the property, which is believed to be one of the oldest forested areas in Allen County. Stately oak trees with trunks 4 feet in diameter and huge sycamores dominate a small, heavily wooded area that is bisected by Willow Creek, a quiet tributary of scenic Cedar Creek. The property has two designated hikes—the Dogwood Trail and the Eagle Trail, the latter of which is described here.

To begin the hike, locate the path on the south edge of the parking lot. Walk the trail into the preserve, staying left at the fork, and make a gradual descent along the face of a low ridge that slopes to the right. Reach another T intersection at 0.1 mile. Here you can turn left (east) to access the Willow Creek footbridge. Take an optional short spur to the right (northwest) to the Arnold oaks, a half-dozen gigantic trees named in honor of the family that preserved the area before it was purchased by ACRES.

Return to the main trail, turn right and walk 50 yards to the footbridge over Willow Creek. Cross the footbridge and take an immediate right (southwest) turn; walk along the edge of the creek for 0.3 mile before turning left (southeast). Go 200 feet to a wooden staircase. Climb the steps and go about 100 yards to a T intersection. Turn left (northeast) to begin a counterclockwise loop that leads back to the inbound trail and connects to two optional loops of 0.3 mile each.

The trail leads back to another wooden staircase at 1.3 miles. Go down the steps to reach the Willow Creek footbridge. Cross the bridge and return to the parking lot.

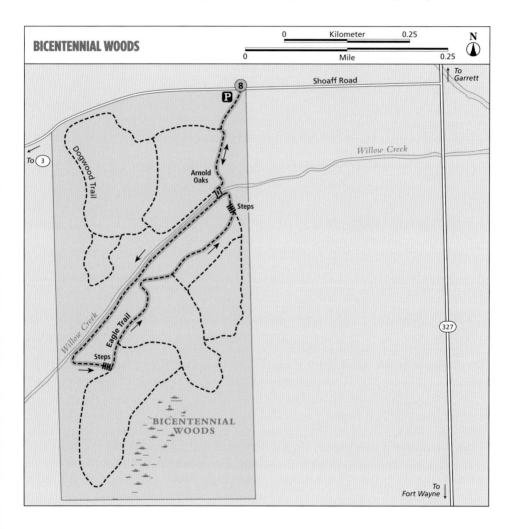

MILES AND DIRECTIONS

0.0 Begin at the trailhead on the south edge of the parking lot.

0.1 Reach the Eagle Trail/Dogwood Trail junction; turn left (east). (**Option:** Turn right and walk 20 yards to view the Arnold oaks.)

0.2 Cross the Willow Creek footbridge and turn right (southwest).

0.6 Turn left (southeast).

0.9 Climb a wooden staircase to reach a trail junction and turn left (northeast) at the T intersection. (**Option:** Turn right for an optional loop past a wetland.)

1.0 Pass the first of two more optional loops connecting from the right.

1.3 Arrive at a wooden staircase that leads back to the Willow Creek footbridge.

1.4 Arrive back at the trailhead.

9 DYGERT WOODS NATURE PRESERVE

WHY GO?
A short trail through high-quality forest offering a diversity of hardwood trees and wildflowers.

THE RUNDOWN

Location: Near Columbia City
Distance: 1.9-mile lollipop loop
Elevation change: Minimal
Hiking time: About 1 hour
Difficulty: Moderate
Jurisdiction: ACRES Land Trust
Fees and permits: No fees or permits required

Maps: USGS Lorane, Columbia City
Special attraction: Spring displays of wildflowers
Camping: No camping permitted
Trailhead facilities: Parking lot only at the trailhead; no potable water or restrooms

FINDING THE TRAILHEAD

From US 30 in Columbia City, go north 3.5 miles on IN 109 to Whitley CR 400 North. Turn left (west) and go 0.5 mile to CR 50 West. Turn right (north) and go a quarter mile to the trailhead parking lot on the left.

THE HIKE
A large stone inscribed with the names Evelyn and Wendell Dygert and the brief message "Who shared this peaceful place" pays tribute to the couple who once owned this land and left portions relatively untouched. The memorial marker sits in the shadow of a large chestnut oak at the start of the preserve's Outer Loop Trail.

To get there, begin at a gravel parking lot and follow a beeline west for 0.4 mile along the edge of an open field on the left and a thin band of woods on the right. A brief uphill climb precedes entry to the main woods where the memorial marker, a bench, and preserve sign are located.

The Dygerts acquired the property and adjacent farmland in 1968. They often hosted school groups at the wooded area and eventually donated 134 acres to ACRES Land Trust in 2001.

In July 2009 the 56-acre Dygert Woods parcel was named a state-dedicated nature preserve. The request for nature preserve status presented to the Indiana Natural Resources Commission described the site as "high quality forest in a part of the state where there isn't much of that left."

Dygert Woods contains a diversity of tree species—beech, cherry, hickory, and a variety of maples and oaks—spread across a landscape of ridges and ravines adjacent to

Blue Babe Branch, a 4-mile stream flowing south to the Blue River just outside of Columbia City.

As impressive as the trees are, they are outdone by a wildflower array considered among the best in northeast Indiana, especially in early May when bursts of blue-eyed Mary dominate the forest floor. Others you are apt to see during the spring or summer include bird's-foot trefoil, blue phlox, butterweed, Canada violet, cluster black-snakeroot, Jack-in-the-pulpit, spring beauty, white-flowered leafcup, wild geranium, yellow sweet clover, and yellow wood sorrel, to name a few.

The Outer Loop can be taken either direction but is described here as a clockwise route.

Marked with white blazes on trees, the Outer Loop reaches the first of several short footbridges just a few steps past the starting point. Nearing the half-mile mark, pass a small pond on the right and then the Inner Loop connector trail (marked with blue blazes).

Stay left on the Outer Loop as it meanders through dense woods, up and down ridges in a westerly direction before curling back to the east. At 1.1 miles, veer right when

Wild phlox at Dygert Woods Nature Preserve

DYGERT WOODS NATURE PRESERVE

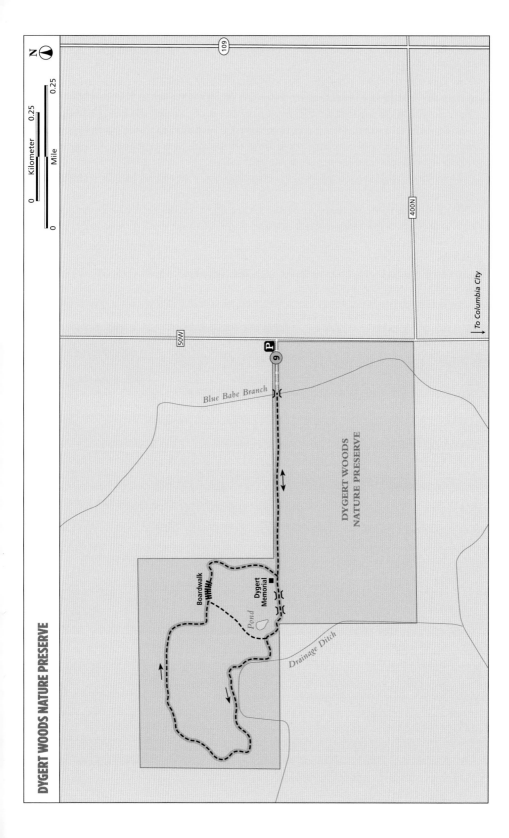

approaching a farm field on the edge of the preserve. At 1.2 miles, a sharp left reaches the north end of the Inner Loop connector trail, followed immediately by a 60-foot-long boardwalk. After taking a sharp right turn, your path parallels a deep ravine on the right before returning to the Dygert memorial marker and the start of the Outer Loop.

From here, turn left (east) and return to the parking lot.

MILES AND DIRECTIONS

0.0 Begin at the trailhead on the west edge of the parking lot.

0.4 Outer Loop start, go left.

0.5 Trail juncture with Inner Loop, stay left.

1.1 Veer right at edge of farm field.

1.2 Trail juncture with Inner Loop north end, stay left.

1.3 Long boardwalk.

1.4 Edge of farm field.

1.5 Return to start of Outer Loop, go left to trailhead parking lot.

1.9 Return to trailhead parking lot.

10 PISGAH MARSH

WHY GO?
A short out-and-back on shaded boardwalk over geographically significant glacial esker overlooking a diverse wetland.

THE RUNDOWN

Location: Near North Webster,
northern Indiana
Distance: 0.5 mile out and back
Elevation change: Minimal
Hiking time: About 30 minutes
Difficulty: Easy
Jurisdiction: Indiana Department of
Natural Resources, Division of Fish &
Wildlife

Fees and permits: No fees or permits
required
Maps: USGS North Webster
Special attractions: Boardwalk,
viewing areas, birdwatching
Camping: No camping permitted
Trailhead facilities: Small parking lot
with 4 spaces, 2 designated ADA;
restrooms

FINDING THE TRAILHEAD

From IN 13 in North Webster, go south 1.3 miles. Turn left (east) on Kosciusko
CR 500 North and go 1.3 miles. Turn right (south) on CR 925 East and go 0.5
mile to CR 450 North. Turn left (east) and go 1.2 miles to IN 5. Turn right
(south) and go 0.5 mile to West CR 850 North. Turn right (west) at Pisgah Marsh sign
and go 0.4 mile on gravel road between two fields to the sign for Pisgah Marsh Wildlife Diversity Area. Turn right on the paved road and go uphill to the parking lot and
trailhead.

THE HIKE
It might not seem as if a half-mile walk is worth the time, but this one is.

Short but sweet, the Pisgah Marsh "trail" is fully accessible with a 1,500-foot-long
boardwalk that is 6 feet wide, has railings on both sides, and is relatively flat from start to
finish—perfect for wheelchairs or strollers or introducing little ones to nature.

Pisgah Marsh is a three-unit, 445-acre property managed by the DNR Division of Fish
& Wildlife and its staff at nearby Tri-County Fish & Wildlife Area.

The boardwalk trail is in Unit 1, a 130-acre parcel with biological and geological significance. It is the only access to Pisgah Marsh and Pisgah Lake. Fishing and hunting are
not allowed on this unit but are regulated activities on Units 2 and 3.

Boardwalk hours are sunrise to sunset with a solar-powered gate timed to open and
close at those times.

The boardwalk was built in 2004 and sits on an esker, a narrow ridge of sand and gravel
left by streams of meltwater flowing below receding glaciers. The same runoff deposited
clay on glacial rocks and boulders to form pockets where water collected. The high
ground created by the esker also explains the site's name—Pisgah is derived from the
Hebrew word for "summit."

Boardwalk at Pisgah Marsh, perfect for young hikers

The surrounding area provides diverse upland habitat for many wildlife and plant species. Large oak, maple, and hickory trees dominate the ridgetop while the marsh and lake present an array of cattails, bullrush, lily pads, and spatterdock.

Interpretive signs along the boardwalk detail animals, insects, and plants present in the area. Two rare species documented here are the Blanding's turtle and eastern massasauga rattlesnake. Both are on the state endangered-species list, so any sighting by you would be considered most fortunate. You are more apt to see sandhill cranes, ducks, geese, squirrels, raccoons, wild turkeys, or deer. Maybe even a red fox.

Pisgah Marsh is an especially good location for seeing—or hearing—such songbirds as eastern wood-pewee, yellow warbler, Baltimore oriole, swamp sparrow, rose-breasted grosbeak, and many others.

Benches are located along the boardwalk, providing ample opportunity to stop, look, listen, and enjoy the peaceful surroundings.

An overlook at the end of the boardwalk offers clear views of Pisgah Marsh and adjacent 5-acre Pisgah Lake. A beaver lodge is nestled between the two bodies of water. Sit quietly on one of the benches here and watch for beavers to emerge from their home.

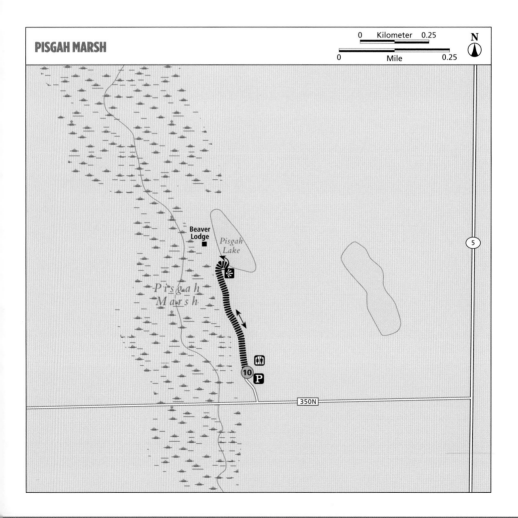

MILES AND DIRECTIONS

0.0 Begin at the boardwalk trailhead, go north.

0.25 Arrive at the boardwalk terminus overlooking Pisgah Marsh and Pisgah Lake.

0.5 Arrive back at the trailhead.

11 CROOKED LAKE NATURE PRESERVE

WHY GO?

A double-loop trail through old fields, along a bluff, and along the lakeshore.

THE RUNDOWN

Location: North of Columbia City on Crooked Lake

Distance: 2.0-mile double loop

Elevation change: A 45-foot decline from the trailhead to the lakeshore

Hiking time: About 45 minutes

Difficulty: Easy

Jurisdiction: Indiana Department of Natural Resources, Division of Nature Preserves

Fees and permits: No fees or permits required

Maps: USGS Merriam; Crooked Lake Nature Preserve brochure

Special attractions: Phil M. McNagny Jr. Tall Trees Memorial Grove, Leaman Cemetery, Crooked Lake

Camping: No camping permitted

Trailhead facilities: Parking space for 6 to 8 vehicles; no potable water available

FINDING THE TRAILHEAD

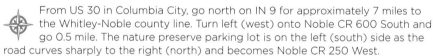

From US 30 in Columbia City, go north on IN 9 for approximately 7 miles to the Whitley-Noble county line. Turn left (west) onto Noble CR 600 South and go 0.5 mile. The nature preserve parking lot is on the left (south) side as the road curves sharply to the right (north) and becomes Noble CR 250 West.

THE HIKE

It is practically impossible to find a lake in northern Indiana that is not completely encircled by either summer cottages or year-round homes. This state-designated nature preserve protects about 3,500 feet of the north shoreline of Crooked Lake. The spring-fed lake is one of the most pristine in Indiana and, at 108 feet, one of the deepest.

It was on the shores of Crooked Lake that the Leamans, a pioneer family, were forced to interrupt their westward journey when a teenage daughter became ill. The daughter died, and legend has it that the mother was so distraught at her tragic loss that she wouldn't resume travel. The Leamans buried their daughter on a hillside overlooking the lake and built a home nearby. Over time, several other family members were buried in the small cemetery that lies on the east loop through the nature preserve.

The 145-acre preserve features old farm fields, ridges, hardwood forests, a pine plantation, and a 0.5-mile walk along the north shore of Crooked Lake. The woodlands feature green ash, beech, dogwood, hickory, ironwood, red oak, white oak, and sassafras trees.

Begin the hike by passing through the entry at the small parking lot. Pick up an interpretive brochure and walk the mowed path through fields that were farmed until the late

Violet

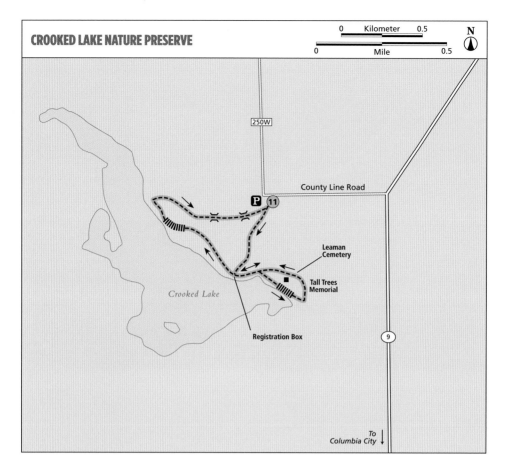

CROOKED LAKE NATURE PRESERVE

0   Kilometer   0.5

0   Mile   0.5

N

250W

County Line Road

P 11

Leaman
Cemetery

Tall Trees
Memorial

Crooked Lake

Registration Box

9

To
Columbia City

1970s. Already the natural progression of vegetation is taking place as small trees pop up among Queen Anne's lace, goldenrod, wild berries, and prairie grasses. It is about 0.3 mile from the trailhead through the fields and down a gradual slope to a registration box near the lakeshore. The preserve's east and west loops begin here, and together they make a pleasant hike.

Start with the east loop to keep in sequence with the numbered signs along the trail. Walk the shoreline for about 0.25 mile, crossing boardwalks in two marshy areas before curving left for an uphill climb. Along the right side of the trail is a broad ravine featuring a winding creek and the Phil N. McNagny Jr. Tall Trees Memorial Grove, which is at the top of the ridge at 0.6 mile. Turn left (west) and at 0.7 mile pass what remains of the Leaman Cemetery along the left (south) side of the path.

Continue along the ridgetop, which features large red oak trees, before descending toward the lake and to the registration box at 0.9 mile, where you will start the west loop. The path winds along the lakeshore, crossing two ravines and one boardwalk before turning right (east) and heading uphill at 1.4 miles. Cross a footbridge at the back end of a ravine before passing a pine plantation on the left (north). Just past the pines, cross another footbridge and then reenter the old farm fields. At 1.9 miles link up with the main path and turn left to return to the parking lot.

MILES AND DIRECTIONS

0.0 Begin at the trailhead, passing through the entry.

0.3 Pass the registration box at the start of the east loop. Turn left onto the loop.

0.6 Reach the Phil M. McNagny Jr. Tall Trees Memorial Grove.

0.7 Pass the Leaman Cemetery.

0.9 Arrive at the registration box and the start of the west loop. Turn left onto the loop.

1.4 Reach the west end of the west loop trail.

1.9 Return to the junction with the main trail; turn left.

2.0 Arrive back at the trailhead.

12 MERRY LEA ENVIRONMENTAL LEARNING CENTER

WHY GO?
A network of trails through meadows and forests, past Bear and Cub Lakes, and circling a large wetland.

THE RUNDOWN

Location: North of Columbia City
Distance: 4.7 miles of interconnecting loops
Elevation change: Minimal
Hiking time: About 2.5 hours
Difficulty: Easy
Jurisdiction: Merry Lea Environmental Learning Center of Goshen College

Fees and permits: No fees or permits required to use trails; donations encouraged
Maps: USGS Ormas; Merry Lea map sheet
Special attractions: Peaceful meadows, wetlands
Camping: No camping permitted
Trailhead facilities: Nature displays, reference books, water fountain, and restrooms at the learning center

FINDING THE TRAILHEAD

From Columbia City, drive north 10 miles on IN 109, passing between Crooked and Big Lakes, to Noble CR 350 South. Turn left (west) and go 1.5 miles to Noble CR 500 West. Turn right and go 0.5 mile to the south gate leading to the Learning Center.

THE HIKE

More than fifty years ago, Mary Jane and Lee A. Rieth were inspired by their love of nature to establish the Merry Lea Environmental Learning Center as a way of preserving habitat and creating a site for environmental study. Twenty years later the Rieths began turning over the 1,150-acre property to Goshen College, which now owns and manages Merry Lea for educational and scientific purposes.

The area includes wetlands, prairies, meadows, and forest environments that are ideal for quiet hikes, wildlife watching, or plant study. The trails are generally well groomed but sometimes can be confusing to follow in spots where trails have been cleared by mowers. Picking up a map at the trailhead will make it easier to follow the path. Merry Lea is a popular location for school trips, so weekdays can be quite busy during spring and fall.

Begin the hike by walking west past the learning center to a mowed path behind the building. Go about 0.1 mile to an intersection with a signpost marked with an "A." This signpost, the first of many on the hike, is in the southeast corner of Mary's Meadow. Take the left path and swing around the southwest corner of the meadow, turning north to enter the Maple Bottom at post E. The path can be muddy in wet weather.

At 0.4 mile reach signpost H and turn right (east) onto Hickory Ridge. Walk to post C and turn left (north) to wind through Rieth Woods toward Shew Meadows. At 0.7 mile (post D), turn right (east) and go to signpost O (0.8 mile), where the trail splits. Stay straight (east) as a gravel path winds between two drastically different environments—dry and sparse Bear Lake Prairie on the left and Onion Bottom, a large wetland and pond, on the right.

At 1.1 miles (post M) turn left (east) and walk along the north side of Wilmer Meadows for a little more than 0.3 mile to post P, on the north shore of Cub Lake. Several paths merge here. Go left (east) from Cub Lake and cross a bridge over a drainage ditch

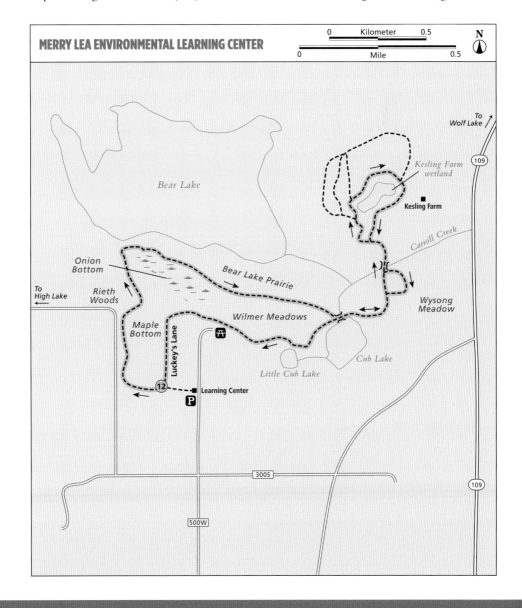

between Cub and Bear Lakes. Continue east to post Q, where the trail splits again at the southwest corner of Wysong Meadow. Turn left (north).

At 1.9 miles cross a footbridge over Carroll Creek to signpost R, turn left (northwest), and split South Kesling Meadow by going slightly uphill. At 2.1 miles (signpost S), turn left (west) and make a clockwise loop around Kesling Wetland to signpost T (2.5 miles).

In 2006 Merry Lea added Rieth Village, a biological field station for undergraduate education northwest of the Kesling Wetland. This also is the site of the Merry Lea Sustainable Farm. The three cottages earned Indiana's first platinum-level LEED rating for a variety of green building strategies (see www.goshen.edu/merrylea/about/facilities-directions/).

At signpost T, continue right to complete the loop around the wetland and return to signpost S (2.7 miles). Go left to signpost R (2.9 miles) and cross the footbridge over Carroll Creek before reaching Wysong Meadow. Turn left (east) and take the outer loop of the meadow back to signpost Q at 3.2 miles.

Continue retracing the outbound path past Cub Lake, now on the left (south), to return to signpost P (3.6 miles). Turn left (southwest) to cover the south edge of Wilmer Meadows, reaching signpost N and a gravel road at 4.0 miles. Cross the road and through a picnic area to enter the woods and continue the westbound trail.

Shortly after entering the woods, a side trail on the right leads to a two-tiered observation deck overlooking Onion Bottom. It's worth a stop.

After returning to the main trail, turn right (west) and go 0.1 mile (signpost J); turn left (southwest), going another 0.1 mile to signpost F at Luckey's Lane (4.3 miles). Turn left (south) and follow the old roadbed to signpost A (4.6 miles). Turn left (east) and make a clockwise arc through the woods to return to the south trailhead parking lot and the learning center at 4.7 miles.

MILES AND DIRECTIONS

0.0 Begin at the south trailhead, at the west end of the learning center.

0.1 Turn left at signpost A.

0.3 Pass Maple Bottom (post E).

0.5 Reach signpost H and turn right (east) onto Hickory Ridge. Turn left (north) at post C for Rieth Woods.

0.7 Signpost D; turn right.

0.8 Signpost O; stay left to skirt Bear Lake and north side of Onion Bottom.

1.1 Turn left (east) at post M and walk along Wilmer Meadows to signpost P.

1.4 Signpost P near Cub Lake.

1.9 Cross a footbridge over Carroll Creek to post R; stay straight.

2.1 Signpost S; turn left (west).

2.5 Signpost T; go straight (southeast) to the Kesling Farmstead.

2.7 Return to signpost S; go left (south).

2.9 Signpost R; go left to circle Wysong Meadow.

3.2 At signpost Q, turn left (south) to retrace your steps west past Cub Lake to signpost P.

3.6 Signpost P; turn left to pick up the trail running along the south side of Wilmer Meadows.

4.0 Signpost N; cross the picnic area and pick up the trail on the other side.

4.2 Signpost J; turn left (southwest).

4.3 Turn left onto Luckey's Lane (signpost F) and walk to post B.

4.6 At signpost A, turn left to trailhead and parking lot.

4.7 Arrive back at the parking lot.

13 CHAIN O'LAKES STATE PARK

WHY GO?
A network of connecting trails winds around a chain of glacier-formed lakes.

THE RUNDOWN

Location: Near Albion in Noble County
Distance: 4.9-mile loop
Elevation change: Lots of up-and-down terrain
Hiking time: About 1.5 hours
Difficulty: Moderate
Jurisdiction: Indiana Department of Natural Resources, Division of State Parks
Fees and permits: Park entry fee, higher for nonresidents; season passes available
Maps: USGS Merriam; Chain O'Lakes State Park brochure

Special attractions: Kettle lake system, Glacial Esker Nature Preserve, one-room Stanley Schoolhouse
Camping: Chain O'Lakes State Park—331 modern electric and 82 non-electric campsites; youth tent areas
Trailhead facilities: The Stanley Schoolhouse, a one-room brick schoolhouse built in 1915, is on the National Register of Historic Places. It is open to visitors on weekends from Memorial Day through Labor Day. Drinking water is available at the nature center near Sand Lake and other water sources throughout the park.

FINDING THE TRAILHEAD
Chain O'Lakes State Park is located midway between Albion and Churubusco. From Albion, go 4 miles south on IN 9 to the park entrance; turn left (east) and drive 1 mile to the park gate. From the gate go 1 mile on the main park road; turn left (northeast) and drive another 1.25 miles. The Stanley Schoolhouse is on the right (west) side of the road; the parking lot is on the left (east) side. The trail begins at the "Trail 8" sign near the northeast corner of the schoolhouse.

THE HIKE
Chain O'Lakes State Park is exactly what the name implies—a park featuring a series of eleven small lakes, nine of which are connected to one another by channels. The park's 29 miles of trails are wide, well maintained, and well marked. There are a few potentially muddy spots near the lakes.

The lakes are what remain of the Pleistocene ice age, whose glaciers retreated from this area thousands of years ago. Beneath the melting glacier, streams deposited sand and gravel, while detached blocks of ice formed deep depressions that became the park's kettle lakes.

A portion of this hike goes through the Glacial Esker Nature Preserve. The nature preserve was dedicated in 2012 to protect the glacial features in two parcels of the park totaling 732 acres. An esker is a long, winding ridge of sand and gravel deposited by a retreating glacier.

Native Americans settled here on the north shore of what now is Bowen Lake— named for William Bowen, one of the first white settlers in the area in the 1830s.

The hike begins at the Stanley Schoolhouse, near the east end of the park. First built in 1915, it is the fourth school building at this site. Students attended the school until it closed in the early 1950s.

Start on the north side of the schoolhouse at Trail 8, a self-guided interpretive nature trail that forms a loop around Big Finster Lake. Walk around the north side of Big Finster Lake and turn right at 0.3 mile onto a non-numbered path that leads across a ridge overlooking Big Finster Lake to the left (south).

At 0.7 mile the path connects with Trail 2. Turn right (north) and walk counterclockwise on a ridge overlooking Bowen Lake to reach the junction with Trail 7. Turn right (west) on Trail 7 as it hugs a ridgetop before gradually descending and turning left (south). At 1.4 miles, Trail 7 splits left and right. Go right (west), exit the dense woods, and cross the park road.

Continue straight until Trail 7 merges with Trail 4 at 1.7 miles. Turn left (south) and zigzag over several small ridges and along a channel that connects Sand and Weber Lakes. Reach the junction of Trails 7 and 5 on the north shoreline of Sand Lake and turn left

1915 Stanley Schoolhouse is now used for special programs.
INDIANA DEPARTMENT OF NATURAL RESOURCES

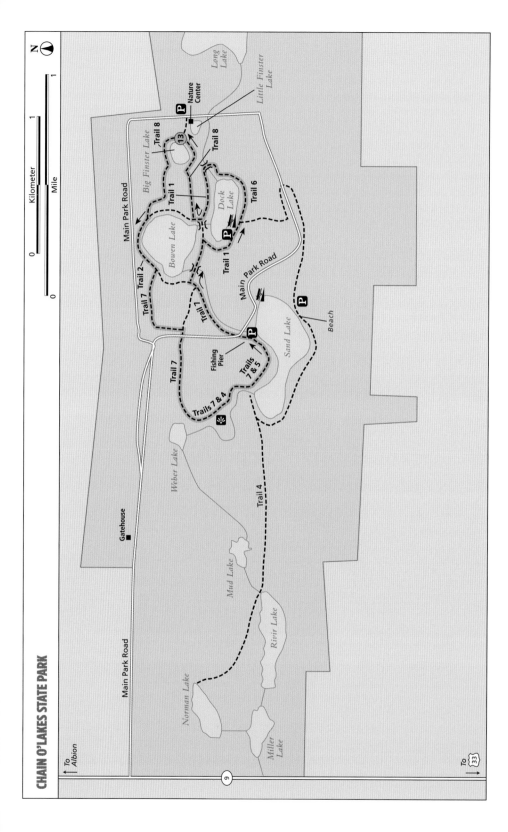

(east). Skirt the shoreline for a short distance to a fishing pier where Trails 7 and 5 split at 2.8 miles. Turn left (north) to stay on Trail 7 and cross the main park road again to reenter the woods. Trail 7 runs in a northeasterly direction along a channel that connects Sand Lake to Bowen Lake. At 3.3 miles Trail 7 ends at a junction with Trail 2 at the southwest corner of Bowen Lake.

Turn right (east) onto Trail 2 and cross a footbridge over the Sand–Bowen channel. At 3.5 miles turn right (south) off Trail 2 onto Trail 1 as it skirts the west shore of Dock Lake. When Trail 1 joins Trail 6, turn left and follow Trail 6 around the south and east shores of Dock Lake to a footbridge that crosses the channel connecting Dock Lake to Long Lake. Cross the footbridge at 4.1 miles and turn left (west) on Trail 1. Walk along the north shore of Dock Lake for 0.2 mile to the next trail intersection. Turn right (east) and go another 0.2 mile along a ridgeline to rejoin Trail 8 on the south side of Big Finster Lake at 4.5 miles. Turn right (east) and head back uphill to the trailhead at Stanley Schoolhouse.

MILES AND DIRECTIONS

- **0.0** Begin at the trailhead at the "Trail 8" sign.
- **0.3** Turn right on non-numbered trail to a ridge.
- **0.7** Trail 2 junction; turn right (north) overlooking Bowen Lake.
- **1.0** Trail 7 junction; turn right (west).
- **1.4** Turn right (west) at Trail 7 sign and cross main park road.
- **1.7** Turn left (south) at junction of Trails 7 and 4.
- **2.5** Turn left (east) onto Trails 7 and 5 and reach Sand Lake.
- **2.8** Pass a small fishing pier; cross the park road to Trail 7 and reenter the woods.
- **3.3** Turn right (east) onto Trail 2 and cross a footbridge over the channel between Sand and Bowen Lakes.
- **3.5** Turn right (south) onto Trail 1.
- **3.7** Trail 6 junction at Dock Lake; turn left (west) on Trail 6.
- **4.1** Cross a footbridge and turn left (west) on Trail 1.
- **4.3** Turn right (east) on unnumbered trail.
- **4.5** Trail 8 junction; turn right (east).
- **4.9** Arrive back at the schoolhouse and the trailhead.

14 EDNA W. SPURGEON NATURE PRESERVE

WHY GO?
This trail loops up, over, and through rolling glacial kames.

THE RUNDOWN

Location: West of Kendallville in Noble County, northeast Indiana
Distance: 1.3-mile lollipop loop
Elevation change: Minimal
Hiking time: About 45 minutes
Difficulty: Easy
Jurisdiction: ACRES Land Trust
Fees and permits: No fees or permits required

Map: USGS Ligonier
Special attractions: Glacial kames, vernal pond, large tulip poplar trees
Camping: No camping permitted
Trailhead facilities: Gravel parking lot for about a dozen vehicles; no drinking water or restrooms

FINDING THE TRAILHEAD

From I-69 north of Fort Wayne, take exit 134 and drive west on IN 6 for 25 miles, passing through Kendallville, Brimfield, and Wawaka. Turn right (north) onto Noble CR 600 West and go 2.2 miles to the ACRES Land Trust parking lot on the right (east).

THE HIKE

In 1961 Edna W. Spurgeon donated this 65-acre piece of real estate to a fledgling organization called ACRES Land Trust. Since then, ACRES has grown to 119 sites totaling just over 7,600 acres across twenty-one counties and three states (Indiana, Michigan, and Ohio). Thirty-one of the sites offer hiking trails.

This preserve was ACRES's first, and it does not take long to encounter its special characteristics.

Known by locals as "The Knobs," the area is a remnant of the glacial age that shaped much of Indiana's terrain, especially northeast Indiana. What appear to be a series of irregular, rolling hills are kames, or cone-shaped sediment deposits. Sand, gravel, and till were collected by glacial meltwater and deposited on the ice. As the glaciers continued to melt, the kame deltas collapsed onto the land below to form these hilly knobs. State nature preserve status ensures the land will remain this way.

The hike begins at the northeast corner of the parking lot. Go through the fence opening and walk along a flat stretch for about 200 yards before going downhill and then uphill to reach a trail junction at 0.2 mile. Turn right (southeast) and start what becomes a roller-coaster stroll up, down, and through the kames in a counterclockwise direction.

Along the way you will pass some of the biggest tulip poplar trees in the state. Large beech and maple trees also grace the woodland, which is home to an array of wildflowers, including bloodroot, trillium, Dutchman's breeches, and blue-eyed Mary.

At 0.7 mile reach a trail junction. Take the right (northeast) fork and follow a ridge that curls around a vernal pond before reconnecting with the main trail at 0.9 mile. Turn right (west) and return to the parking lot.

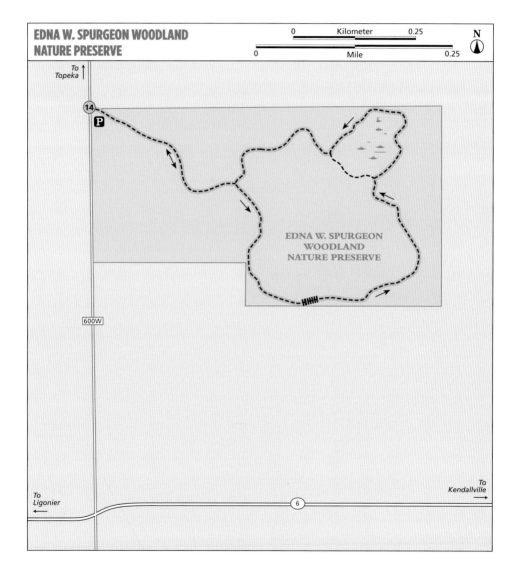

MILES AND DIRECTIONS

0.0 Begin at the trailhead at the northeast corner of the parking lot.

0.2 Reach a trail junction; turn right (south) to begin the main trail outer loop.

0.5 Cross a boardwalk.

0.7 Arrive at a trail junction; turn right (northeast) to begin the Vernal Pool Loop.

0.9 Reach a trail junction with the main trail; turn right (east).

1.1 Arrive at the first trail junction; turn right (northeast) to return to the parking lot.

1.3 Arrive back at the trailhead.

15 OLIN LAKE NATURE PRESERVE

WHY GO?

An interlocking loop trail through mixed woods leads to a lake with undeveloped shoreline.

THE RUNDOWN

Location: North of Kendallville in LaGrange County, northeast Indiana
Distance: 1.8-mile lollipop loop with a spur trail
Elevation change: Minimal
Hiking time: About 1 hour
Difficulty: Easy
Jurisdiction: Indiana Department of Natural Resources, Division of Nature Preserves

Fees and permits: No fees or permits required
Maps: USGS Oliver Lake; Olin Lake Nature Preserve brochure
Special attraction: Olin Lake, the largest lake in the state with an undeveloped shoreline
Camping: No camping permitted
Trailhead facilities: Gravel parking lot for about a dozen vehicles; no drinking water available

FINDING THE TRAILHEAD

From Kendallville, drive west for 4 miles on IN 6 to IN 9. Turn right (north) onto IN 9 and go north 7 miles, passing through Rome City and Wolcottville. Turn left (west) onto LaGrange CR 660 South and go 2 miles to a T intersection with LaGrange CR 125 East. Turn right (north) and go 0.5 mile to LaGrange CR550 South. A parking lot for the nature preserve is on the right as the road curves to the left (west).

THE HIKE

Olin Lake is a rarity in Indiana because not one single cottage can be found on its entire shoreline. Although this 103-acre lake is 82 feet deep in one spot, its low, marshy shore contributes to it being the largest undeveloped lake in the state. State nature preserve status for the 269 acres that surround the lake will keep it that way.

Olin is one of several lakes in a glacial chain connected by channels. To the northeast is tiny Martin Lake; to the northwest is Oliver Lake, a popular fishing lake stocked annually with brown and rainbow trout and home to a remnant population of lake trout.

The hike begins at the east end of the parking lot. Picture a figure eight on its side for a mental image of the trail layout. The east loop of the figure eight is lightly used, since the main attraction, Olin Lake, is near the midpoint of the trail. Traffic is minimal, with the most use coming in spring, when wildflowers put on an early show.

Walk between the fence posts to a registration box, where you can pick up a copy of the interpretive brochure. The preserve is abundant with wildflowers—large-flowered trillium, false rue anemone, trout lily, Dutchman's breeches, bloodroot, spring beauty, hepatica, cut-leaved toothwort, and Jack-in-the-pulpit. At 0.3 mile the trail crosses a boardwalk through a mucky area where two other plants are prominent—jewelweed, also called touch-me-not, and skunk cabbage. Look for a small tree that has smooth, gray bark with ripples. It's called musclewood. Many other trees grow in the low, wet soil, including silver maple, green ash, tamarack, and red elm. Large beech, hackberry, and red oak are present in other areas of the preserve.

After crossing a footbridge, the trail splits at signpost 2, at 0.4 mile. Turn right (southeast) and walk through an upland woods featuring large beech, sugar maple, tulip, walnut, and oak trees.

At 0.6 mile a crossroad marks the center point of the figure-eight trail. Turn right (southeast) and follow the east half of the figure eight as it loops counterclockwise through more upland woods before reconnecting near the crossroads at 1.0 mile. Turn right (north) and walk less than 0.1 mile through a thick zone of shrubs to Olin Lake. Retrace your steps to the crossroads one more time and turn right (west) to walk the west loop of the figure eight in a counterclockwise direction.

At 1.4 miles come to signpost 2 again. Turn right (northwest), heading back over the footbridge and the boardwalk to the parking lot.

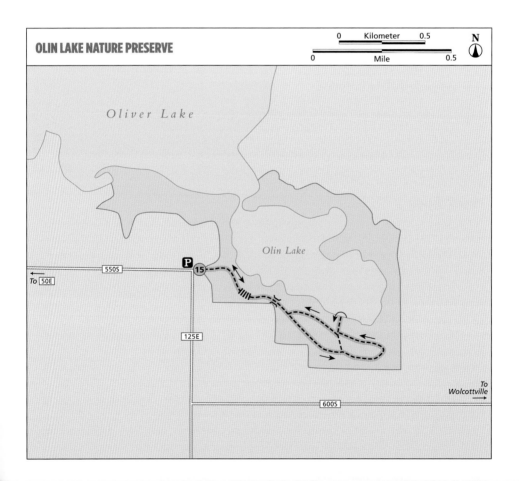

OLIN LAKE NATURE PRESERVE

MILES AND DIRECTIONS

0.0 Begin at the trailhead at the east end of the parking lot.

0.3 Cross a boardwalk.

0.4 Cross a footbridge and reach the junction with signpost 2; turn right (southeast).

0.6 Reach the center point of the figure eight; turn right (southeast).

1.0 Turn right (north) to Olin Lake.

1.2 Return to figure eight and turn right (west).

1.4 Return to the junction with signpost 2; turn right (northwest).

1.8 Arrive back at the trailhead.

Trillium

16 POKAGON STATE PARK

WHY GO?
A hike over varied terrain skirts the outer perimeter of Pokagon State Park.

THE RUNDOWN

Location: North of Angola
Distance: 8.0-mile loop; 3 optional loops of 1.8 miles, 1.0 mile, and 1.7 miles
Elevation change: 135 feet from Lake James to Hell's Point
Hiking time: About 3 hours
Difficulty: Mostly moderate, except for distance and stairway at Hell's Point
Jurisdiction: Indiana Department of Natural Resources, Division of State Parks
Fees and permits: Park entry fee, higher for out-of-state vehicles; season passes available
Maps: USGS Angola West; Pokagon State Park brochure; Pokagon Trail brochure

Special attractions: Hell's Point, Lake Lonidaw, Potawatomi Inn, historical structures built in the 1930s and 1940s by the Civilian Conservation Corps
Camping: Pokagon State Park—200 modern electric, 73 non-electric campsites
Trailhead facilities: Large paved parking lot at the nature center, which is open most of the year; restrooms and drinking water at nature center. There are numerous other water sources in the park, including campgrounds, picnic areas, the Potawatomi Inn, and the Spring Shelter, built by CCC workers in the 1930s.

FINDING THE TRAILHEAD

From exit 354 on I-69, turn left (north) onto IN 127 and go about 100 yards to a stoplight at the intersection with IN 727. Turn left (west); pass underneath I-69 and follow IN 727 about 1 mile to the park gatehouse. Follow park signs to the nature center. The trail begins behind the nature center on a paved path.

THE HIKE

At 1,260 acres, Pokagon State Park is one of the smallest parks in Indiana, but it is also one of the most popular. More than a million annual visitors partake of its various attractions, including hiking trails, camping, horseback riding, cross-country skiing, an 1,800-foot refrigerated toboggan slide, the Potawatomi Inn and cabins, and one of the largest natural lakes in the state—Lake James. The park was established in 1925, and most of its early buildings were constructed by the Civilian Conservation Corps (CCC) in the 1930s and 1940s.

The park is named for father and son Leopold and Simon Pokagon, two former leaders of the Potawatomi Indian people. The Potawatomi sold about 1 million acres in northern Indiana, southern Michigan, and northeast Illinois to the US government for 3 cents an acre, including a deed to the site of present-day Chicago.

The park owes its geographic legacy to the most recent ice age, which left in its tracks piles of rocky debris known as glacial till and the many lakes that dot the Steuben County landscape. Two of the most noticeable glacial remnants in the park are Hell's Point, located in the park's northeast corner, and Lake Lonidaw, named for Simon Pokagon's wife.

The hike described visits both locations and covers all or part of Trails 1, 2, 3, 4, 5, and 6. Hikers have the option of an additional 1.8-mile loop on Trail 7, a 1.0-mile loop on Trail 8, and a 1.7-mile option on Trail 9.

The park trails are heavily used and thus easy to follow. Some trail segments—around the nature center, campgrounds, and Lake Lonidaw—can be busy, but other areas can seem remote. Major holiday weekends are the busiest.

To begin the hike, walk around to the back side of the nature center and down a paved path that joins a dirt trail marked "Trail 1." Turn right and hike south and then north as the trail parallels privately owned cottages that line Lone Tree Point on Lake James.

Just beyond the 0.5-mile mark, hike uphill into a clearing that at one time was a fenced pen for bison and elk, which no longer exist in the wild in Indiana. Various trails converge on Trail 1 as it continues north to the Apple Orchard Picnic Area; ignore these and remain on Trail 1.

The east end of the Pokagon Trail is spotted with wetlands like this.

You will reach the picnic area at 1.3 miles. Cut northeast diagonally across the picnic area to a path that leads downhill to a bridge passing over the main park road. Go under the bridge to find a paved bicycle trail that parallels the paved road leading to the park campground area. Continue north, passing the campground gatehouse at 1.8 miles, and walk about 50 yards to Trail 4.

Turn left (west) onto Trail 4, cross the campground road, and climb a short set of wooden steps. Walk northwest on the trail, crossing a path that connects the group camp to the park's general store. Trail 4 heads downhill and twice connects with other paths. Stay to the right each time and connect with Trail 5 near the shore of Lake James. Turn right (north) and go uphill, cross a paved road, and pass along the east edge of a string of small cabins that compose the group camp. Trail 5 ends at a paved road leading to Campground 1.

Cross the road and pick up Trail 2 on a gravel road that passes the park's water-treatment plant and swings out to a point overlooking Snow Lake, one of a handful of smaller lakes in the James chain of lakes. When Trail 2 turns south away from Snow Lake, you are about 3.0 miles into the hike. Continue along Trail 2 as it slips behind the tent camp area. At 5.0 miles reach the Spring Shelter, a small shelter built by the CCC in 1938 next to

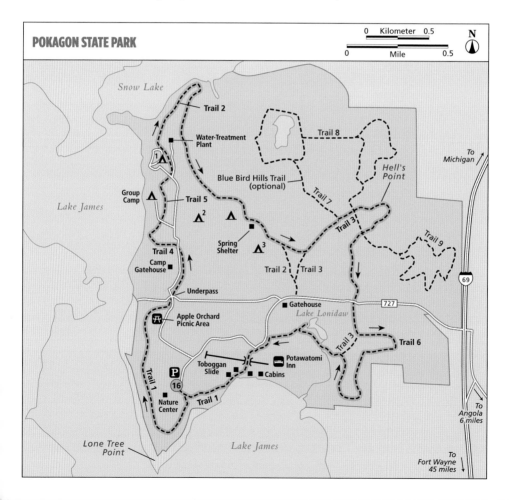

POKAGON STATE PARK

a natural spring that produces potable water. (Park personnel check the water for purity each week.)

Southeast of the shelter, Trail 2 forks; take the left fork, which leads to Trail 3. Turn left (northeast) onto Trail 3 and walk about 0.25 mile to the intersection with Trail 7. Another 50 yards on Trail 3 takes you to a crossroads with Trail 8 to the left and Trail 9 to the right.

Go straight (east) on Trail 3 for another 0.25 mile to Hell's Point, the highest point in the park and the third-highest point in the county. A wooden staircase of eighty-four steps makes the climb easier, plus cuts down on erosion of the hill. This hill is a glacial deposit of sand and stone known as a kame. The elevation change from the top of Hell's Point to the shore of Lake James is 135 feet.

From Hell's Point hike south as Trail 3 descends into a series of small marshes and streams that dot the eastern area of the park at the northern edge of Potawatomi Nature Preserve. You will remain in the preserve until passing Lake Lonidaw. The 256-acre preserve features cattail marshes, sedge meadows, and a tamarack–black ash swamp. The high glacial ridges that surround this area feature stands of red and white oak, shagbark hickory, and maple trees.

Stay on Trail 3 to cross IN 727, the entry road to the park, and walk less than 0.25 mile to the intersection with Trail 6. Turn left (east) and take Trail 6 as it skirts the park border for 1.0 mile before rejoining Trail 3. Turn left (west) and reach Lake Lonidaw at 7.3 miles. A wooden pier extends into the lake, which is partly encircled with tamarack trees.

From Lonidaw, a deep glacier-formed kettle lake, walk southwest and then west to the main park road. Turn left (south) and walk along the road past the Potawatomi Inn to a parking lot entrance with a "Boat Rental" sign. Turn left (south) and cross the parking lot to a bridge across the toboggan slide. Cross the bridge to a set of cabins. Walk between Cabins 64 and 65; cross the parking lot and pick up Trail 1 behind the parking space for Cabin 73. Turn right (southeast) and follow Trail 1 for a little more than 0.25 mile along the shore of Lake James to the paved path that leads back to the nature center.

MILES AND DIRECTIONS

0.0 Begin at the trailhead behind the nature center.

0.5 Hike uphill into a clearing.

1.3 Reach the Apple Orchard Picnic Area. Cut across the picnic area to pick up a path; head downhill to a bridge over the park road.

1.8 Pass the campground gatehouse. Walk 50 yards and turn left (west) onto Trail 4. Stay to the right at two trail junctions.

2.0 Turn right (north) onto Trail 5.

2.5 Pick up Trail 2 on a gravel road.

5.0 Reach the Spring Shelter.

5.4 Turn left (northeast) onto Trail 3; stay on Trail 3 to reach Hell's Point.

5.8 Climb to Hell's Point; continue right (south) on Trail 3.

6.2 Cross IN 727.

6.3 Turn left (east) onto Trail 6.

7.3   Arrive at Lake Lonidaw. Walk southwest and then west to the main park road and turn left (south) onto the road.

7.7   Turn left (south) at a parking lot and cross a bridge to a group of cabins. Pick up Trail 1 behind Cabin 73 and turn right (southeast).

8.0   Arrive back at the trailhead.

OPTIONS

The first of three optional loops off Trail 3 is Trail 7, also known as the Blue Bird Hills Trail (1.8 miles). Trail 7 leads to a large hillside meadow, loops around a wetland area, and returns to its trailhead on Trail 3. There's also a short spur on the northeast side of the Trail 7 loop that connects with Trail 8.

A short 50 yards up Trail 3 from the Trail 7 trailhead is the start of Trail 8.

Trail 9, the third option, begins across from the Trail 8 trailhead. If you choose this option, prepare for lots of hills over a 1.7-mile loop that takes you to the far eastern border of the park.

From Trail 8, there is even one more option, but it leads off-property to ACRES Land Trust's Beechwood Nature Preserve.

WABASH VALLEY

Oh, the moonlight's fair tonight along the Wabash,
From the fields there comes the breath of new-mown hay;
Through the sycamores the candle lights are gleaming,
On the banks of the Wabash far away.

With these lines, Paul Dresser celebrated the Wabash River with his 1913 song "On the Banks of the Wabash," which was named the official state song the same year. The river, on the other hand, endured years of neglect. That changed in 1996 when Indiana's General Assembly declared the Wabash the "official state river," a deserving title for a variety of reasons.

From its origin just over the Ohio border, the Wabash cuts a swath across north-central Indiana to its western border and then flows south past Terre Haute and Vincennes to merge with the Ohio River. The third-longest tributary of the Ohio River, the Wabash covers 475 miles from start to finish and forms almost 200 miles of the border with neighboring Illinois.

The river has played an integral role in Indiana history. Long before the French and British arrived, Native Americans were drawn to the fertile river valley, home to bountiful wild game, including buffalo and deer. The Miami, Shawnee, Wea, Piankashaw, Kickapoo, Pepikokia, and Osage all established villages along the Wabash. They were not the first. Archaeological evidence indicates that humans lived along the Wabash as far back as 10,000 years ago.

The name given to the river by local indigenous peoples, *Wah-bah-shik-a,* means "water flowing over white stones." The French, who had arrived as fur traders by 1700, altered the name, calling it Ouabache (pronounced WAU-*bash*). Later, pioneer settlers kept the French pronunciation but changed the spelling to "Wabash."

Because the river provided an obvious transportation route, the French established trading posts and military forts at Kekionga (now Fort Wayne), Ouiatenon (near Lafayette), and Sackville (near Vincennes). Replicas of those forts remain today as historic sites where the past is celebrated. One of the biggest annual events is the Feast of the Hunter's Moon at Fort Ouiatenon, held each October, which re-creates an eighteenth-century gathering of French traders and Native Americans.

Over time, more than two dozen towns were located along the Wabash, including Harmonie near the southern terminus. Harmonie was established in 1814 as a religious commune.

At about the same time, state leaders embarked on their own dream—a statewide network of canals for transporting farm goods as well as people. It was several decades before work began in 1832 in Fort Wayne, and it took more than thirty years to finish. Areas that were completed flourished, but soon after the Wabash & Erie Canal was completed, it was rendered obsolete by the development of railroads.

The river has not always been a friendly neighbor. Massive floods wreaked havoc on river towns, but flooding is minimized today by three dams. One forms J. Edward Roush Lake; the others are on tributaries of the Wabash: the Mississinewa and Salamonie Rivers.

Impacted by agricultural and industrial runoff, the Wabash River has become a focal point of a different sort in recent years. The Wabash River Heritage Commission is a coalition of groups working to develop recreational opportunities along the river, including hiking trails.

In 2004 the Department of Natural Resources opened Prophetstown State Park, restoring hundreds of acres of native prairie bordered by the Wabash and Tippecanoe Rivers and the town of Battle Ground. It was in this area in 1811 that the Battle of Tippecanoe took place—a confrontation between Native Americans assembled by Tecumseh and US troops under the direction of Gen. William Henry Harrison.

Today the area is a 2,000-acre state park featuring camping, hiking, and bicycle trails wrapped around a rolling tallgrass prairie.

Trails in this section are presented from Eagle Marsh in Fort Wayne, south to the Ouabache Trail near Bluffton, then west to the Portland Arch Nature Preserve near Lafayette.

17 EAGLE MARSH

WHY GO?

This loop travels partly atop an earthen berm constructed to block passage of invasive aquatic species.

THE RUNDOWN

Location: Eagle Marsh Wetland Preserve, southwest side of Fort Wayne
Distance: 3.1-mile loop
Elevation change: Minimal
Hiking time: About 1.5 hours
Difficulty: Easy

Jurisdiction: Little River Wetlands Project, Indiana Department of Natural Resources
Fees and permits: No fees or permits required
Map: USGS Fort Wayne West
Special attraction: Restored wetlands
Camping: No camping permitted
Trailhead facilities: None

FINDING THE TRAILHEAD

From the US 24 exit on I-69, go east 0.9 mile to Engle Road and turn right (southeast). Go another 0.3 mile past the Towpath trailhead sign and copper-roofed gazebo to a gravel parking lot on the right side of the road. Additional parking is available at a gazebo that is one of the trailheads for the Towpath Trail. The Continental Divide trailhead is about midway between the gravel parking lot and the gazebo and is marked by a sign.

THE HIKE

Continental divides usually are natural boundaries that direct precipitation runoff in two different directions. The Continental Divide at Eagle Marsh Wetland Preserve was created instead by bulldozers, backhoes, and other heavy equipment to prevent the mixing of floodwaters from two different watersheds: the Maumee and Wabash Rivers.

The culprits that prompted the $3.5 million project in 2015 were Asian carp, a non-native invasive fish species that threatens to migrate into the Great Lakes. Eagle Marsh was a potential pathway.

The marsh is the centerpiece of the Little River Wetlands Project, which acquired 500 acres of farmland in 2005 and began restoration of wetlands in an area once part of the Great Marsh that covered 25,000 acres before it was drained in the late 1800s for agriculture.

Eagle Marsh has grown to 831 acres and has become a community treasure, but the possibility of Asian carp passing through threatened to give it a black eye.

Fort Wayne has three rivers. The St. Joseph meets the St. Marys to form the Maumee, which flows northeast to Lake Erie. Historically, Eagle Marsh was the headwaters of the Wabash River, which flows across Indiana then south to meet the Ohio River.

Under certain conditions, floodwaters from the two watersheds back up into Eagle Marsh and mingle. If Asian carp were to move up the Little River, a tributary connecting Eagle Marsh to the Wabash River, they had a clear path to Lake Erie.

There's no evidence the carp ever did, and when federal, state, and local partners built a 2-mile-long earthen berm through the marsh in 2015, it blocked their path and created a barrier to prevent other invasive species already in the Great Lakes from using Eagle Marsh as a pathway into the Wabash watershed. Little River Wetlands Project took advantage of the opportunity to declare the top of the berm the Continental Divide Trail. On a map, the trail is a parallelogram—a rectangle that's leaning to the right with four sides that are relatively straight.

The trail begins at a sign that encourages hikers to take a selfie atop a continental divide.

More than a dozen Leopold benches are scattered along the berm—not so much as places to rest on the flat, easy trail but more as places to sit and observe the abundant bird life that frequents Eagle Marsh. Canada geese and mallard ducks are the most common, but more than 250 species have been documented there, including bald eagles, sandhill

Beginning of the Continental Divide Trail

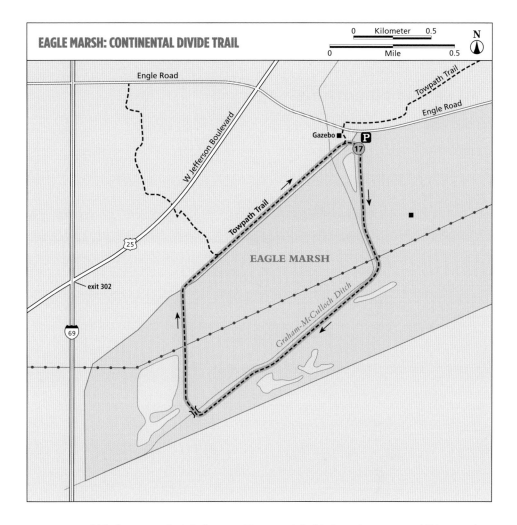

EAGLE MARSH: CONTINENTAL DIVIDE TRAIL

cranes, and black-crowned night herons. Twenty-eight bird species, two amphibians, and one reptile species are endangered or of special concern in Indiana.

From the trailhead sign, go straight south for 0.5 mile atop the berm. To the left is a wetland prairie section of Eagle Marsh; on the right is a large pond that was created when soil was removed to construct the berm. In between the pond and the berm is the Graham-McCulloch Ditch, which drains into Little River.

After passing under a power line, the trail makes a gentle right curve to begin one of the longest stretches—a nearly straight line over the next 1.0 mile.

At 1.6 miles a footbridge over Graham-McCulloch begins the inbound portion of the trail. As you step off the bridge, a gravel service road heads north between a series of ponds. The service road ends at a double gate at 2.1 miles. Pass through the gate and turn right (northeast) on a gravel path.

At 2.4 miles reach a paved trail that is part of the Towpath Trail, a 5.5-mile linear trail that follows the corridor of the Wabash & Erie Canal that operated in the mid-1800s. Near a water filtration plant at 2.9 miles, the paved path veers left toward a gazebo while a gravel access road to the filtration plant is on the right. Proceed either way for another 100 yards to reach the trailhead.

If you go, be advised that dogs are not allowed at Eagle Marsh.

MILES AND DIRECTIONS

0.0 Begin at the trailhead next to the "selfie" sign and head clockwise.

0.5 Pass under a power line.

1.6 Cross a footbridge over the Graham-McCulloch Ditch.

2.1 Reach a metal gate; pass through the gate and turn right (northeast) on a gravel path.

2.4 Connect with the paved Towpath Trail.

2.9 Pass a water filtration plant.

3.1 Arrive back at the trailhead.

18 FOX ISLAND PARK

WHY GO?
The loop travels along a wooded dune to a marsh overlook and back.

THE RUNDOWN

Location: Southwest side of Fort Wayne
Distance: 2.6-mile lollipop loop
Elevation change: A minor elevation increase at the upper dune
Hiking time: About 1.5 hours
Difficulty: Easy
Jurisdiction: Allen County Parks & Recreation Department

Fees and permits: Gate entry fee per vehicle; additional fee to hunt mushrooms
Maps: USGS Fort Wayne West; Fox Island Park trail sheet
Special attractions: Bog, marsh
Camping: No camping permitted
Trailhead facilities: Nature center with restroom and drinking fountains

FINDING THE TRAILHEAD
From Fort Wayne go 0.4 mile west from I-69 on US 24 to the third stoplight. Turn left (south) onto Ellison Road, following the directional signs pointing to Fox Island Park and the state police post. Follow Ellison Road for 1.9 miles as it parallels I-69, crosses over the interstate, and becomes Yohne Road. Go another 0.8 mile to the park entrance and turn left (north). From the gatehouse turn right (east) to the nature center parking lot.

THE HIKE
When the Wisconsin glacier began its retreat more than 10,000 years ago, wind shaped a sand dune rising 40 feet high in the heart of a sluice that carried away glacial meltwaters. Today that dune is at the heart of Fox Island Park.

Unfortunately, Fox Island sustained major damage in June 2022 when a derecho with 98 mph winds tore through the property, downing or damaging more than 3,000 trees and forcing temporary closure of the park. The 605-acre property was the largest continuous block of woodlands in Allen County, and more than half the site is protected as a state-dedicated nature preserve.

The park remained closed through 2023 for ongoing cleanup before reopening on a limited basis in 2024. It is hoped that the pre-storm trails will be unchanged except for the missing trees.

If the original trails are restored, visitors will see a marsh, wetlands, meadows, a peat bog, and what remains of a dune forest that provides varied habitat for wildlife and an abundance of wild plants. Nearly 200 species of birds have been seen at Fox Island.

Despite the uncertainty, Fox Island County Park remains in this edition of *Hiking Indiana* with the trails as they once were and, hopefully, how they will be once the storm recovery is complete.

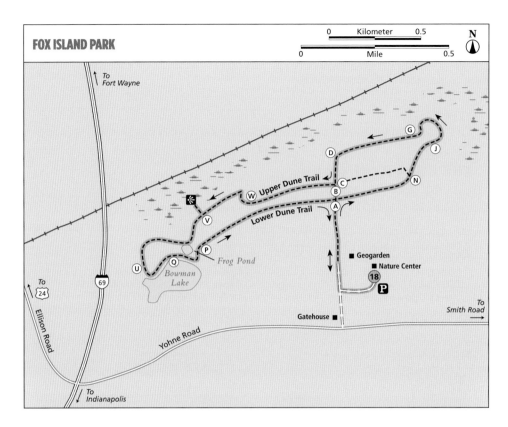

FOX ISLAND PARK

To Fort Wayne

To 69

To 24

Ellison Road

Yohne Road

To Indianapolis

Upper Dune Trail

Lower Dune Trail

Frog Pond

Bowman Lake

Geogarden

Nature Center

Gatehouse

To Smith Road

Morel mushrooms are a coveted prize in springtime.

MILES AND DIRECTIONS

0.0 Begin at the trailhead at the nature center.

0.1 Turn right (north) at the Geogarden.

0.2 Turn right (east) at the Lower Dune crossroads and post B.

0.6 Reach the post N intersection and go straight (north) past posts O and K.

0.7 Go right (northeast) at post J to the bog.

0.8 Turn right (west) at post G.

1.1 Go left (south) at post D.

1.2 Go right at post C onto Upper Dune Trail.

1.4 Pass post X.

1.5 Go right at post W.

1.7 Go right to the marsh observation deck at post V.

1.9 Reach post U; turn left (east).

2.1 Reach post Q; turn right (east).

2.2 Pass post P.

2.4 Go right at post A.

2.5 Return to the Geogarden; go straight and then left to the nature center.

2.6 Arrive back at the trailhead.

19 VERONICA'S TRAIL

WHY GO?
A short linear trail traverses a wetland nature preserve.

THE RUNDOWN

Location: Loblolly Marsh Nature Preserve, Jay County
Distance: 0.5 mile out and back
Elevation change: Minimal
Hiking time: About 30 minutes
Difficulty: Easy
Jurisdiction: Indiana Department of Natural Resources, Division of Nature Preserves

Fees and permits: No fees or permits required
Maps: USGS Domestic; Limberlost State Historic Site
Special attractions: Marsh, additional trails
Camping: No camping permitted
Trailhead facilities: Parking area; seasonal restrooms nearby

FINDING THE TRAILHEAD

From Bryant, take IN 18 west for 3.6 miles to CR 250 West. Turn right (north) and go about 0.75 mile to a parking lot on the left side of the road. The trailhead is off the northwest corner of the parking area.

THE HIKE
Although this trail is short, there's a long story behind it.

Present-day Loblolly Marsh is a 450-acre restored wetland that is a remnant of the larger Limberlost Swamp that covered 13,000 acres straddling Adams and Jay Counties. When Gene Stratton-Porter moved to nearby Geneva in 1888, Limberlost Swamp became the backdrop for her career as a famous author.

She spent countless hours exploring the Limberlost during the eighteen years she lived in a thirteen-room home in Geneva, and her experiences provided fodder for six of her twelve novels and five of her seven nature books, among them the best-selling novels *Freckles* and *A Girl of the Limberlost*. She wrote nearly thirty books in all and was a regular contributor to national magazines. Her books have been translated into several languages and read worldwide by tens of millions. Nine books have been turned into movies.

After the swamp was drained in 1913 and converted to agriculture, Stratton-Porter and her husband, Charles, moved to northern Indiana and built a new home on Sylvan Lake. Both homes—Limberlost in Geneva and Cabin at Wildflower Woods on Sylvan Lake—are preserved as state historic sites.

Eight decades later, local farmer Ken Brunswick formed Limberlost Swamp Remembered, a citizens group that became the catalyst for restoration of the swamp made famous by Stratton-Porter. Backed by a coalition of state and federal agencies, other partners, and local patrons, the initiative acquired five farms enrolled in the federal Wetland Reserve Program.

Loblolly Marsh was back. And in 2012 the 440-acre site was unveiled as the 250th state-dedicated nature preserve.

Loblolly Marsh is a mixture of small potholes, upland prairie, and meadows that provide habitat for waterfowl, shorebirds, and frogs and other amphibians.

Veronica's Trail is one of several trails at Loblolly and has its own special story. It is named for Veronica Rambo, who was born with spina bifida. During a fourth-grade field trip to Loblolly Marsh nearly twenty-five years ago, Veronica refused to stay on the school bus because she wanted to see the marsh with her classmates. There was no trail at the time, so it took several people to help get her and her wheelchair through the muddy marsh.

A couple of years later, Brunswick called Veronica to tell her that an accessible trail meeting Americans with Disabilities Act standards had been built and he wanted to name it for her. She approved.

Veronica's Trail is only 0.25 mile long, double that for the out-and-back trip. It begins on a paved path, crosses a footbridge overlooking a pothole, continues over crushed stone,

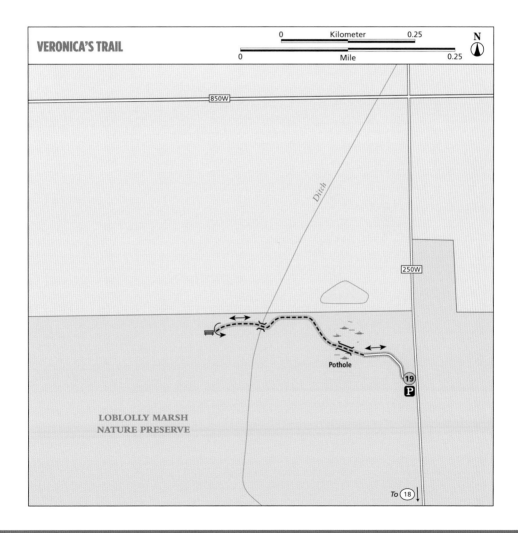

crosses another footbridge, and ends at a bench overlooking a depression where Engle Lake was before being drained in the early 1900s.

Prairie grasses, wildflowers, raspberries, blackberries, and wild strawberries are on either side of the trail.

MILES AND DIRECTIONS

0.0 Begin at the trailhead in the northwest corner of the parking area.

0.25 Reach the end of the linear trail; return on the same path to the trailhead.

0.5 Arrive back at the trailhead.

Gene Stratton-Porter home at the Limberlost State Historic Site

20 **OUABACHE STATE PARK**

WHY GO?

A combination of park trails forms a perimeter loop through refor-ested sections in various stages of regrowth.

THE RUNDOWN

Location: East of Bluffton, northeast Indiana

Distance: 6.0-mile loop

Elevation change: Minimal

Hiking time: About 3 hours

Difficulty: Easy

Jurisdiction: Indiana Department of Natural Resources, Division of State Parks

Fees and permits: Park entry fee, higher for out-of-state vehicles; season passes available

Maps: USGS Linn Grove; Ouabache State Park brochure

Special attraction: Small herd of bison kept in a 20-acre pen

Camping: Ouabache State Park—124 modern electric campsites, youth group areas

Trailhead facilities: Gravel parking lot on the south edge of Kunkel Lake for two dozen vehicles; no drinking water at trailhead; water fountains around Kunkel Lake

FINDING THE TRAILHEAD

From IN 1 in Bluffton go east 2 miles on IN 124 to the junction of IN 201. Turn right (south) onto IN 201 and drive a little more than 0.5 mile to a four-way stop. IN 201 turns left (southeast) and goes directly into Ouabache State Park. It is 0.8 mile from the park gatehouse to a parking lot (left) on the south edge of Kunkel Lake. As you face the lake levee, the trail begins on the right (east) side of the parking lot.

THE HIKE

The area around Ouabache State Park was once the home of Miami Indians, whose villages flanked the banks of the nearby Wabash River. Ouabache is the French Jesuit spelling of the Miami name for Wabash (*Wah-bah-shik-a*), but some people today pro-nounce it *Oh*-BA-*chee*. Even the Division of State Parks has capitulated to using the mispronunciation.

The present property was acquired by the state in the 1930s and established as the Wells County State Forest and Game Preserve. The area had been stripped of its mature timber and was heavily eroded, but the Civilian Conservation Corps and the Works Progress Administration reforested the area. Other projects included construction of buildings and development of a game preserve, considered the "greatest wildlife laboratory in the United States," in which pheasants, quail, rabbits, and raccoons were raised for release elsewhere in the state.

The state phased out the game-raising program in the early 1960s and converted the property to a state park. Remnants of the game pens can still be seen along some portions of the trail. Another key attraction is a 20-acre wildlife exhibit pen near the midway point of the trail. The pen is home to American bison, an animal that years ago roamed freely across Indiana.

From the Kunkel Lake parking lot, pick up Trail 5 at the east edge of the lot and walk east. The flatness of the trail that greets the hiker does not change much over the next 6.0 miles, but the trail surface does—sometimes gravel, sometimes crushed stone, sometimes grass, and sometimes just dirt.

Almost immediately you come to the first of several footbridges, but most are not as elaborate as this one. At 0.3 mile cross the main park road and pick up Trail 5 on the other side. At 0.8 mile cross another paved road and at 1.0 mile turn left (north) to squeeze between Campground B and the east boundary of the park.

At 1.3 miles Trails 3/5 make a right (east) turn before separating. Trail 5 continues east through a stand of mature hardwood trees, then bends back west to merge with Trail 2 and turn right (north) along the park boundary to the northeast corner of the park where the trail turns left (west).

One of the bison that can be seen at Ouabache State Park. The small herd is a popular draw at the park.

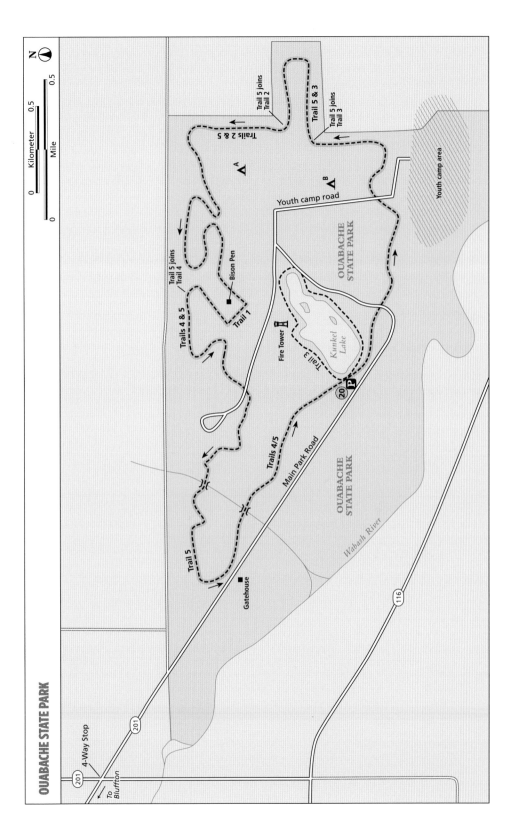

OUABACHE STATE PARK

At 2.4 miles the trail reaches an open field. At this point Trail 2 turns left. Stay on Trail 5 for a wide sweep through the open field that is a good area to spot white-tailed deer if you are on an early-morning hike.

At 3.1 miles Trail 5 hooks up with Trails 1 and 4 at the wildlife exhibit pen, home to about a dozen American bison. Take Trails 1/4 for a 0.75-mile clockwise circle of the pen, providing an opportunity to track down the bison as they roam from one end to the other.

Trails 5 and 4 continue at the northwest corner of the bison pen, heading west on a winding course through periodic stands of pine trees. Near the 4.0-mile mark the trail crosses a paved road that was the park entry road until 1995.

At 4.2 miles Trail 4 breaks off to the left (south) as Trail 5 continues toward the west boundary of the park; stay straight on Trail 5. The trail crosses a creek at 4.5 miles, swings left (southeast) to parallel the main road as it passes the gatehouse, crosses the creek again, and continues toward the parking lot. At 5.5 miles Trail 5 links again with Trail 4. Trail 4 breaks off to the left (north) near the parking lot and makes a 1.0-mile loop around Kunkel Lake. If you don't take the optional lake loop, stay on Trails 4/5 to return to the parking lot.

MILES AND DIRECTIONS

0.0 Begin at the trailhead at the right (east) side of the parking lot and go right.

0.3 Cross the main park road.

0.8 Cross the youth camp road.

1.2 Trail 5 joins Trail 3

1.3 At the split of Trails 3 and 5, go straight (east).

1.8 At the junction of Trails 2 and 5, go right (north).

3.1 Trail 5 meets Trail 1. Go left (south) around bison pen.

3.8 At the junction of Trails 1 and 5, go left (west) on Trails 4 and 5.

4.2 Trails 4 and 5 split; go right (north) on Trail 5.

5.5 At the junction of Trails 4 and 5, go straight. (**Option:** Turn left [north] at parking lot for a 1.0-mile loop around Kunkel Lake.)

6.0 Arrive back at the trailhead parking lot.

21 **BLOODROOT TRAIL**

WHY GO?

A loop hike meanders through meadows, over ravines, and along bluffs overlooking Salamonie Lake.

THE RUNDOWN

Location: Salamonie Lake, south of Huntington, Huntington County
Distance: 11.5 miles of interconnecting loops
Elevation change: Minimal
Hiking time: 4 to 5 hours
Difficulty: Easy to moderate
Jurisdiction: Indiana Department of Natural Resources, Division of State Parks
Fees and permits: Daily entry fee at Lost Bridge West State Recreation Area; season passes available
Maps: USGS Andrews and Mount Etna; Salamonie Lake brochures

Special attraction: Bluffs at Salamonie Lake
Camping: Lost Bridge West State Recreation Area—245 modern electric campsites, 38 non-electric campsites, 51-site equestrian camp, youth group areas; 6 walk-in primitive sites along the trail
Trailhead facilities: Restrooms and water fountains available at both ends of the loop; most conveniences available at the interpretive center in Lost Bridge West

FINDING THE TRAILHEAD

Go 9 miles south on IN 9 from its intersection with US 24 near Huntington. Turn right (west) onto IN 124 and go 2.5 miles to IN 105. Turn right (north) onto IN 105 and go 1.8 miles to Huntington CR 400 South. Turn left (west) and go about 100 yards to the main entry to Lost Bridge West State Recreation Area, just past the property office. Turn right (northwest) and go 0.6 mile, passing the main gatehouse and taking the first right turn (north) to reach the Salamonie Interpretive Center parking lots. Go to the lot on the left, farthest from the interpretive center, and locate the trailhead in the southwest corner of the lot.

An alternate trailhead is at Mount Etna State Recreation Area. From its intersection with IN 9, go west on IN 124 for about 0.4 mile and turn right (north) onto Huntington CR 700 West. Go 0.4 mile to a crossroad and turn left (west) into a small parking lot. The trailhead sign is off the west side of the parking lot.

THE HIKE

The Bloodroot Trail was developed in 2007 as a modification of the former Lakeview and Boundary Trails. The multiuse trail is open to mountain bikes. In winter it is part of the 40.0-mile Salamonie Snowmobile Trail along the south side of the reservoir, a flood-control impoundment of the US Army Corps of Engineers. The lake extends 17 miles during summer months, and the surrounding land is managed by the Indiana Department of Natural Resources (DNR) for a variety of recreational pursuits.

The Bloodroot Trail gets its name from a plant once used by Native Americans to make a yellow paint. Bloodroot was a common plant along the banks of the Salamonie, a named derived from the Native American word *O-sah-mo-nee,* which means "yellow paint."

The trail is easy to follow and easy to hike. It is well marked with frequent directional arrows and distance signage. The early half of the trail is over relatively flat terrain along wide, well-groomed pathways through meadows and sparse woodland.

The trail begins at a wooden trailhead sign in the southwest corner of the Salamonie Interpretive Center parking lot. (**Note:** You will need to pay the entrance fee to reach the parking lot.) From the trailhead, go south along a mowed path that parallels the access road from the main park road. When the trail reaches the main road, turn left (southeast).

Continue southeast, passing the first of two junctions with the Kin-Ti-Onki Mountain Bike Trail before reaching the second junction at 0.5 mile. Go left (northeast) and slightly downhill to enter a meadow that passes behind the Salamonie property office to the right (south) as the trail curls to the east and reaches IN 105 at 1.1 miles.

Cross the highway and reach a trail junction at 1.2 miles that begins a stretch of one-way traffic control. To the right is the outbound leg. To the left, marked by a "Wrong Way" sign, is the inbound leg.

Go right (east). The trail parallels Lost Bridge East Road, weaving along in a zigzag fashion before coming to the first of two old, paved roads. Continue east, crossing Lost Bridge East Road at 2.0 miles.

After crossing, turn right (south). The trail skirts the edge of a patchwork of meadows and farm fields, occasionally slipping into the woods. At 3.1 miles the two trails link for a short distance while passing a large pond. As the trail splits again, go right (south) at the twin yellow and white arrows.

Zigzag along meadow boundaries for another 0.5 mile before crossing a gully. At 4.2 miles cross another gully; at 4.3 miles reach the second spot where the two trails join. Continue straight, dipping into another gully, before reaching the trail turnaround at 5.0 miles and the eastern trailhead near Mount Etna State Recreation Area.

(**Note:** To reach the Mount Etna State Recreation Area facilities—water supply, restrooms—follow the paved road to the right [south] for 0.2 mile to a four-way intersection and turn left [north]. Go 0.1 mile and turn right [east] to reach the facilities. Backtrack to the eastern trailhead.)

From the eastern trailhead you will find the return portion of the trail more scenic as it scallops the edge of several gullies over the next 4.0 miles and crosses several footbridges while offering occasional glimpses of the lake from high bluffs. The best views come near the 9.0-mile mark, where Monument Island can be seen. The island is east of the previous location of Monument City, which is underwater now. Monument City gained widespread media attention in 2012 when local, state, and national media erroneously reported that a prolonged drought exposed the site for the first time in almost sixty years. The site actually is visible most winters when the US Army Corps of Engineers draws down the lake's water levels for flood control purposes.

A monument to twenty-seven men from Polk Township who died in the Civil War and the town cemetery were moved 1 mile north when the reservoir was built.

Go another 0.5 mile before crossing the last footbridge. Go uphill through a stand of younger trees to return to Lost Bridge East Road. Cross over the road again and pick up the right trail option.

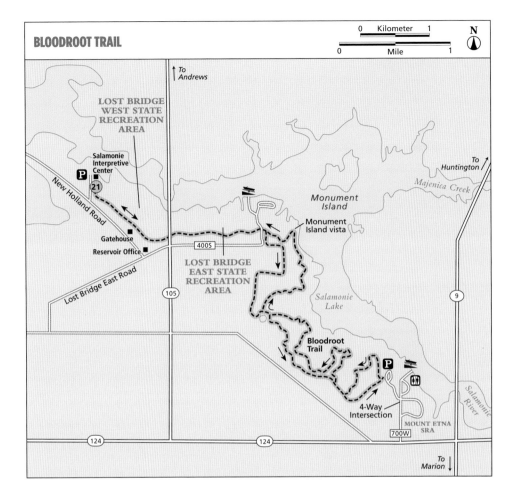

The inbound trail pretty much parallels the outbound leg and comes to IN 105 at 10.5 miles. After crossing the highway and going uphill, the trail splits one last time.

Take the right (northwest) leg and come to a trail junction on the right. Continue straight (west) through the largest meadow portion of the entire trail for another 0.3 mile.

At 11.0 miles reconnect to the outbound leg for the last time. Go uphill and turn right (northwest) to return to the trailhead and parking lot.

MILES AND DIRECTIONS

0.0 Begin at the trailhead at the southwest corner of the parking lot.

0.2 Turn left (south) to cross the access road.

1.1 Cross IN 105.

1.2 Trail junction; go right (east).

1.6 Arrive at access road to former Lost Bridge East State Recreation Area; go straight (east).

2.0 Cross Lost Bridge East Road to trail junction; turn right (south).

3.1 Trails link and pass a large pond.

4.2 Cross a gully.

4.3 Trails join again.

5.0 Reach the east trailhead at Mount Etna State Recreation Area.

9.0 Arrive at the Monument Island vista.

9.5 Return to Lost Bridge East Road; cross the road and continue straight (west).

10.5 Cross IN 105; bear right (northwest) at the trail split, then keep straight at the next junction.

11.0 Reconnect to outbound leg; go uphill and turn right (northwest) to return to the parking lot.

11.5 Arrive back at the trailhead.

22 **LOST SISTER TRAIL**

WHY GO?

A lollipop trail wends through a reforested area of ravines and plateaus on the northern shore of Mississinewa Lake.

THE RUNDOWN

Location: Southwest of Huntington
Distance: 2.5-mile lollipop loop
Elevation change: A couple of 30- to 40-foot changes in ravines
Hiking time: About 1.5 hours
Difficulty: Easy to moderate
Jurisdiction: Indiana Department of Natural Resources, Division of State Parks
Maps: USGS Peoria; Mississinewa Lake property map and trail brochure (available at property office)

Fees and permits: No fees or permits required
Special attractions: Multiple ravines, creek crossings, occasional views of Mississinewa Lake
Camping: No camping permitted near trailhead; campground located at the Miami State Recreation Area on the south side of the lake
Trailhead facilities: Parking and a restroom (open seasonally)

FINDING THE TRAILHEAD

From the courthouse square in downtown Peru, go 0.2 mile south on IN 19 and cross a bridge over the Wabash River; turn left (east) onto IN 124. Go about 6 miles to where IN 124 makes a 90-degree right turn and then a left turn. Go another 0.5 mile on IN 124 to Miami CR 675 East and turn right (south). Go 1 mile to a T intersection with Mississinewa Dam Road (also listed as Miami CR 700 South). Turn right, go about 800 feet, and turn left followed by an immediate right at the "Observation Mound" sign to find parking areas and a seasonal restroom. The trailhead is at a small footbridge about 50 yards east (left) of the restroom.

THE HIKE

It might seem as though the name Frances Slocum is on everything around here—a bank, a cemetery, a road, a state recreation area, and a nearby state forest.

Slocum was 5 years old when she was kidnapped by Delaware Indians from her Quaker home in Pennsylvania in 1778. The Delaware raised her to adulthood, changing her name to *Mahkoonsihkwa* (sometimes spelled *Maconaquah*), meaning "Little Bear Woman." She married the war chief *Siipaakana* and lived among the Indians until she was found in 1837 by her brother, Isaac, who was able to identify her by a scar on her left hand.

Once it was revealed that she was a white woman, Slocum lost her claim to government payments to Indians prescribed in the Treaty of 1826, but John Quincy Adams took her case to Congress. Slocum and her family could remain in Indiana, and two daughters were granted almost 650 acres of land, including the original homesite. A memorial marks the homesite, which is adjacent to the Slocum Cemetery, 4.5 miles east of the trailhead on Mississinewa Road. Frances Slocum died in 1847 and is buried about 8 miles from the Mississinewa Dam.

The Lost Sister Trail on the north shoreline of Mississinewa Lake pays additional tribute to Slocum.

The trail's course meanders over plateaus and into small ravines that owe the surrounding woodlands to the Civilian Conservation Corps (CCC). During summer months from 1937 to 1941, CCC Company 589 camped at the site while constructing roads and a shelter house and planting more than a half-million trees in the Frances Slocum State Forest.

The trail winds through the mature forest, up and down small ravines, over small creeks, and across paved roads that access picnic shelters and a boat ramp. Each year, every fifth-grade student in Miami County, where the Lost Sister Trail is located, takes a field trip to hike the trail and learn about the area's soil, water, wildlife, and plants. Brown, numbered signs mark the twenty-four learning stations on the trail. A brochure explaining the stations is available at the park office on the south side of the lake.

A sign along the Lost Sister Trail

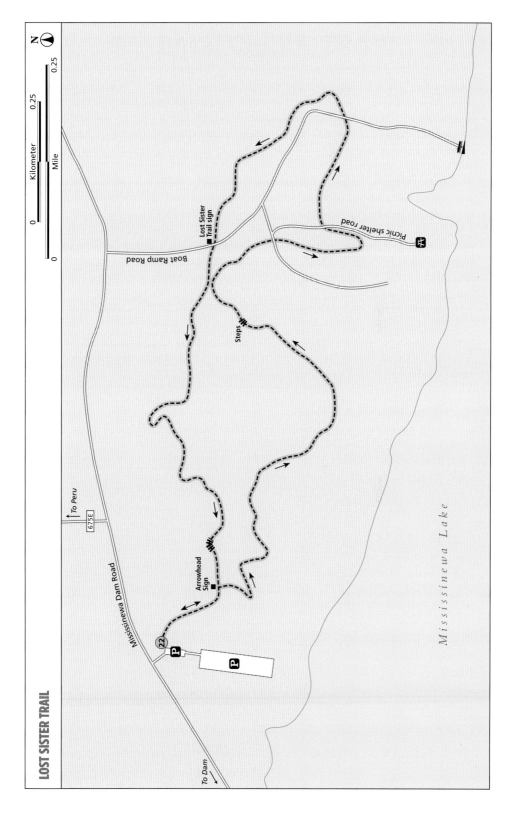

LOST SISTER TRAIL

N

Kilometer
0   0.25

Mile
0   0.25

To Peru

675E

Mississinewa Dam Road

To Dam

22

P

P

Arrowhead
Sign

Steps

Boat Ramp Road

Lost Sister
Trail sign

Picnic shelter road

Mississinewa Lake

The hike begins at the trailhead about 50 yards left (east) of the restroom near the first parking lot after turning off Mississinewa Dam Road. An interpretive sign gives a brief history of Frances Slocum and displays a trail map.

After crossing the footbridge, a gravel-covered path winds through trees to another parking area and a large arrow-shaped sign that once served as the trailhead. Veer right from this sign to continue a counterclockwise circuit.

At about 0.4 mile (near post 7), cross a paved road to resume the trail. At 0.6 mile the longest set of rustic steps—about two dozen—leads into another of the ravines on the outbound part of the trail.

Cross another paved road at 0.9 mile, after which the trail turns lakeward to reach another road and a shelter house for picnicking. The trail resumes across the parking lot and about 50 yards up the entry road.

The trail section from here to the next road crossover is wide and gravel-covered. The road crossover is the entry road to the Frances Slocum boat ramp. After crossing the road, enter the woods and continue a route bordered on the left by the road and on the right by an open field. Exit the woods at 1.5 miles to cross the boat ramp road again to continue the inbound hike.

The trail is relatively flat from here to the finish, with two boardwalks at about 1.9 miles that provide dry access through ephemeral wetlands.

At 2.3 miles you return to the arrow-shaped sign for the original trailhead. Proceed across the parking lot to the northwest to reach the final leg back to the restroom parking area at 2.5 miles.

MILES AND DIRECTIONS

0.0 Begin at the trailhead at the footbridge; turn left.

0.2 Reach an old trailhead marked by arrow-shaped sign and benches; turn right.

0.4 Cross a paved road.

0.6 Go down steps to a footbridge.

0.9 Cross another paved road; veer right (south) toward the lake.

1.0 Reach the picnic shelter road and parking lot.

1.2 Reach the boat ramp road.

1.5 Exit the woods and cross the paved boat launch road again; veer right 30 yards to the "Lost Sister Trail" sign.

1.9 Reach the first of two boardwalks.

2.3 Arrive back at the old trailhead marker (arrow-shaped sign); turn right.

2.5 Arrive back at the trailhead.

23 KOKIWANEE

WHY GO?

This trail meanders through woodlands and along a creek, takes a side trip past several scenic waterfalls, and loops through forests and meadows.

THE RUNDOWN

Location: Southwest of Huntington
Distance: 2.5-mile loop with side spur
Elevation change: 60 feet
Hiking time: About 1.5 hours
Difficulty: Moderate to strenuous
Jurisdiction: ACRES Land Trust
Maps: USGS Lagro; ACRES Land Trust map

Fees and permits: No fees or permits required
Special attractions: Waterfalls, rock formations
Camping: No camping permitted
Trailhead facilities: Small parking lot; no drinkable water or restrooms at trailhead

FINDING THE TRAILHEAD

From the intersection of IN 9 and US 24 near Huntington, go south on IN 9 for 3.5 miles to Division Road. Turn right (west) and go 7.5 miles to Wabash CR 600 East. Turn left (south) and go 0.4 mile to Wabash CR 50 South. Turn right (west) and go 0.2 mile to the trailhead parking lot on the left (south).

THE HIKE

Native American place names—Kekionga, Salamonie, Mississinewa, etc.—are common in this area of the state.

Kokiwanee has a similar ring but is not Native American. Instead, it is a spin on the Kiwanis Club of Kokomo, which donated the land for a Girl Scout camp in 1945. The camp closed in 1996 and was acquired in 2003 by ACRES Land Trust. The Kokiwanee site contains a forested upland, small creeks, and an array of small waterfalls spilling off a bluff overlooking the north bank of the Salamonie River.

The Girl Scout era at Kokiwanee left an abundance of trails and other vestiges, but the natural settings are relatively undisturbed. ACRES dropped the Girl Scouts trail names (e.g., Little Fox, Waterfall, River, Riding Ring, Fawn Lake, etc.) because they caused confusion for hikers. Still, it is advised to view or print a map from the ACRES website (https://acreslandtrust.org/preserve/kokiwanee/) to supplement this guide.

The hike described here begins about 70 yards south of the parking lot on the left (east) side of the gravel road that once served as the main entry into the Girl Scout camp.

Pass through the woods and across a meadow to a stand of pine trees. After passing the first of several footbridges, turn left (east) along the side of a hill. The trail turns right (south) and descends into a gully.

Follow a similar course into and out of gullies and across footbridges until you reach a trail junction at 0.5 mile. Go left (south) and continue for about 0.25 mile to cross over the smooth rock that forms the top of Kissing Falls. Only a small amount of water trickles over the 20-foot-high falls most of the year.

Once on the other side of the falls, turn left (southwest) and descend wooden steps to the base of the bluff. Proceed northwest along the trail, passing the Stairwell Crevice, Riding Ring Crevice, Daisy Low Falls, Broken Falls, and Skunk Cabbage Falls.

At Skunk Cabbage Falls turn left (southwest) toward the river and a T intersection. Turn right (northwest) and go through Skunk Cabbage Marsh, past Sponge Rock and Sleepy Hollow Bluff to reach Frog Falls at 1.1 miles.

Backtrack on the outbound trail, climb back up the wooden steps and turn left (northwest) at the top of the bluff.

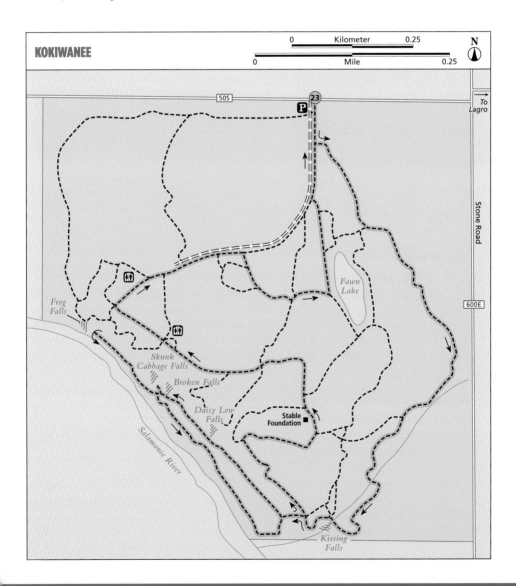

Follow the well-mowed path to reach a T intersection at 1.6 miles. Turn right (north) and go 0.1 mile. Look to the left of the trail for the stone foundation of the camp's former riding stable.

Turn left (northwest) and continue past a series of trail junctions on the wide, gravel main trail as it passes through deep woods.

At 1.9 miles the trail turns sharply right (northeast) and uphill to eventually reach the main gravel road. At 2.1 miles, turn right (south) and go 0.1 mile to Fawn Lake, a 1-acre pond. A bench provides a good resting spot to sit quietly and wait for wildlife to show up.

From the west edge of the lake, go north about 0.1 mile to reconnect with the main gravel road. Turn right (north) and return to the parking lot.

MILES AND DIRECTIONS

0.0 Begin at the trailhead on the left (east) side of the gravel road; turn left (east).

0.5 Trail junction; go left (south).

0.7 Cross over the creek above Kissing Falls; turn left (west) at the trail junction.

0.8 Trail junction; turn left (southwest) and go downhill.

0.9 Arrive at Daisy Low Falls.

1.1 Come to Frog Falls.

1.4 Complete the waterfall trail loop; go uphill.

1.5 Trail junction; turn left (northwest).

1.6 Trail junction; turn right (north).

1.7 Trail junction; turn left (northwest).

2.1 Trail junction to Fawn Lake; turn right (southeast).

2.3 Reconnect to the main trail; turn right (north).

2.5 Arrive back at the trailhead.

24 HATHAWAY PRESERVE AT ROSS RUN

WHY GO?

This trail skirts a high bluff over a tributary of the Wabash River and passes through woods and meadows.

THE RUNDOWN

Location: Southwest of Huntington
Distance: 1.7-mile loop
Elevation change: Minimal; mostly level
Hiking time: About 1 hour
Difficulty: Easy to moderate
Jurisdiction: ACRES Land Trust
Fees and permits: No fees or permits required

Maps: USGS Wabash; ACRES Land Trust map
Special attraction: Trail rim views of Ross Run
Camping: No camping permitted
Trailhead facilities: Parking at the trailhead; no drinking water or restrooms

FINDING THE TRAILHEAD

From the intersection of IN 9 and US 24 near Huntington, go west 14 miles on US 24 to Wabash CR 300 East, also listed as Lagro Road. Turn left (south) onto CR 300 East and go 0.8 mile to the intersection with IN 524. Go straight to pick up IN 524; pass through Lagro Road and continue south approximately 1.3 miles to Baumbauer Road. Turn right (west) and go 2.2 miles to the trailhead on the right (north).

THE HIKE

ACRES Land Trust has been acquiring and preserving unique natural areas since 1960, and Hathaway Preserve at Ross Run is one of the finest. Added to the ACRES roster in 2007, the preserve is named for Dr. Harvey Hathaway Jr., whose family helped fund protection of the site. The eastern boundary of the 72-acre property is Ross Run, a tributary of the Wabash River.

Though small, Ross Run performed its magic on the area by carving an impressive gorge with 75-foot cliffs and exposing the stream's bedrock. Because the trail skirts the rim of the gorge, much of the geologic artistry is viewed from above.

The trail begins at the northeast corner of the parking lot near a stone marker. Go 0.1 mile to a trail junction and turn right (north).

The gorge is to the right, and it deepens as the trail progresses over relatively flat terrain. A connecting trail intersects the main trail from the left. Stay on the main trail to reach the southeast corner of a meadow at 0.6 mile.

The trail makes a counterclockwise loop along the edge of the meadow. At the northern edge of the property, the trail cuts diagonally across the meadow and uphill to reach the northwest corner of the property's main woods at 1.0 mile.

Continue south along the edge of a farm field on your right to the southwest corner of the main woods and turn left (east) through another meadow. There's another trail juncture here that dips farther south in the preserve but stay to the left and continue east.

Reach another trail junction at 1.5 miles and turn right (south), skirting the edge of the woods and a farm field before coming to a junction with the outbound trail. Turn right and return to the parking lot.

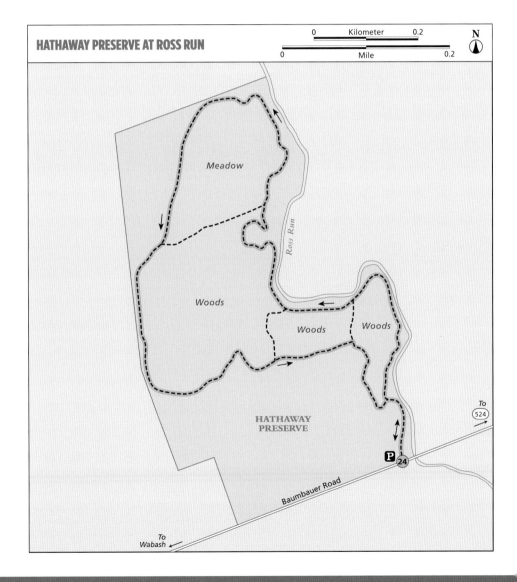

MILES AND DIRECTIONS

0.0 Begin at the trailhead by a stone marker at the northeast corner of the parking lot.

0.1 Trail junction; turn right (north).

0.3 Trail junction; continue straight (west).

0.4 Trail junction; turn right (northwest).

0.6 Arrive at the meadow; go straight (north).

1.0 Finish the meadow loop at the woods; go straight (southwest).

1.4 Trail junction; turn right (east).

1.5 Trail junction; turn right (southeast).

1.6 Trail junction; turn right (east) and return to parking lot.

1.7 Arrive back at the trailhead.

25 PROPHETSTOWN STATE PARK

WHY GO?
This loop trail crosses a wooded hillside and a restored prairie and offers views of two major rivers—Tippecanoe and Wabash.

THE RUNDOWN

Location: Near Lafayette
Distance: 3.5-mile loop
Elevation change: 75 feet
Hiking time: 1.5 hours
Difficulty: Moderate
Jurisdiction: Indiana Department of Natural Resources, Division of State Parks
Fees and permits: Gate entrance fee (includes access to The Farm at Prophetstown)

Maps: USGS Brookston, Lafayette East; Prophetstown State Park brochure
Special attractions: Restored prairie, 1920s-era farmstead, Native American village, Circle of Stones
Camping: 55 full-hookup sites, 55 electric sites
Trailhead facilities: Parking only at the trailhead; no drinking water or restrooms

FINDING THE TRAILHEAD
From exit 178 on I-65 north of Lafayette turn onto IN 43 and go south for 0.1 mile to Burnett Road. Go 0.4 mile to Ninth Street and turn right. Go 0.5 mile to Swisher Road and turn left. Once on Swisher Road, go 2.5 miles to the park gatehouse. Continue from the gatehouse on the main park road for 3 miles to the trailhead parking lot.

THE HIKE
Established in 2004, Prophetstown is Indiana's newest state park. It is loaded with ecological, cultural, and historical significance.

The 2,000-acre property includes a meticulously restored prairie, a replica 1920s-era farmstead, and a reconstructed Native American village.

Thousands of years ago, three glaciers plowed through the landscape, leaving deposits of boulders and gravel while forming two of the park's natural boundaries—the Tippecanoe River on the east end and the Wabash River along the south end.

The rich resources therein proved attractive to indigenous people, and various tribes settled here over time. In 1808 Shawnee brothers Tecumseh and Tenskwatawa established a village, which drew its name—Prophet's Town—from Tenskwatawa's role as a spiritual leader, for which he was called "The Prophet."

Tecumseh saw it as an opportunity to build a confederation of tribes that would resist the advance of white settlers that pushed them out of their lands in Ohio. The multi-tribal community grew to fourteen tribes, which drew the attention of Gen. William Henry Harrison, territorial governor of Indiana. Perceiving it as a growing threat, Harrison

Jerusalem artichoke and giant ironweed are part of Prophetstown State Park's colorful prairie restoration.

marched 1,000 soldiers 150 miles from Vincennes in southern Indiana to Prophet's Town to confront the tribes in late 1811.

While Tecumseh was away on a mission to recruit more tribes, Tenskwatawa launched an attack on Harrison's troops on November 7. The clash—known as the Battle of Tippecanoe—lasted about two hours. Both sides suffered significant casualties and Prophet's Town was burned. Tenskwatawa lost his influence with the tribal confederation, Tecumseh continued leading the fight against Americans until he was killed in 1813, and Harrison went on to be elected US president in 1840.

The nearby town of Battle Ground has a museum commemorating the US military presence at the Battle of Tippecanoe, but Prophetstown State Park counters with a Circle of Stones.

The Circle of Stones is located off the south end of the parking lot for Trail 3. Each of the large stones honors a tribe that lived at Prophet's Town—Creek, Delaware, Fox, Kickapoo, Menominee, Miami, Ojibwe, Ottawa, Potawatomi, Sac, Shawnee, Wea, Winnebago, and Wyandot.

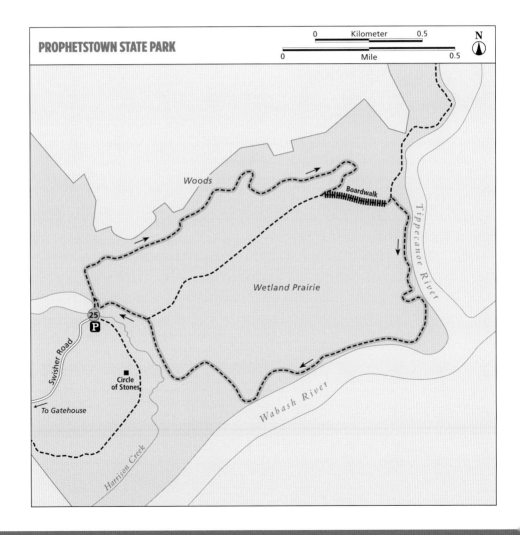

Trail 3 begins about a quarter mile north of the parking lot. Hiking and trail running are popular activities, and the area is designated part of the Indiana Birding Trail by the Indiana Audubon Society.

The trail's elevation is in the first mile after the trailhead. It runs along a wooded hillside overlooking the prairie on the right. Once out of the woods at 1.1 miles, an elevated boardwalk stretches over the prairie to the south to intersect with a paved bike path that runs from here to the gatehouse at the west end of the park.

Here, too, is the start of Trail 4, an optional add-on extending to the northeast along the banks of the Tippecanoe River to the far eastern end of the park before returning to this spot. Because of its proximity to the river, Trail 4 is often closed due to high water.

The same conditions can affect the next mile of Trail 3, which hugs the north bank of the Tippecanoe to its confluence with the Wabash River before turning north along a gravel road through the prairie and back to the parking lot.

The prairie itself is a sight to see. Depending on the season, its profusion of wildflowers includes bergamot, black-eyed Susan, brown-eyed Susan, butterfly weed, various coneflowers, coreopsis, evening primrose, great blue lobelia, hoary vervain, ironweed, Jerusalem artichoke, milkweed, obedient plant, orange jewelweed, royal catchfly, wild indigo, wingstem, and a whole lot more.

MILES AND DIRECTIONS

0.0 Begin at the parking lot and go north.

0.3 Trailhead sign; turn right to enter wooded hillside.

1.1 Exit wooded hillside, turn right and go 100 yards to boardwalk over prairie.

1.3 Exit boardwalk at paved bike path. (**Note:** Optional Trail 4 begins here.)

1.3 Go right off the paved bike path to enter woods.

1.8 Confluence of Tippecanoe and Wabash Rivers.

2.3 Turn right and go north through prairie.

3.2 Return to path back to parking lot.

3.5 Reach the parking lot.

26 WABASH HERITAGE TRAIL

WHY GO?

This linear trail along the Wabash River is full of historic locations, from Battle Ground to Fort Ouiatenon.

THE RUNDOWN

Location: Near Lafayette, west-central Indiana
Distance: 13.0-mile shuttle
Elevation change: Minimal
Hiking time: About 7 hours
Difficulty: Moderate
Jurisdiction: Parks Departments for Lafayette, West Lafayette, and Tippecanoe County
Fees and permits: No fees or permits required
Maps: USGS Brookston, Lafayette East, and Lafayette West; Wabash Heritage Trail brochure

Special attractions: Prophetstown State Park, Prophet's Rock, Davis Ferry Bridge, Tapawingo Park, Fort Ouiatenon, Purdue University
Camping: No camping permitted
Trailhead facilities: Tippecanoe Battlefield Museum (open 10 a.m. to 5 p.m. Mon through Sat; noon to 5 p.m. Sun; admission fee); seasonal nature center; drinking fountain available seasonally at Tippecanoe Battlefield Park; no other sources of potable water available until Tapawingo Park in West Lafayette

FINDING THE TRAILHEAD

Go 3 miles northeast on US 25 from the I-65 interchange to IN 225. Turn left (northwest) onto IN 225 and go over the one-lane bridge that crosses the Wabash River. The highway passes between the two sections of Prophetstown State Park before reaching the village of Battle Ground. Cross the railroad tracks at the center of town; take an immediate left (southwest) turn and go 0.4 mile farther to the Tippecanoe Battlefield Park. The trailhead is at the Wah-bah-shik-a Nature Center at the north end of the parking lot.

THE HIKE

As noted in the introduction, this is where Shawnee leader Tecumseh attempted to establish a confederacy of Native American tribes to resist the advancement of white settlers. Military forces directed by Gen. William Henry Harrison confronted the Indians at Prophet's Town on November 7, 1811, and the outcome—considered a draw on the battlefield—effectively ended Tecumseh's ambitions for the confederacy. Harrison was elected US president in 1840 but died after only thirty days in office.

Two landmarks commemorate the famous battle—Prophetstown State Park and a local historic park at the battlefield site on the west edge of Battle Ground. Thirteen miles downstream from the battlefield is Fort Ouiatenon, the first military outpost in Indiana. The French established the fort in 1717 to counter British expansion.

The hike begins at Tippecanoe Battlefield Park. Before heading out on the trail, explore the 104-acre battlefield and military graveyard or visit the museum or nature center.

Any part of the trail is vulnerable to flooding (especially riverside segments from Tapawingo Park to Fort Ouiatenon), so it's recommended to check weather forecasts and Wabash River levels before starting.

The linear nature and distance of this trail will require you to arrange a vehicle shuttle or be willing to backtrack—and that's a long trek back to Battle Ground. There are additional trailheads along the route—at Davis Ferry Park, Lafayette Municipal Golf Course, Tapawingo Park, and Fort Ouiatenon. Spring rains can flood out some sections of the trail, but rerouting has taken care of most problems. Trail conditions sometimes are posted at the Battle Ground nature center. The busiest segments are at the battlefield and paved areas in downtown Lafayette.

To start the hike, walk down a concrete stairway near the nature center to a footbridge over Burnett's Creek, named for William Burnett, a French trader and early settler. Just short of 0.1 mile arrive at a marked junction of the Wabash Heritage and Prophet's Rock Trails. An optional side trip, Prophet's Rock Trail leads 0.2 mile to the rock. Popular legend relates that the Prophet chanted encouragement and instructions to the Indian warriors during the 1811 battle. Native American historians dispute this tale.

From the junction with Prophet's Rock Trail, turn left (southwest) at the Wabash Heritage Trail marker and follow a path that hugs the north bank of Burnett's Creek as it cuts a southwesterly path toward its confluence with the Wabash River. Interpretive sign-posts help mark the way on what begins as an easy walk, with only three minor inclines over the entire stretch to Fort Ouiatenon.

Two short footbridges cross drainage ditches that feed Burnett's Creek before the path passes under I-65 at 1.4 miles. Go 0.1 mile to another footbridge, followed by a climb of 30 feet up a steep bank. Drop back down to the creek bed and at 1.8 miles pass under a bridge at Burnetts Road.

The trail crosses Burnett's Creek at Burnetts Road on a boardwalk built on the side of the bridge. It then continues along the southeast bank of the creek for another 1.8 miles to Davis Ferry Bridge (3.6 miles). Pass behind private homes and along a farm field to a paved road, following trail markers that point to the iron suspension bridge built over the Wabash in 1912. John Davis, who married William Burnett's daughter, operated a ferry at this location until the bridge was built. Davis charged 6 cents per person and 12½ cents per car or horse. Today the bridge is restricted to pedestrian use. Cross the bridge and turn right (west) as the path proceeds along the southeast bank of the Wabash. At 4.1 miles pass Heron Island, a 12-acre wildlife refuge in the Wabash that is accessible only by boat. Continue along the banks of the Wabash for about 1.7 miles to another footbridge before passing under the US 52 bridge at 5.8 miles.

From here the trail parallels the river, Lafayette Municipal Golf Course, and an open field that is home to a local model airplane club. At 6.5 miles you will come to McAllister Park and a paved section of trail that is also open to bicycles. Bikes are not allowed on the unpaved portion of the trail. Walk past several ball fields on the left (east) and under another bridge to reach the final leg into downtown Lafayette.

Trailhead of the Wabash Heritage Trail at Burnett's Creek, its northern terminus

At 9.3 miles reach the Big Four Depot, a restored train stop at the foot of the John T. Myers pedestrian bridge, which crosses the Wabash River into West Lafayette, home of Purdue University. After crossing the bridge, go left around the circular fountain and take a left turn down the paved walkway away from the bridge to a T intersection with a paved trail. Go right (south) and pass underneath highway and railroad overpasses.

After about 0.25 mile, the trail passes through an area of borrow pits from which soil was taken for three purposes: to construct dikes around the nearby wastewater treatment plant, to provide storage for floodwater, and to create wildlife habitat.

It is in this area, at 9.7 miles, that the trail splits in more ways than one. A paved trail to the right is managed by the West Lafayette Parks Department and feeds to a sidewalk adjacent to South River Road but stops at the intersection with US 52/231. Walkers, joggers, and bicyclists can use the paved trail.

The left fork is a natural surface trail managed by the Tippecanoe County Parks & Recreation Department. It is open to hikers only. Although the county portion is prone to flooding, when dry enough it offers a more scenic trip on the banks of the Wabash River almost all the way to Fort Ouiatenon, including passage under a four-lane bridge at US 52/231. The last 0.25 mile is on a paved trail alongside South River Road.

At Fort Ouiatenon the most dominant feature is a replica blockhouse the Tippecanoe County Historical Association operates as a museum. Historical programs are conducted at the park, the most notable being the annual Feast of the Hunter's Moon each October, which re-creates French and Indian life here during the 1700s.

Horses, bikes, and motorized vehicles are prohibited on the trail.

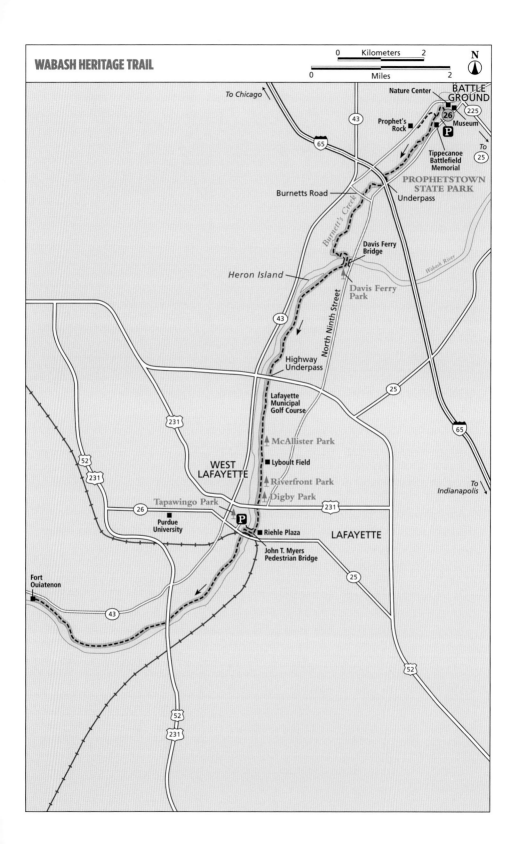

0   Kilometers   2

0   Miles   2

N

To Chicago

BATTLE GROUND

Nature Center

43

Prophet's Rock

26

225

P

Museum

To 25

Tippecanoe Battlefield Memorial

PROPHETSTOWN STATE PARK

Burnetts Road

Underpass

Burnett's Creek

Davis Ferry Bridge

Wabash River

Heron Island

Davis Ferry Park

North Ninth Street

43

25

Highway Underpass

Lafayette Municipal Golf Course

65

McAllister Park

231

Lyboult Field

52

231

Riverfront Park

WEST LAFAYETTE

Digby Park

Tapawingo Park

26

231

To Indianapolis

Purdue University

P

Riehle Plaza

LAFAYETTE

John T. Myers Pedestrian Bridge

25

Fort Ouiatenon

43

52

52

231

MILES AND DIRECTIONS

0.0 Begin at the trailhead near the nature center and go straight.

0.1 Reach the Prophet's Rock Trail junction; turn left. (**Option:** Take the 0.4-mile round-trip to Prophet's Rock.)

1.4 Reach the I-65 underpass.

1.8 Arrive at the Burnetts Road underpass.

3.6 Cross the Davis Ferry Bridge.

4.1 Pass the Heron Island Wildlife Preserve.

5.8 Take the US 52 underpass to the Lafayette Municipal Golf Course.

6.5 Reach McAllister Park.

9.3 Cross the John T. Myers Bridge.

9.5 Go left at Myers Bridge fountain; turn left at the first opening and then right at a T on the paved trail.

9.7 Trail junction; take the left fork and follow the trail 3.3 miles to Fort Ouiatenon.

13.0 Arrive at Fort Ouiatenon, trail's end.

27 PORTLAND ARCH NATURE PRESERVE

WHY GO?
This short loop trail has several creek crossings.

THE RUNDOWN

Location: Southwest of Lafayette near Attica, west-central Indiana
Distance: 0.8-mile loop
Elevation change: Less than 50 feet
Hiking time: About 30 minutes
Difficulty: Moderate
Jurisdiction: Indiana Department of Natural Resources, Division of Nature Preserves

Fees and permits: No fees or permits required
Maps: USGS Stone Bluff; Portland Arch Nature Preserve brochure
Special attractions: Portland Arch, Bear Creek Ravine
Camping: No camping permitted
Trailhead facilities: Small gravel parking lot; no drinking water available

FINDING THE TRAILHEAD
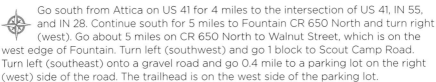
Go south from Attica on US 41 for 4 miles to the intersection of US 41, IN 55, and IN 28. Continue south for 5 miles to Fountain CR 650 North and turn right (west). Go about 5 miles on CR 650 North to Walnut Street, which is on the west edge of Fountain. Turn left (southwest) and go 1 block to Scout Camp Road. Turn left (southeast) onto a gravel road and go 0.4 mile to a parking lot on the right (west) side of the road. The trailhead is on the west side of the parking lot.

THE HIKE
Legend has it that following the confrontation between American soldiers and his Indian confederacy at the Battle of Tippecanoe in 1811, Shawnee chief Tecumseh sought refuge at this site. If true, it was a good hiding place. Bear Creek already had carved a deep but narrow channel through layers of rock when a small adjoining stream—Spring Creek—punched a hole in the sandstone to create a natural bridge.

A Boy Scout troop from Illinois owned the property from 1938 until 1966 when it was sold to The Nature Conservancy. The troop relocated to another site after a Boy Scout died accidentally when he fell off a cliff. So, be advised, stay on marked trails, and rock climbing is prohibited.

The archway that Spring Creek formed is the focal point of the North Trail hike, but it's not the only attractive feature of the state-protected nature preserve, which is listed as a National Natural Landmark by the US Department of the Interior.

Plant life is abundant in the moist ravine environment, where steep slopes host a mix of oak, hickory, and native white pine trees. Berry bushes, lichens, and mosses grow in the thin soil, and a variety of other plants cling to small crevices in the surrounding cliffs. This is the only place in the state where Canada blueberry grows.

The trail alternates between being rugged, muddy, steep, and level.

Begin the hike by passing through the fence opening at the west end of the parking lot to pick up an interpretive brochure at the registration box. Brochures are also on the DNR website at www.in.gov/dnr/nature-preserves/files/Portland_Arch.pdf.

Turn right (north) and begin a short walk toward the ravine before making a sharp descent at 0.1 mile. Cross a footbridge and continue downhill to Spring Creek at 0.2 mile. The trail turns left (west) beside a cliff, with Spring Creek on the right (north). Walk over two footbridges to reach the sometimes-muddy passageway beneath the arch.

Once through the archway, turn left (south) and follow the pathway beside the sandstone ridge to begin a fairly straight walk alongside Bear Creek. At about 0.6 mile turn left and climb uphill to a ledge along the east side of the ravine, eventually turning toward the east to return to the parking lot.

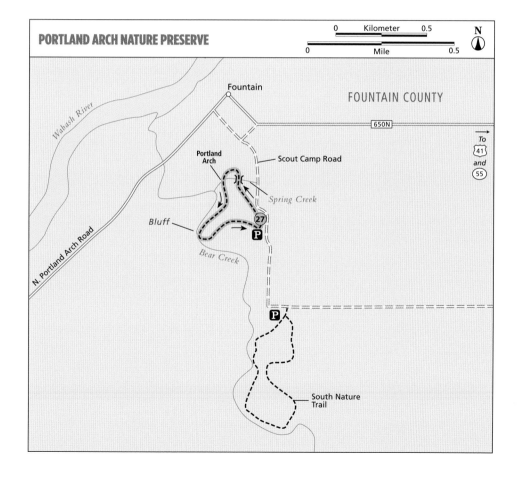

PORTLAND ARCH NATURE PRESERVE

Fountain

FOUNTAIN COUNTY

650N

To 41 and 55

Portland Arch

Scout Camp Road

Spring Creek

Bluff

Bear Creek

27

South Nature Trail

Wabash River

N. Portland Arch Road

MILES AND DIRECTIONS

0.0 Begin at the trailhead on the west side of the parking lot and go right.

0.2 Reach Spring Creek; turn left (west).

0.3 Reach Portland Arch.

0.6 Climb the rocky ledge on Bear Creek.

0.8 Arrive back at the trailhead.

OPTION

The 0.9-mile South Nature Trail is also available in the preserve. Access the trail by turning right (south) from the Portland Arch parking lot and going 0.3 mile to its parking area.

CENTRAL PLAIN

Among the various geographic regions in Indiana, this is the largest. It also gives the impression of being the most featureless area of the state. Nothing could be further from the truth.

Three unique properties in Indiana are located here—Shades State Park, Turkey Run State Park, and Pine Hills Nature Preserve. Each is marked by deep ravines, canyons, flowing water, and lush vegetation. Even the state capital, Indianapolis, has its share of scenic locations, including those along Fall Creek at Fort Benjamin Harrison State Park and at Eagle Creek Park on the northwest side. It's also home to two new hike descriptions in this book—Meltzer Woods and Shrader-Weaver Nature Preserves. Both display some of the last remaining old-growth woodlands in Indiana.

The area is bounded on the north by the Wabash River and on the south by a jagged line just below mid-state that marks the farthest advance of the last glacier thousands of years ago. Rolling plains and flat farmland typify most of the Central Plain, but Shades and Turkey Run, on the western edge of the region, are notable exceptions.

Sandy sediment was dumped here, at the mouth of the ancient Michigan River, and it solidified like cement. Later the exposed sandstone was carved and gouged by glacial meltwaters to create a maze of canyons and ravines.

Nearby Pine Hills further exemplifies the erosive power of water. Two small, winding creeks—Clifty and Indian—have sliced through the bedrock to create four narrow backbone ridges. The formations are 100 feet high and as much as 1,000 feet long. Devil's Backbone is a scant 6 feet wide at one spot.

The splendor of Shades, Turkey Run, and Pine Hills is unmatched in the state.

The trails in this section are presented in a clockwise sweep, heading south from Mounds State Park near Anderson to Shrader-Weaver near Connersville and Meltzer near Shelbyville, then west through Indianapolis toward Crawfordsville.

28 MOUNDS STATE PARK

WHY GO?
A loop trail passes prehistoric earthworks and ceremonial mounds.

THE RUNDOWN

Location: Near Anderson
Distance: 1.5-mile loop
Elevation change: About 70 feet from White River to the Great Mound
Hiking time: About 1 hour
Difficulty: Easy to strenuous
Jurisdiction: Indiana Department of Natural Resources, Division of State Parks
Fees and permits: Park entry fee, higher for out-of-state vehicles; season passes available

Maps: USGS Anderson South and Middletown; Mounds State Park brochure
Special attractions: The Great Mound and several smaller earthworks
Camping: 75 modern electric campsites in the park; youth camp area
Trailhead facilities: Large parking lot near the pavilion; water and restrooms located throughout the park

FINDING THE TRAILHEAD
From I-69 drive 1.1 miles north on IN 9. Turn right onto IN 232 and go about 0.75 mile to the Mounds State Park entrance on the left (northwest). Past the gatehouse, follow the main park road less than 0.1 mile to the pavilion parking lot on the left.

THE HIKE
As state parks go in Indiana, Mounds is a tiny one. At just over 290 acres, it is about one-tenth the average size of Indiana parks. With an annual average of more than 400,000 visitors, it ranks middle of the pack for all Indiana state parks.

Despite its size, the park has several attractions—picnic areas, a swimming pool and splashpad—plus the extensive earthworks and ceremonial mounds for which the park is named. These mounds are circular, fiddle-shaped, or rectangular and were constructed from about 160 BC to AD 50 by Adena and Hopewell peoples. The largest is the Great Mound, more than 1,200 feet around, 9 feet high, and 60 feet wide at the base. An archaeological excavation of the mound in the late 1960s uncovered bone awls, a ceremonial stone pipe, pottery shards, projectile points, and a log tomb.

The park also is purported to be home to pukwudgies (also spelled puk-wud-jies)—mysterious human-like creatures about 2 to 3 feet tall who wander the forest and are prone to mischievous behavior. Part of Delaware Indian folklore, pukwudgies and their alleged encounters with humans are the subject of a 1998 book by Paul Startzman that's available at the park's nature center. Park staff occasionally lead hikes to look for pukwudgies.

These trails get heavy use . . . usually from human hikers but maybe by pukwudgies too.

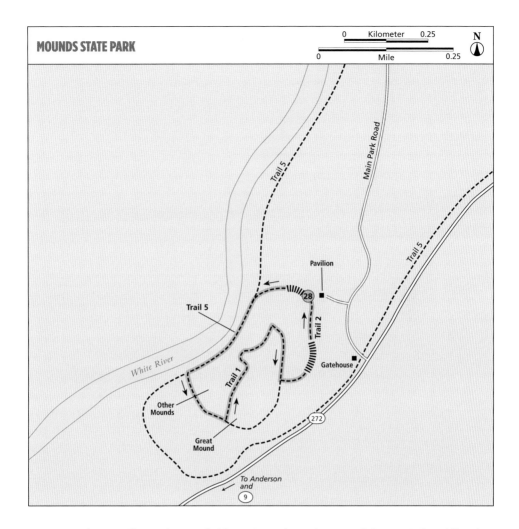

MOUNDS STATE PARK

0   Kilometer   0.25

0   Mile   0.25

N

Main Park Road

Trail 5

Trail 5

Pavilion

28

Trail 5

Trail 2

Gatehouse

White River

Trail 1

Other Mounds

272

Great Mound

To Anderson and

9

Crowds normally can be avoided by visiting the park on weekdays or in late fall and winter. People are not alone in swarming this small park. Mosquitoes can be a problem too, especially along the river portion of the trail.

Trail 2 begins across a grassy area behind the park's main pavilion. Cross a boardwalk, go down a wooden staircase and cross a small creek to reach the White River. At 0.2 mile, Trail 2 joins Trail 5, which circles the perimeter of the park. Turn left (south) and go 0.3 mile along the riverbank to where Trail 1 turns left (southeast); a bench sits at this junction. Trail 1 goes uphill to a plateau where the mounds complex is located. Here you will find the Great Mound, Fiddleback Mound, and other earthworks.

Between Fiddleback Mound and the Great Mound, at 0.7 mile, bear left (north) on Trail 1 for a winding walk along bluffs and around the high side of a ravine. Circle back to the intersection with Trail 2 (1.2 miles) near the northeast side of the Great Mound.

Turn left (east) at Trail 2 and cross a multitiered boardwalk and staircase above a moist ravine through which a small creek flows. At the end of the boardwalk, at 1.5 miles, enter the grassy area near the pavilion.

MILES AND DIRECTIONS

0.0 Begin at the trailhead behind the pavilion and go right.

0.2 At the junction of the boardwalk path (Trail 2) and Trail 5, turn left onto Trail 5.

0.5 At the trail junction turn left and go uphill on Trail 1.

0.7 Trail 1 continues behind Fiddleback Mound.

1.2 Trails 1 and 2 meet; turn left onto Trail 2 (boardwalk).

1.5 Arrive back at the pavilion and trailhead.

OPTION

The park has six trails. Trail 5, the longest, is a 2.5-mile loop around the outer edges of the park and past Circle Mound.

The Great Mound is 1,200 feet around and 9 feet high.

29 SHRADER-WEAVER NATURE PRESERVE

WHY GO?

A double-loop trail wanders through old-growth woodland designated National Natural Landmark.

THE RUNDOWN

Location: Near Connersville in east-central Indiana
Distance: 1.95 miles
Elevation change: 65 feet
Hiking time: About 1 hour
Difficulty: Easy to moderate
Jurisdiction: Indiana Department of Natural Resources, Division of Nature Preserves

Maps: USGS Connersville; DNR Nature Preserves interpretive brochures
Fees and permits: No fees or permits required
Special attractions: Several ancient trees estimated at 250 years old or older; spring wildflower outburst
Camping: No camping permitted
Trailhead facilities: Parking only

FINDING THE TRAILHEAD

From US 40 in Cambridge City go south 5 miles on IN 1 through the town of Milton to Bentonville Road (also known as Fayette CR 700 North). Turn right (west) and go 4.4 miles to CR 450 West. Turn left (south) and go 1.6 miles to the preserve's trailhead parking lot on the right (west) side of the road.

THE HIKE

Shrader-Weaver Nature Preserve offers visitors a visual contrast between an old-growth upland forest and an area in transition from an old farm field into a lowland forest.

Think of it this way—one area was farmed and plowed; the other was left relatively undisturbed.

Separate loops of less than a mile each cover the two areas in the 100-acre site that was dedicated as a state nature preserve and National Natural Landmark in 1974. Laz and Edith Weaver gifted the property to The Nature Conservancy, which then transferred ownership to DNR Nature Preserves. The pioneer homestead beyond a fence west of the parking lot belonged to the Weavers' great-grandfather, Philip Shrader, who settled here in 1823 and built the home in 1830.

Despite its small size, the nature preserve represents a portion of Indiana's remaining 2,000 acres of old-growth forest, which the Indiana DNR defines as forests untouched by human presence or unnatural disturbance and containing trees 150 to 200 years old or older. Shrader-Weaver has numerous beech, oak, and tulip poplar meeting that age threshold and a couple of bur oaks that likely top 400 years.

The biggest concentration of large trees is on the Woods Trail loop. Although there are some mature trees in the Succession Trail loop, the difference between the two loops can be seen in their contrasting understory. The Succession Trail is thick with shrubs and secondary-growth trees that have emerged in the former farm field over the past fifty years. The Woods Trail is more shaded because of the mature canopy, making for an understory with smaller saplings and blanketed with wildflowers.

To see for yourself, head south from the parking lot to a double gate on a feeder trail that leads to the two loops.

At 0.2 mile, reach a "crossroads" of the loops. Feel free to sign in at a registration box or continue left (south) for a little more than a quarter mile to the start of the Succession Trail and another optional registration box.

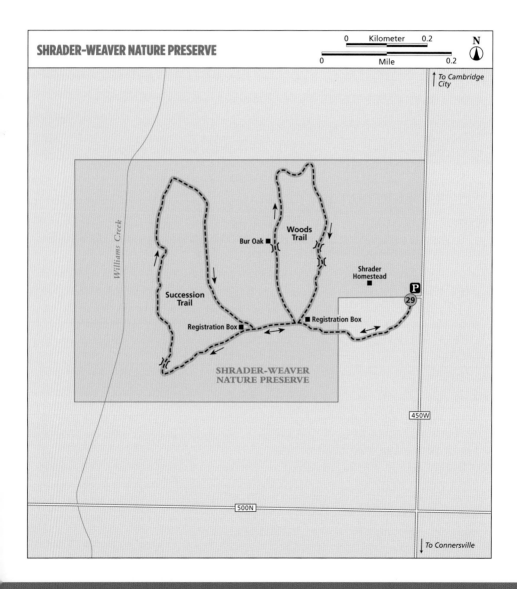

Lush understory surrounds a fallen tree at Shrader-Weaver Nature Preserve.

An interpretive brochure (available on the DNR website under Fayette County at www.in.gov/dnr/nature-preserves/publications) explains the transitional succession occurring here—farm field to forest—but you will be hard-pressed to find any of the interpretive marker posts on this loop. Either they have been removed or they are covered by vegetation. Regardless, what you can look for on a clockwise walk of this loop are the abundance of emerging trees, a bur oak that is over 5 feet thick, a massive Shumard oak that likely was part of the original forest, and a big white ash.

Go left (south) to begin the Succession Trail, which gets noticeably narrower over the next 0.1 mile before taking a sharp right turn for a northerly jaunt that parallels Williams Creek. Cross an L-shaped boardwalk built in 1989 by a Boy Scout to meet requirements for Scouting's highest rank, Eagle Scout.

At just under 1.0 mile the trail takes an almost 180-degree right-hand swing back to the east and eventually to the Succession Trail registration box.

Turn left (east) from here and head back to the "crossroads" to pick up the Woods Trail at 1.1 miles.

Go left (north) for a clockwise route of the Woods Trail to follow the numbered sequence of interpretive signposts, which are still in place, unlike on the Succession Trail.

This 28-acre old-growth section has countless tall, straight beech, tulip poplar, cherry, and oaks, but a bur oak at the No. 7 marker is the biggest tree in the forest with a girth approaching 6 feet. It is found to the left of a short footbridge that crosses a dry creek bed.

The apex of the Woods Trail is between trail markers 12 and 14 at 1.4 miles. Exiting the curve, head south for another quarter mile and then go downhill about 20 yards to a footbridge over a creek bed. Hit another smaller footbridge, head uphill, and return to the "crossroads" at 1.75 miles.

Turn left (east) and return to the parking lot.

MILES AND DIRECTIONS

0.0   Pass through a wooden gate to begin at the trailhead.

0.2   Reach the "crossroads" for the Succession Trail and Woods Trail; go left (southeast) for the Succession Trail.

0.3   Go left to begin a clockwise loop of the Succession Trail.

0.5   Reach the west end of the Succession Trail; make a sharp right turn (north).

0.8   L-shaped footbridge.

1.1   Complete the Succession Trail; turn left (east).

1.2   Arrive at "crossroads"; turn left (north) to begin Woods Trail.

1.4   No. 7 marker at massive bur oak.

1.6   First of two footbridges on Woods Trail.

1.75   Arrive at "crossroads"; turn left (northeast) to return to parking lot.

1.95   Arrive at parking lot.

30 MELTZER WOODS NATURE PRESERVE

WHY GO?
One of the few remaining stands of old-growth forest in Indiana.

THE RUNDOWN

Location: Northeast of Shelbyville in east-central Indiana
Distance: 1.3-mile loop
Elevation change: Minimal
Hiking time: About 30 minutes
Difficulty: Easy
Jurisdiction: Central Indiana Land Trust

Maps: USGS Rays Crossing, Waldron; Central Indiana Land Trust website (https://conservingindiana.org)
Fees and permits: No fees or permits required
Special attraction: National Natural Landmark with trees estimated to be hundreds of years old
Camping: No camping permitted
Trailhead facilities: Parking only

FINDING THE TRAILHEAD

From exit 119 on I-74 southeast of Shelbyville, take IN 244 East (also posted as CR E 200 S) for 1.5 miles to Shelby CR S 600 E and turn left. Go 0.4 mile to the trailhead parking lot on the right. The trailhead is across the road from the north end of the parking lot.

THE HIKE

A stroll through Meltzer Woods is akin to time travel, giving visitors a glimpse of what much of Indiana looked like before pioneer settlers moved in and began clearing land for farming and towns.

Alton Lindsey, a Purdue University professor, wrote in his 1969 book, *Natural Areas in Indiana*, that "although not the largest original forest in Indiana, Meltzer Woods is not surpassed as a museum-piece forest with particularly fine, large individual specimens."

Lindsey's survey documented forty trees measuring at least 30 inches in diameter, with the largest being a Shumard oak just shy of 65 inches. That was more than fifty years ago!

Lindsey noted that at the time of his survey there had been no cutting of live trees in the previous ninety years. Tack on the fifty-plus years since his research and much of this woodlot is pushing 150 years or more. Central Indiana Land Trust boasts that some of the trees date to the 1600s.

Ironically, original landowner Brady Meltzer operated a sawmill during the Depression but left these woods untouched and enrolled it in Indiana's Classified Forest Program in 1928.

The US Department of Interior designated the woods as a National Natural Landmark In 1974.

Central Indiana Land Trust purchased the site in 2014 with financial assistance from the state's Bicentennial Nature Trust, a funding program aimed at conserving land for public recreation in celebration of Indiana's 200th anniversary of statehood in 2016.

In May 2016 the Indiana Department of Natural Resources added Meltzer Woods to a growing list of state-designated nature preserves, forever protecting it from any development.

Meltzer Woods is two forests in one—a well-drained section and a wetter section.

After crossing CR S 600 E from the parking lot, enter an opening in the woods to reach the trail.

Go straight (west) for a counterclockwise route that will bring you back to the trail-head 1.3 miles later. Less than one-tenth of a mile into the drier section of Meltzer

Meltzer Woods' old-growth forest is a National Natural Landmark.

Woods, reach a footbridge over a drainage ditch that eventually feeds into Lewis Creek just east of Shelbyville. Cross the footbridge and continue straight to the second footbridge at 0.2 mile.

Turn left (south) when the trail reaches the west end of the preserve at 0.3 mile, then turn left (east) in a few yards. Metal signs with white arrows mark both turns. Continue straight, crossing footbridges at 0.4, 0.5, and 0.55 mile.

You're now in the wetter section of the forest, but the path stays dry with the aid of boardwalks in two places. The second boardwalk is long, with a combination of forty 4-foot and 8-foot sections.

Once off this lengthy boardwalk, it is less than a quarter mile back to the trailhead.

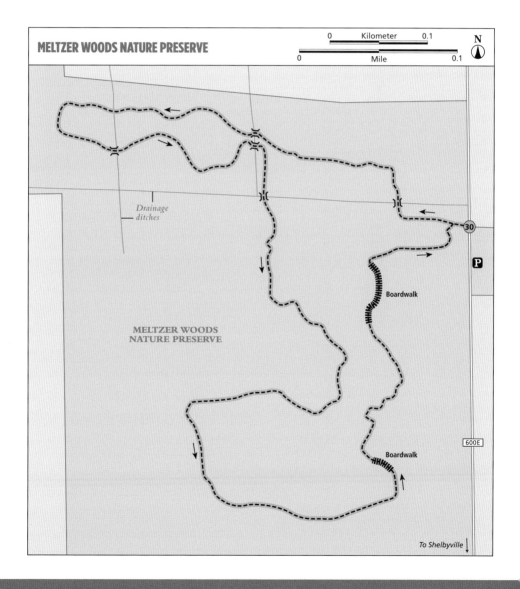

MELTZER WOODS NATURE PRESERVE

Kilometer
Mile
N

Drainage ditches

MELTZER WOODS
NATURE PRESERVE

Boardwalk

Boardwalk

30

P

600E

To Shelbyville

MILES AND DIRECTIONS

0.0   Begin at the trailhead informational sign.

0.05 Footbridge.

0.2   Second footbridge.

0.3   Trail turns left at arrow sign.

0.35 Trail turns left again at arrow sign.

0.4   Third footbridge.

0.5   Trail junction; stay right and cross fourth footbridge.

0.55 Fifth footbridge.

0.6   Turn left (north).

0.7   Boardwalk.

1.1   Longer boardwalk.

1.3   Arrive at trailhead.

31 **FALL CREEK TRAIL**

WHY GO?
A loop trail travels along the banks of Fall Creek and through woodlands of a former military base.

THE RUNDOWN

Location: Fort Harrison State Park, northeast Indianapolis, central Indiana
Distance: 2.2-mile lollipop loop
Elevation change: 75 feet
Hiking time: About 1.5 hours
Difficulty: Moderate
Jurisdiction: Indiana Department of Natural Resources, Division of State Parks
Fees and permits: Park entry fee, higher for out-of-state vehicles; season passes available

Maps: USGS Fishers and Indianapolis; Fort Harrison State Park brochure
Special attraction: Secluded woodland along Camp Creek
Camping: No camping permitted in park
Trailhead facilities: Large parking lot; modern restrooms nearby equipped with drinking fountains

FINDING THE TRAILHEAD

From I-465 take exit 40 and go 2 miles east on 56th Street to Post Road. Turn left (north) and drive 0.5 mile to a 3-way stop at the main park road. Turn left (northwest) and go to the park gatehouse. From the gate travel 0.7 mile to a T intersection. Turn right (east) and go 0.2 mile to the Delaware Lake Picnic Area parking lot.

THE HIKE
Fort Benjamin Harrison, or "Fort Ben," is one of Indiana's newer state parks, established in 1996 after the Indiana Department of Natural Resources acquired about two-thirds of the former military post from the US government. Fort Ben was dedicated in 1906 by President Theodore Roosevelt and was used by the military until its closure in 1991. It is named for Benjamin Harrison, who followed in his grandfather's footsteps by being elected US president.

The 1,700-acre state park contains several large tracts of hardwood forest, three small lakes, Fall and Lawrence Creeks, and a championship golf course. Low spots along Fall Creek can be muddy in wet weather. A popular urban park, Fort Ben drew more than 1 million visitors for the first time in 2021, many of them taking to the park's six trails.

To begin the Fall Creek Trail, leave the northeast corner of the main parking lot at the Delaware Lake Picnic Area and walk 0.25 mile on the crushed-stone path to the junction with the loop trail. Take the left (northeast) path, sticking to the south bank of Fall Creek as the trail passes through Warbler Woods Nature Preserve, one of four state-dedicated nature preserves in the park.

At 0.7 mile the connector trail from the paved Harrison Trace Bike Trail joins on the right (southeast) side. Continue straight (northeast) ahead for 0.1 mile to where the trail bends right (south). Climb an extensive wooden staircase system to reach a flat ridgetop and the highest point on the trail—about 75 feet above Fall Creek. Along the trail, look for signs of the former military post, including a sandbag bunker and concrete markers.

At 1.2 miles reach a gravel road that crosses the paved Harrison Trace Bike Trail at 1.4 miles. Walk through a series of small forest openings to Duck Pond and cross a small footbridge at 1.5 miles; reenter the woods on a gravel lane.

At 1.8 miles begin a downhill walk on the winding gravel lane to a quiet ravine containing Camp Creek. The area is home to some of the largest trees—oak, hickory, and maple—in the park plus a variety of wildflowers.

Cross the bike path one more time at 2.0 miles and turn left (southwest) at the connecting leg of the Fall Creek Trail to return to the parking lot.

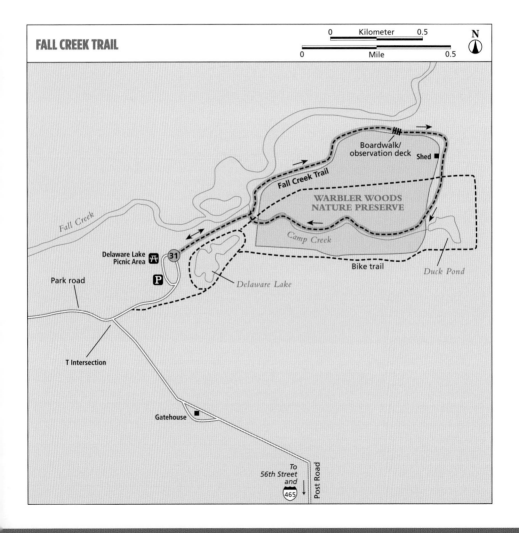

MILES AND DIRECTIONS

0.0   Begin at the trailhead at the northeast corner of the parking lot.

0.7   Reach the trail intersection and go straight (northeast).

1.2   Reach a gravel road.

1.4   Cross the Harrison Trace Bike Trail.

1.5   Pass Duck Pond and cross a footbridge to reenter woods.

1.8   Reach the gravel road; follow Camp Creek west.

2.0   Cross bike trail again and turn left (southwest) onto connecting leg of Fall Creek Trail.

2.2   Arrive back at the trailhead.

32 PINE HILLS NATURE PRESERVE

WHY GO?
A passage traverses two narrow backbone ridges above a deep gorge in the state's first dedicated nature preserve.

THE RUNDOWN

Location: Near Shades State Park, southwest of Crawfordsville
Distance: 1.8 miles of lollipop loops
Elevation change: 100 feet to Devil's Backbone
Hiking time: About 1.5 hours
Difficulty: Moderate to strenuous
Jurisdiction: Indiana Department of Natural Resources, Division of State Parks
Fees and permits: No fees or permits required

Maps: USGS Alamo; state park nature preserve brochure
Special attractions: Turkey Backbone, Devil's Backbone, Honeycomb Rock
Camping: No camping permitted on-site; camping available at Shades and Turkey Run State Parks
Trailhead facilities: Water fountain and pit toilet in the parking lot located across the road from the trailhead

FINDING THE TRAILHEAD

Go 7.5 miles southwest from Crawfordsville on IN 47 to IN 234 and turn right (west). Drive 6 miles to a gravel parking lot on the left (west) side of the road. Cross the road and climb over a stile to access the trailhead.

THE HIKE
Don't be fooled by the easy pace with which this trail begins. The deep gorge the entry trail leads to may be the most spectacular piece of natural landscape in Indiana.

Dedicated in 1971 as the first state nature preserve, Pine Hills presents perhaps the finest examples of "incised meanders" in the eastern United States. Glacial meltwater formed two meandering streams—Clifty Creek and Indian Creek—that carved two deep gorges through the bedrock, leaving four narrow ridges, or backbones, that rise 70 to 100 feet. The pathway over Devil's Backbone is a mere 6 feet wide, with a sheer drop-off on both sides. Caution should be used in this area.

In his book *Natural Areas of Indiana*, Alton Lindsey cited an Indiana Academy of Science report from 1933 stating that the backbones and streams at Pine Hills "without exaggeration . . . may be considered as the most remarkable examples of incised meanders in the eastern United States." Incised meanders occur when flowing water erodes the riverbed into the bedrock. A classic example of an incised meander is Horseshoe Bend on the Colorado River near Grand Canyon National Park.

Two other geologic features at Pine Hills are The Slide, a smooth patch on Clifty Creek created by constant rockslides, and Honeycomb Rock, a wall of sandstone where the two creeks meet.

There is more to the preserve than rocks, however. When the last glacier receded thousands of years ago, Indiana had a Canada-like environment in which white pine, hemlock, and Canada yew thrived. They remain as prominent features of the preserve.

Despite its uniqueness, the area did not avoid human intervention. Timber interests removed many large hardwoods in the 1850s, and in 1868 the Pine Hill Woolen Company dammed Clifty Creek and cut a notch in one of the backbones through which water flowed to power the mill. The business pulled out five years later, and the area has been mostly undisturbed since then.

That didn't stop the US Army Corps of Engineers from plotting in the early 1960s to build a reservoir that would have inundated this area. Opposition from the DNR and the public stopped the idea.

Part of Shades State Park, the Pine Hills site covers 480 acres. Portions of the trail are steep and hazardous, so proceed with caution.

An entrance trail begins at the stile on IN 234 and proceeds east along a gravel road for 0.4 mile to the Turkey Backbone. At the east end of the backbone, descend a set of

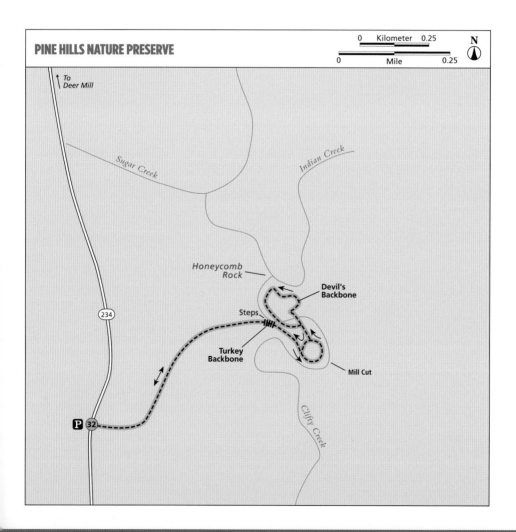

wooden steps to the floor of the gorge at 0.6 mile. Turn right (southeast) to make a loop along the banks of Clifty Creek past the old woolen mill site, the mill cut, and The Slide. At 0.8 mile the loop intersects the trail leading to Devil's Backbone. Bear right (north) at another trail fork at 0.9 mile. Take the right (northeast) fork and scramble up the steep slope to the east end of Devil's Backbone at 1.0 mile.

Use extreme caution in crossing the narrow, steep-sided ridge to a hemlock grove. Descend the western slope of the ridge to Honeycomb Rock, where the two creeks merge and flow north to Sugar Creek. Turn left and follow the path along Clifty Creek before crossing the creek to link up with the main trail near the base of Turkey Backbone. Climb the staircase to begin backtracking to the trailhead parking lot.

Note: Pine Hills Nature Preserve also can be accessed via a 1.5-mile trail (Trail 10) that begins at the Dell Shelter in Shades State Park.

MILES AND DIRECTIONS

0.0 Begin at the trailhead by climbing over the stile.

0.4 Reach the Turkey Backbone.

0.6 Arrive at the base of the gorge; turn right (southeast).

0.8 Turn right (northeast) at the trail fork.

0.9 Bear right (north) at the trail fork.

1.0 Reach the Devil's Backbone.

1.1 Arrive at Honeycomb Rock.

1.4 Reach the Turkey Backbone staircase. Climb the staircase and backtrack to the trailhead.

1.8 Arrive back at the trailhead.

33 RAVINE TRAILS

WHY GO?
A combination of loop trails follows the streambeds of rocky ravines.

THE RUNDOWN

Location: Southwest of Crawfordsville
Distance: 3.5 miles of lollipop loops
Elevation change: A drop of 150 feet from the trailhead to Sugar Creek
Hiking time: About 2 hours
Difficulty: Strenuous
Jurisdiction: Indiana Department of Natural Resources, Division of State Parks
Fees and permits: Park entry fee, higher for out-of-state vehicles; season passes available
Maps: Alamo USGS; Shades State Park brochure

Special attractions: Kintz, Frisz, and Kickapoo Ravines; Inspiration Point; Silver Cascade Falls; Devil's Punch Bowl
Camping: 101 non-electric campsites; 10 canoe sites and 7 backpacking sites; youth camp area
Trailhead facilities: Water spigot at trailhead parking lot, plus a pit toilet nearby; water supply and restroom facilities located elsewhere in the park

FINDING THE TRAILHEAD

From Crawfordsville go 7.5 miles southwest on IN 47 to IN 234 near Waveland. Turn right (north) and go 5 miles to where IN 234 curves to the right. Turn left (west) onto Montgomery CR 800 South, passing a "Shades State Park" sign. Go 0.8 mile to the entrance road to the park. From the gatehouse take the first paved road to the right (north) and go 0.4 mile to a parking lot northwest of Dell Shelter at the end of the road. The trail begins at a metal gate.

THE HIKE

Long before it became a state park in 1947, the dark, shadowy forest along the banks of Sugar Creek was called "Shades of Death." Stories vary on origins of the name, but the eerie legends it evoked led to its being simplified to "The Shades."

In 1887 a forty-room inn was built as part of a health resort on a hill just south of the Devil's Punch Bowl. The inn later closed due to fire damage, but Joseph W. Frisz gained financial control of the association that owned the surrounding property. Frisz protected the natural features while adding more land.

The park now covers nearly 3,500 acres and includes the adjacent Pine Hills Nature Preserve. The remote location of Shades and the popularity of nearby Turkey Run State Park make Shades an overlooked jewel in the state park system. Although fifth in size among Indiana parks, Shades is one of the least visited with annual attendance around 110,000 compared to an average for all Indiana state parks of almost 600,000.

Perhaps another reason for the park's relative lack of visitors is that hiking the trails here is a challenge, particularly along the ravine streambeds. However, Shades is popular with hard-core hikers despite—or because of—the challenge of rugged ravines. Most visitors congregate at the Devil's Punch Bowl and Silver Cascade Falls, where the multitiered wooden staircases reduce the difficulty of the steep climbs. Trail sections that follow ravine streambeds can be wet and hazardous after heavy rain. The following hike links Trails 1, 4, 5, and 7, traveling through four ravines and passing two scenic overlooks more than 200 feet above Sugar Creek.

Begin at the parking lot just north of Dell Shelter, site of the old inn. Pass a metal gate on Trail 1 and go 0.1 mile to a wood deck above the Devil's Punch Bowl. From the deck, hike left (west) over two gullies on a pair of footbridges. Climb a set of stairs to a gravel road that circles Hickory Shelter. Turn left (west) onto the gravel road at 0.2 mile and follow markers leading to Trail 7, passing the starting points of Trails 5 and 4.

Turn right (north) at the Trail 7 junction at 0.4 mile to make a counterclockwise loop of Kickapoo Ravine. The narrow dirt path descends to Sugar Creek through a dense forest. Stairs aid the downhill walk in a couple places, including one set of eighty-five steps. Two sets of steps go uphill; take the left set to continue uphill through Kickapoo Ravine

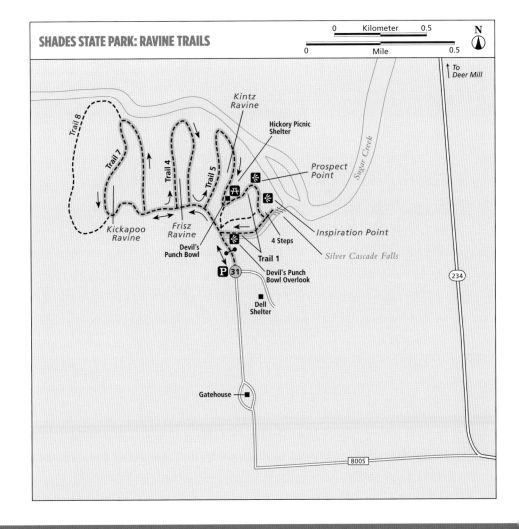

A hiker descends a staircase at Shades State Park.
INDIANA DEPARTMENT OF NATURAL RESOURCES

(the right set leads to Shawnee Canyon and Trail 8). Stay left (east) when the trail joins Trail 8 at 1.3 miles and return to the starting point of Trail 7.

Backtrack to the first Trail 4 marker at 1.4 miles and turn left (north) onto Trail 4, which begins as a wide gravel path leading downhill. Upon reaching Sugar Creek, turn right (east, then south) to Frisz Ravine, a more rugged uphill scramble than Kickapoo Ravine. The narrow passage of Frisz Ravine follows a streambed and requires climbing a staircase and two ladders in some of the roughest spots.

After exiting the top of the ravine at 2.0 miles, turn left (east) onto the feeder trail and go to the first Trail 5 marker. Turn left (north) and go downhill once more to Sugar Creek. Several sets of steps lead to the creek. Turn right (east, then right/south) at the creek and begin another scramble through Kintz Ravine. A set of stairs bypasses a small waterfall in Kintz Ravine.

Climb a ladder near the top end of the ravine and enter an open area near Hickory Picnic Shelter at 2.9 miles. Rejoin the feeder trail at a Trail 5 marker on the right (west) side of the shelter restroom and turn left (southeast) to backtrack to Trail 1. Follow Trail 1 uphill to the east side of the Hickory Shelter area and take the left fork of Trail 1 (northeast) to Prospect Point, the first of two overlooks high above Sugar Creek.

After passing the second overlook—Inspiration Point—at 3.0 miles, turn left and climb down the stairs to get a view of Silver Cascade Falls at 3.1 miles. At the base of the stairs, turn left (northeast) and take a spur trail about 30 yards to get a full view of the falls. Backtrack on the spur trail to the main trail and follow the creek through a sandstone canyon to get a ground-level view of Devil's Punch Bowl at 3.4 miles. A set of stairs leads up from the canyon to the wood deck. Backtrack from here to the parking lot.

MILES AND DIRECTIONS

0.0   Begin at the trailhead at the metal gate.

0.1   Reach the Devil's Punch Bowl overlook.

0.2   Turn left (west) on the trail to Trail 7.

0.4   Turn right (north) at the Trail 7 junction.

1.3   Stay left at the Trail 8 junction.

1.4   Turn left (north) at the Trail 4 junction.

2.0   Turn left at the trail junction.

2.1   Turn left at the Trail 5 junction.

2.9   Reach the Hickory Picnic Shelter.

3.0   Visit Prospect and Inspiration Points.

3.1   Go down the stairs to Silver Cascade Falls.

3.4   Reach the Devil's Punch Bowl. Climb the stairs up from the canyon and backtrack from the wood deck to the parking lot.

3.5   Arrive back at the trailhead.

34 TURKEY RUN STATE PARK

WHY GO?

A combination of park trails loops through canyons and along scenic Sugar Creek.

THE RUNDOWN

Location: Southwest of Crawfordsville
Distance: 3.0-mile loop
Elevation change: About 150 feet from the north bank of Sugar Creek to the ridgetops above the various canyons
Hiking time: About 2.5 hours
Difficulty: Strenuous
Jurisdiction: Indiana Department of Natural Resources, Division of State Parks
Fees and permits: Park entry fee, higher for out-of-state vehicles; season passes available
Maps: USGS Wallace; Turkey Run State Park brochure

Special attractions: Ice Box, Falls Canyon, Boulder Canyon, 140 Steps, Punch Bowl, Rocky Hollow, Wedge Rock
Camping: Campground entrance located about 0.5 mile west of the main park entrance on IN 47; 209 modern electric campsites; youth camp area
Trailhead facilities: Parking lot accommodates cars and buses; water available at the nature center and at other locations throughout the park; restrooms located around the park; no water supply or restrooms on the north side of Sugar Creek

FINDING THE TRAILHEAD

From Crawfordsville go 23 miles west on IN 47 to the Turkey Run State Park entrance on the right (north) side of the highway. Go about 0.25 mile from the gatehouse to the main parking lot near the nature center. The trailhead is on the north side of the nature center and leads to a suspension bridge that crosses to the north bank of Sugar Creek.

THE HIKE

Already popular with Hoosiers, Turkey Run State Park earned outside recognition in 2023 when TravelAwaits website named it the seventh-best state park in America, and *Midwest Living* magazine called it the best place in the Midwest for hiking.

It is easy to see why.

The sandstone cliffs of Turkey Run State Park had their origins 320 million years ago when the ancient Michigan River left behind sandy deposits as it spilled into a great inland sea. A few thousand years ago, postglacial streams carved the canyons that are distinguishing characteristics of the park. The retreating glacier also left two other notable features: boulders carried here from Canada and the eastern hemlock. A native species in colder regions of North America, this tree makes one of its rare Indiana appearances here.

Turkey Run was set aside as a state park in 1916. Pioneers are responsible for the name. Wild turkeys were abundant and known to congregate in the warmer canyon bottoms, or runs, during winter. Legend has it that the pioneers took advantage of the situation by herding the turkeys together for an easy hunt.

Turkeys still roam the park, as do white-tailed deer. Pileated woodpeckers are common. Warblers pass through during their spring and fall migrations, and turkey vultures have used the park as a winter roost since the late 1800s. The park contains sycamore, walnut, oak, and hemlock trees that are several hundred years old. Wildflowers are abundant, and more than half the varieties of mosses and lichens in the state can be found here. The park is bisected by scenic Sugar Creek, considered one of the cleanest streams in Indiana. The fish population of the creek is quite diverse, including seven different species of darters, further evidence of a clean, cool aquatic environment.

The spectacular nature of the sandstone canyons and their accessibility are major factors in the popularity of the state park. Although smaller than neighboring Shades State Park, Turkey Run draws eight times as many annual visitors and usually ranks among the top five most-visited parks in the system. Trails can be jam-packed on weekends, especially at features north of the suspension bridge. At the busiest times, waiting lines form to pass through some areas, but the scenery and the challenge are worth it.

There are eleven trails in the park, and elements of three are included in the following description that is almost entirely within the park's Rocky Hollow–Falls Canyon Nature Preserve.

To begin, follow the path from the north side of the nature center and cross the suspension footbridge at Sugar Creek to a Trail 3 marker on the north bank. Turn left (west); climb over a large rock formation and then over a boardwalk. A gravel path leads uphill to a platform overlook above Sugar Creek. The trail descends from here across a footbridge and downhill over stone steps to the Ice Box, an eroded opening in the cliff at 0.2 mile.

Continue west along Sugar Creek, walking over a couple of footbridges and through virgin forest featuring gigantic beech and walnut trees. Where Trails 3 and 5 intersect at 0.6 mile, continue straight (west) on Trail 5. Hike along the creek through pine and hemlock stands to where Trails 5 and 9 intersect in a hemlock grove. Go straight (west and north) on Trail 9 to the first of two ravines at 0.9 mile. Falls Canyon, a moss- and fern-covered ravine, follows the creek bed uphill to wooden steps that lead to a ridgetop. At 1.2 miles head downhill on wooden steps to Boulder Canyon. Passing through this canyon requires climbing over large boulders and exposed tree roots.

Stone steps lead out of the canyon to an upland forest. Head right (east) from the canyon across a broad ridge to a wooden staircase with sixty-four steps. At the junction with Trail 5, which comes in from the right (south), stay left (east) and go about 0.1 mile to "140 Steps" at 1.8 miles. This stone staircase descends to the end of Trail 5 at its junction with Trail 3 and a set of ladders at the north end of Bear Hollow. Skip the ladders and stay left (northeast) on Trail 3, passing through a canyon and streambed before climbing over a ridge to the first of two junctions with Trail 10.

Go straight (north and then east) on Trail 3 and cross several footbridges and stairways to the second Trail 10 junction on the left (north). Go straight (east) on Trail 3 to the wooden steps leading into Rocky Hollow Canyon at 2.4 miles and the junction with Trail 4, which breaks off to the left (north). Go right (south) on Trail 3 and proceed through Rocky Hollow, passing the Punch Bowl—a pothole scoured by glacial boulders—on the left (east) side of the trail.

Slip through narrow passages in which you can either walk through the stream or along a sometimes slippery ledge of sandstone. The canyon becomes wider and the walls steeper. Pass picturesque Wedge Rock on the left (east) side of the canyon before you arrive at the end of Trail 3 near the suspension bridge over Sugar Creek at 2.8 miles.

Punch Bowl is a popular stop on the ravine trails at Turkey Run State Park.
INDIANA DEPARTMENT OF NATURAL RESOURCES

MILES AND DIRECTIONS

0.0 Begin at the trailhead at the north side of the nature center.

0.1 Cross the suspension bridge and turn left (west) at the Trail 3 marker.

0.2 Reach the Ice Box.

0.6 At the junction of Trails 3 and 5, continue straight (west) on Trail 5.

0.9 Walk through Falls Canyon.

1.2 Arrive at Boulder Canyon.

1.8 Descend "140 Steps."

2.4 Reach Rocky Hollow Canyon.

2.8 Turn left to return to the suspension bridge.

3.0 Arrive back at the trailhead.

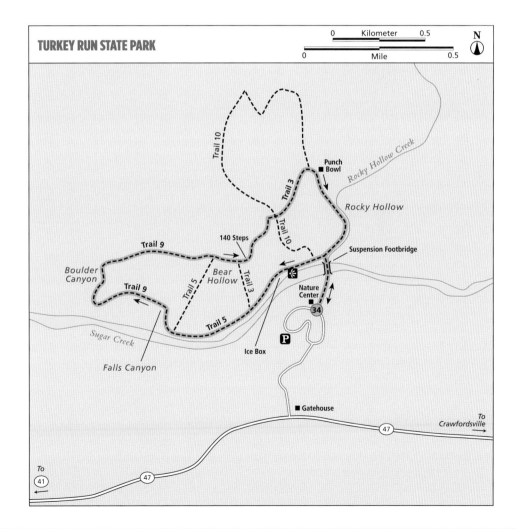

35 TALL TIMBERS TRAIL

WHY GO?

This trail skirts a bluff before looping through a broad, deep ravine.

THE RUNDOWN

Location: Big Walnut Creek Nature Preserve near Bainbridge, west-central Indiana
Distance: 1.7-mile lollipop loop with spur
Elevation change: 90 feet
Hiking time: About 1 hour
Difficulty: Moderate
Jurisdiction: The Nature Conservancy; Indiana Department of Natural Resources, Division of Nature Preserves
Fees and permits: No fees or permits required
Map: USGS Roachdale
Special attractions: Rolling hills, deep ravines, large trees, and a bluff overlooking Big Walnut Creek
Camping: No camping permitted
Trailhead facilities: Gravel parking lot; no drinking water or restrooms

FINDING THE TRAILHEAD

 From its intersection with I-465 on the west side of Indianapolis, go west on US 36 for 21 miles to a stoplight in Bainbridge. Turn right (north) and go 1 mile to where the road curves right (east) and becomes Putnam CR 800 North. Go 0.5 mile to where the road curves left (north) and becomes Putnam CR 250 East. Go 1.5 miles, passing North Putnam High School, and turn right (east) at the first gravel road, Putnam CR 950 North. Continue for 1.4 miles, making several left and right turns to reach the trailhead parking lot on the right side of the road.

THE HIKE

If not for the perseverance of a few folks who recognized the unique qualities of this area, this site would be a large reservoir managed by the US Army Corps of Engineers. Instead, the few hundred acres that encompass the Tall Timbers Trail form a small part of the larger Big Walnut Nature Preserve, which stretches along this valley dug by the flowing waters of Big Walnut Creek.

The Corps of Engineers had plans to dam the creek to create a 1,000-acre impoundment, but conservation and environmental groups fought the idea and gained critical support when the National Park Service designated the valley a National Natural Landmark in 1968.

The designation was granted for a variety of reasons. The area was formed by glacial melt and postglacial water erosion, producing an environment where plant species flourish that are otherwise rare in Indiana—most notably eastern hemlock and Canada yew trees. Some of the largest hemlock trees in the state can be found on north-facing slopes; and large beech, walnut, and oak trees are sprinkled throughout the preserve. Wildflowers are abundant as well, and the area is considered a treasure trove for birders.

Piece by piece, The Nature Conservancy and the IDNR Division of Nature Preserves have worked with private landowners to assemble a 3,000-acre tract known as the Big Walnut Creek Natural Area.

Begin the Tall Timbers Trail on the south side of the parking lot near a registration box. The trail splits a wide buffer zone between a farm field to the right (west) and the gravel road to the left (east) before reaching a wooden trail post. Turn left (southeast), hike in a short clockwise sweep, and come to a wooden bridge at 0.1 mile. After going over the bridge, turn left (south); cross a utility corridor, reenter the woods, and continue straight (southeast).

At 0.3 mile reach a bluff that provides a dramatic view from 100 feet above Big Walnut Creek. Pause for a moment to soak up the scenery before continuing as the trail

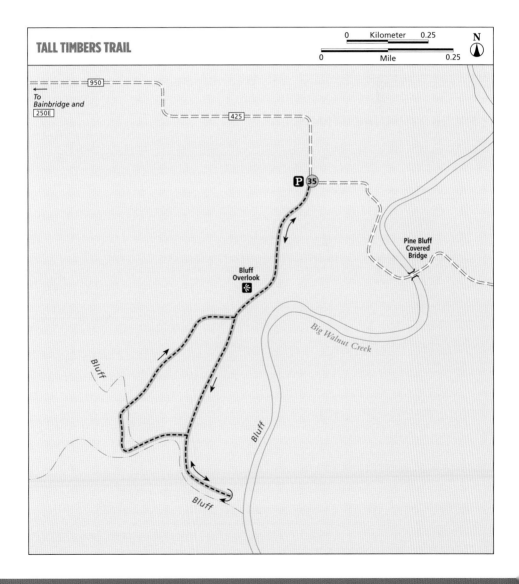

curves right (southwest) and comes to a trail junction with the inbound loop. Go straight (southwest) and come to a sign marking the entrance to Big Walnut Natural Area.

The 120-acre area was preserved for years by Eileen and Ralph Hultz (the log cabin where he was born in 1837 is still on the property) and later given in perpetuity to The Nature Conservancy by Jane H. and William L. Fortune on their fifty-fifth wedding anniversary.

Turn left (southeast) and descend to the point of a ridge leading to an overlook of Big Walnut Creek. Turn right (southwest) and continue downhill into a valley seemingly boxed in by bluffs on all sides. Cross a footbridge and two short boardwalks to reach a trail junction at 0.7 mile. Turn left (southeast) for a short out-and-back spur trail to Big Walnut Creek.

After returning to the trail junction, go straight (northwest) to a shallow creek whose branches must be crossed three times in the next 0.25 mile. Pick your way across this first creek crossing and turn right (northwest) before bending to the southwest and the second crossing. Descend a staircase at 1.1 miles; cross the creek one last time and climb the forty-five-step wooden staircase on the other side to return to high ground.

Back on the ridgetops, turn left (north) and continue back to the trail junction with the outbound loop. Turn left (north) and return to the parking lot.

MILES AND DIRECTIONS

0.0 Begin at the trailhead near a registration box at the south side of the parking lot.

0.1 Cross a wooden bridge and turn left (south).

0.3 Reach a bluff overlooking Big Walnut Creek.

0.4 At a trail junction go straight (southwest). When you complete the loop portion, you'll rejoin this main trail from the right.

0.5 Enter the Big Walnut Natural Area and turn left (southeast).

0.7 Reach a trail junction; turn left (southeast) onto a spur loop to Big Walnut Creek.

0.8 Return to the trail junction; go straight (northwest) to continue the loop trail.

0.9 Make the first of three creek crossings and turn right (northwest).

1.1 Descend wooden steps; cross the creek and turn left (north) to reach a wooden staircase.

1.3 Return to the first trail junction; turn left (north).

1.7 Arrive back at the parking lot and the trailhead.

SOUTHEAST

Diversity is the calling card of this region of the state. Whether it is the rugged hills of Clark State Forest, the marshes and meadows of Muscatatuck National Wildlife Refuge, the waterfalls and deep canyon of Clifty Falls State Park, or the rivers and bluffs of Harrison-Crawford State Forest and O'Bannon Woods State Park, southeast Indiana has a bit of everything.

Much of this area escaped the influences of the last glacial advance, which accounts for the variety in landscape. The most recognizable feature is the Knobstone Escarpment, a steep slope that runs from the Ohio River at a northwest angle for more than 100 miles. The ridge separates two land features—the Norman Upland to the west and the Scottsburg Lowland to the east. The Southeast region chapter of this book encompasses both areas.

This chapter includes hikes in several of Indiana's state forests, which were established in the early 1900s to rebuild what had been ravaged during pioneer settlement. The initial intention of the Indiana legislature, which created a State Forestry Board in 1901, seemed to be directed toward ensuring Indiana's place in the timber industry. The goals were twofold—to preserve remnants of Indiana's once-great forests and to explore methods of reforestation. Purdue University in West Lafayette began offering courses in forestry management in 1905, and Charles C. Deam was named the state's first forester in 1909.

Clark State Forest, located southwest of Scottsburg, was established in 1903. It initially covered 2,000 acres but now exceeds 25,000 acres. Harrison-Crawford State Forest, located west of Corydon, was established in 1926 and has 24,000 acres within its boundaries, including O'Bannon Woods. Both forests, along with Jackson-Washington State Forest to the north, are primarily of hardwoods with occasional stands of white pine.

The Indiana Department of Natural Resources Division of Forestry still operates with its original primary mission of managing sustainable forests, but it also has embraced many recreation opportunities, including hiking, camping, hunting, fishing, and horseback riding.

Clifty Falls, outside Madison, was dedicated as a state park in 1920. Five waterfalls splash over the cliffs of the 3-mile-long canyon. The four primary falls—Big Clifty, Little Clifty, Hoffman, and Tunnel Falls—range from 60 to 83 feet high. The exposed limestone and shale through the canyon is among the oldest bedrock in the state—425 million years old.

John Brough, a local railroad company owner, tried to take advantage of the canyon and its access to the Ohio River during the 1850s. Brough attempted to build two tunnels through the canyon for a rail system. It was a financial failure that became known as Brough's Folly. You can walk through one of the tunnels off Trail 5 from May 1 to October 31, but it is closed from November 1 through April 30 to protect hibernating bats.

Muscatatuck National Wildlife Refuge may lack the geographic splendor of Clifty Falls, but it certainly makes up for it in other ways. A variety of wildlife species make the refuge a year-round home, while hundreds of migratory bird species pass through during spring and fall migrations. Whooping cranes have been high-profile visitors in recent years as part of an effort to reintroduce an eastern population of the giant bird that migrates seasonally between nesting sites in Wisconsin and wintering grounds in Florida.

Hikes in this section are presented heading south in a clockwise sweep from Muscatatuck National Wildlife Refuge near Seymour toward the Ohio River.

36 MUSCATATUCK NATIONAL WILDLIFE REFUGE: TURKEY AND BIRD TRAILS

WHY GO?

A double loop trail wanders through woodlands and along a marsh.

THE RUNDOWN

Location: Muscatatuck National Wildlife Refuge, near Seymour, Jackson County
Distance: 1.8-mile lollipop loop
Elevation change: Minimal
Hiking time: About 1 hour
Difficulty: Easy
Jurisdiction: Muscatatuck National Wildlife Refuge; US Fish & Wildlife Service

Maps: USGS Chestnut Hill; refuge brochure and trail information sheet
Fees and permits: No fees or permits required
Special attractions: Wood Duck pond, Moist Soil Unit 2
Camping: No camping permitted
Trailhead facilities: Parking only

FINDING THE TRAILHEAD

 From I-65 near Seymour, go 2 miles east on US 50 to the Muscatatuck National Wildlife Refuge entrance on the right (south) side of the road. Go 1.8 miles on the main refuge road to the refuge's second interior road. Turn right (west). The trailhead parking lot is on the right (north).

THE HIKE

Muscatatuck is the first national wildlife refuge to be established in Indiana and one of more than 500 across the country whose purchase was funded by revenue from the sale of federal duck stamps required to hunt waterfowl.

Land acquisition at Muscatatuck began in 1966 and encompasses more than 7,800 acres of varied habitat providing sanctuary for an abundance of wildlife. Birds are particularly noteworthy inhabitants, with more than 250 species observed at the refuge, including birds uncommon in Indiana, such as the least bittern, great egret, and yellow-crowned night heron.

The National Audubon Society has named Muscatatuck one of 113 continentally Important Bird Areas in the country.

Muscatatuck also has been a stopover for whooping cranes. Young "whoopers" have been raised at a national wildlife refuge in Wisconsin and led by ultralight plane through Indiana to another refuge in Florida.

Spring and fall bring other migrating waterfowl to Muscatatuck by the thousands. Sandhill cranes, ospreys, and bald eagles can be seen during the fall. Deer, wild turkeys, rabbits, beavers, muskrats, quail, and raccoons are common; and Muscatatuck was the launch site in recent years of restoration efforts for river otters and trumpeter swans. Another refuge inhabitant is the nonvenomous northern copperbelly water snake, so rare nationwide that the US Fish & Wildlife Service lists it as a threatened species.

There are three other maintained hiking trails at the refuge, but most are less than 1.0 mile long. There doesn't appear to be any specific reason for naming the Turkey and Bird Trails, other than the fact that birds of all sorts, including wild turkeys, make the refuge their home or a stopover during migration.

Begin the trail to the right of an informational sign. At 0.1 mile turn right for the outbound leg of the Turkey Trail, which travels through a pine-and-hardwood forest with glimpses of a pond, wetland, and creek. Pause at the pond and look for wood ducks.

At 0.6 mile the Turkey Trail connects to the Bird Trail, which loops through a cedar-and-hardwood forest before curving to the left to pass alongside a large, rectangular pond labeled on the refuge map as "Moist Soil Unit 2."

Reconnect with the Turkey Trail at 1.3 miles; turn right and cross a boardwalk that extends 125 yards.

At 1.7 miles complete the Turkey Trail at the spur leading back to the parking lot.

MILES AND DIRECTIONS

0.0   Begin at the trailhead on the right at an informational sign.

0.1   Junction with the outbound Turkey Trail; turn right.

0.6   Junction with the outbound Bird Trail; turn right.

A sign for Muscatatuck National Wildlife Refuge

1.3 Junction with the inbound Turkey Trail; stay straight.

1.4 Cross a boardwalk.

1.7 Complete the Turkey Trail loop; turn right to return to the trailhead.

1.8 Arrive back at the trailhead.

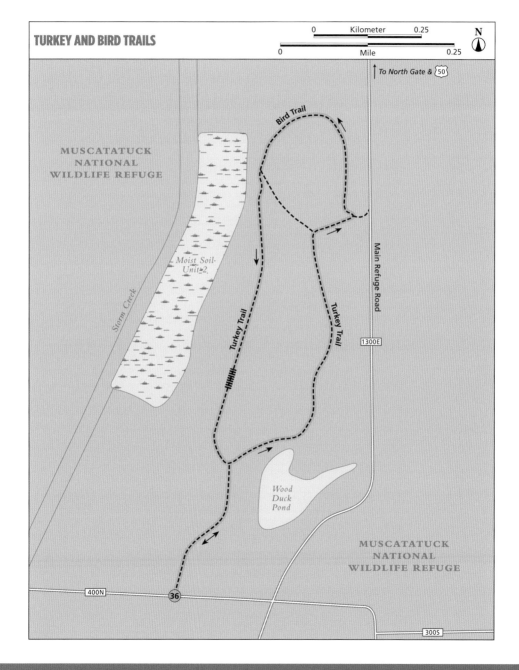

37 VERSAILLES STATE PARK

WHY GO?

A loop trail circles upland woods, ravines, and sinkholes along the eastern bluff of Laughery Valley.

THE RUNDOWN

Location: Southeast Indiana, 24 miles north of Madison
Distance: 2.25-mile loop
Elevation change: One climb of 80 feet
Hiking time: About 1.5 hours
Difficulty: Easy to moderate
Jurisdiction: Indiana Department of Natural Resources, Division of State Parks
Fees and permits: Park entry fee, higher for out-of-state vehicles; season passes available

Maps: USGS Milan; Versailles State Park brochure
Special attractions: Overlook of Laughery Valley, sinkholes
Camping: 220 modern electric campsites; 9 equestrian campsites; youth tent area
Trailhead facilities: Ample parking and restrooms available at Oak Grove Shelter but no potable water; water available at other locations in the park, including the campgrounds, nature center, and camp store

FINDING THE TRAILHEAD

Go east from Versailles for 0.8 mile on US 50/IN 129 to the entrance road to the state park. Turn left (north) and drive 0.7 mile to the gatehouse. Go straight for 0.4 mile and turn right (east) toward the campgrounds. Go 0.6 mile to the Oak Grove Shelter parking lot and turn left (northwest). The trailhead is located on the west side of the shelter house.

THE HIKE

Much of present-day Versailles State Park was marginal farmland when the National Park Service acquired it in the 1930s with intentions of making it a national park. The NPS teamed with the Civilian Conservation Corps (CCC) to develop the property into the Versailles Recreation Demonstration Area before turning it over to the State of Indiana in 1943.

The state's second-largest park at just under 6,000 acres, Versailles is largely undeveloped, with much of the facilities centralized on Versailles Lake except for 24 miles of mountain bike trails in the northern half of the park.

There are four hiking trails in the park, including Trail 1, aka the Old Forest Trail, which is described here. Because there are so few hiking trails in Versailles (which, by the way, Hoosiers pronounce Ver-SALES), they get plenty of use. There is less traffic on this trail because the others are closer to the restrooms. Day hiking is also permitted on 25 miles of bridle trails and the mountain bike trails.

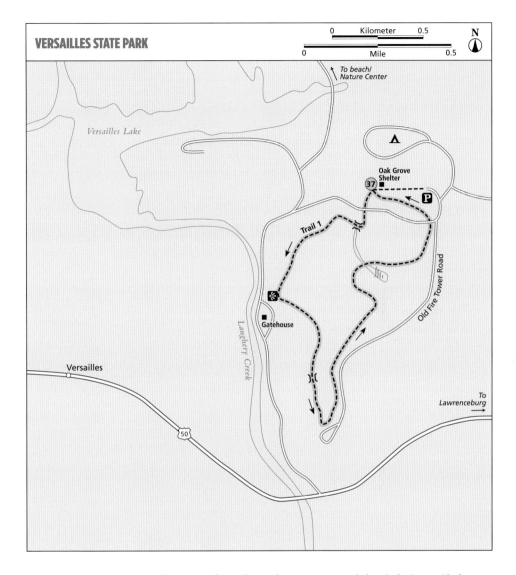

Begin the hike by walking west from the parking area toward the Oak Grove Shelter, one of the original contributions constructed by the CCC. Locate the trail marker off the southwest corner of the building. Descend the hill to the south and cross a footbridge, then the park road. On the opposite side of the road, walk up the ravine and then turn east to cross another footbridge.

Hike uphill out of the ravine and turn south again. It is about an 80-foot climb. Once on top of the ridge, begin looking along the left (east) side of the trail for some of the numerous sinkholes that are sprinkled throughout the woods, or look right and soak up the view of Laughery Valley. Laughery, also the name of the creek below and to the west, is a misprint that has endured. The creek was named for Col. Archibald Lochry, who was killed with half his Pennsylvania volunteer army during a confrontation with Native Americans in 1781. Roughly eighty years later another moment in military history occurred here. In July 1863 Confederate Gen. John Hunt Morgan led a multi-day raid into Indiana during the Civil War before retreating to southern Ohio where he and his troops were captured.

Continue the trail by crossing another bridge and heading uphill. Reach the southern tip of the trail at 1.2 miles near an access path that leads to a parking area at the end of Old Fire Tower Road. The trail turns north at this point and follows a level course for nearly 0.5 mile before dropping down into a ravine that features a picturesque little waterfall. Hike up the other side of the ravine onto a flat area before dropping down once more as the trail intersects the park road. Cross the road, turn left (west) on the trail, and follow it for 0.25 mile parallel to the park road to the Oak Grove Shelter.

MILES AND DIRECTIONS

0.0 Begin at the trailhead at the west side of the shelter house, going south then east (right).

0.7 Reach the Laughery Creek overlook.

1.2 The trail turns north.

2.0 Go straight at the road crossing, and then turn left.

2.25 Arrive back at the trailhead.

38 CLIFTY FALLS STATE PARK

WHY GO?

A combination of park trails forms a loop hike above and through Clifty Falls Canyon.

THE RUNDOWN

Location: Near Madison, southeast Indiana
Distance: 10.5-mile loop
Elevation change: About 400 feet
Hiking time: About 5 hours
Difficulty: Strenuous
Jurisdiction: Indiana Department of Natural Resources, Division of State Parks and Division of Nature Preserves
Fees and permits: Park entry fee per vehicle, higher for out-of-state vehicles; season passes available
Maps: USGS Clifty Falls and Madison West; Clifty Falls State Park brochure

Special attractions: Ohio River overlook; Hoffman, Big Clifty, Little Clifty, Tunnel Falls
Camping: 104 modern electric campsites, 63 non-electric sites; youth tent area
Trailhead facilities: Parking lot and nature center (open 10 a.m. to 4 p.m. daily in summer; 10 a.m. to 4 p.m. Wed through Sun in winter); restrooms and potable water sources available throughout the park at picnic shelter locations

FINDING THE TRAILHEAD

Clifty Falls State Park has gatehouses at the north and south ends. From US 421 in downtown Madison, go 2 miles west on IN 56 to reach the south entrance. From the south gatehouse go 1.1 miles and turn left into the nature center parking lot. To reach the north entrance from US 421 in Madison, go 3.8 miles west on IN 62. From the north gate go 4.2 miles on the main park road and turn right to the nature center parking lot. Trail 1 begins at the south end of the parking lot.

THE HIKE

Most highlights of Clifty Falls State Park can be seen by combining elements of eight of the park's ten trails for a trek into and around the park's rocky canyon. In doing so, you will pass five waterfalls, walk a rock-strewn portion of Clifty Creek, and see the sheer-walled canyon from both above and below.

The canyon is more than 400 feet deep and so narrow in places that it is said sunlight can only reach the canyon floor at noon. Because the Trail 2 portion of this hike is along the streambed of Clifty Creek, it is a rugged hike with difficult footing and some steep climbs. Traffic is heaviest around Hoffman, Big Clifty, and Little Clifty Falls, but it is noticeably lighter on Trail 8 along the west rim of the canyon.

Trail access has changed considerably in recent years, partly due to safety factors and partly due to ecological considerations. A staircase at Big Clifty Falls that once was an exit and entry point for Trail 2 no longer exists. But it is still possible to loop through and around the canyon.

Begin hiking at the nature center on Trail 1. Head south toward the Ohio River, coming to an observation tower at 0.2 mile. The tower provides a spectacular view of the Ohio and the nearby river town of Madison.

From the tower head north on Trail 1 as the trail enters the canyon, hugging a ledge about midway between the top of the canyon and Clifty Creek below. The trail narrows and crosses a couple of footbridges over areas wet with water seeping from the shale and limestone that, at 425 million years old, is among the oldest exposed bedrock in the state.

At 0.5 mile Trail 1 joins Trails 2 and 3 at a three-way fork. Take Trail 3, the middle fork, and continue along the ledge toward Hoffman Falls—at 78 feet the park's third-highest waterfall. At 0.9 mile an unmarked trail breaks off to the left. Stay right, climbing up a steep grade over stone steps toward the canyon lip. Go east along the ledge for another 0.25 mile and cross a footbridge over Hoffman Branch to connect with Trail 4. The trail turns left (west) along the north side of Hoffman Branch and leads to a wooden walkway and platform that extends over the canyon to provide a clear view of Hoffman Falls.

Be advised that areas above, on, and below all of the park's waterfalls are strictly off-limits.

Continue away from the falls on Trail 4 with the canyon to the left of the trail. At 1.5 miles Trail 5 cuts right (north) but go left (south) on a downhill path marked "To Trail 2." This link is steep—a 150-foot drop to the canyon floor in the span of about 0.1 mile.

At the bottom of the canyon turn right (north) to begin a rugged 1.5-mile stretch over loose rocks and running water in Clifty Creek to reach the base of Big Clifty Falls. About two-thirds of the way there, you will first pass Trail 5's entry point and then Dean's Branch, both on the right (east) side of Clifty Creek.

The best sign that the falls are getting closer is the size of the rocks in the stream. They are much bigger, some as big as a compact car. Just before you reach Big Clifty Falls, a branch of Little Clifty Creek breaks off to the right (east). Stay left to get a look at Big Clifty Falls from below.

Backtrack along Big Clifty Creek for 0.5 mile to the Trail 5 junction. Turn left (east) and follow the switchback uphill toward Oak Grove Shelter. Turn left (northeast) before reaching the shelter and continue Trail 5 to an overlook of Tunnel Falls, the tallest falls in the park at 83 feet. From there turn left to reach the main park road. Turn left (northeast) and walk the roadway in a counterclockwise sweep for 0.75 mile to the Hickory Grove parking area and the start of Trail 6.

At 5.3 miles connect with Trail 7. Go left for a spectacular overlook of Little Clifty and Big Clifty Falls before taking a 100-yard jaunt to the Clifty Shelter Picnic Area. The shelter house is the last water source before heading out on the return leg to the nature center.

Turn left on the paved road and follow it north toward the north gatehouse to pick up Trail 8, which is in a clearing west of the gatehouse at 6.0 miles. Cross Big Clifty Creek below a bridge on IN 62 and turn southward as the trail hugs the west rim of the canyon for the next 4.5 miles.

Before reaching Big Clifty Falls, look across to the east side of the creek to see an abandoned stone building. This pumphouse, built by the Civilian Conservation Corps (CCC) nearly ninety years ago, created a reservoir for a water supply for the CCC during their work to develop the park. The building thus has historical significance but cannot

Hikers under Big Clifty Falls at Clifty Falls State Park. Big Clifty is one of five major falls in the park.

be restored, since it now rests in a state nature preserve that encompasses the area north of the falls.

The west-rim hike begins on a relatively flat grade but is punctuated by occasional cuts for small streams that spill and tumble down the canyon walls. Signs stating "No Hikers Beyond This Point" bear witness to the dangers of getting too close to the edge. Continue to ridge-hop to an intersecting trail at 7.0 miles that goes left (east) and down to the canyon floor. Stay straight (south), hugging the west rim, crossing a footbridge, and continuing south over humps and ridges of the canyon rim.

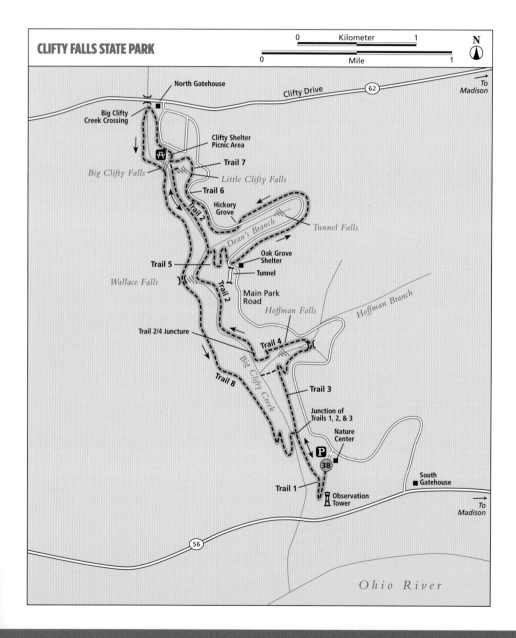

The trail begins to slide easily down from the rim and reaches a switchback at 9.5 miles that leads down to Big Clifty Creek. At 9.9 miles look for a sign hung across the creek by wire pointing to Trails 1, 2, and 8. Follow Trail 2 and begin the climb on the east side of the canyon. When Trail 2 joins Trail 1 at 10.0 miles, turn right (south) and continue uphill past the observation tower to the nature center parking lot.

MILES AND DIRECTIONS

0.0   Begin at the trailhead at the south end of the parking lot.

0.2   Reach the Ohio River observation tower.

0.5   At the intersection of Trails 1, 2, and 3, take Trail 3 (the middle fork).

0.9   An unmarked trail goes left; turn right.

1.4   Reach the Hoffman Falls overlook.

1.5   Turn left at the Trail 2 marker.

3.0   Arrive at Big Clifty Falls; backtrack on Trail 2.

3.5   Reach the junction with Trail 5; turn left (east).

4.0   Arrive at the Tunnel Falls overlook; go to the park road and turn left (northeast).

4.8   Reach the Hickory Grove parking area and Trail 6 trailhead.

5.3   Join Trail 7 to reach overlooks for Big Clifty and Little Clifty Falls; go north toward the park's north gatehouse to join Trail 8.

6.0   Trail 8 begins west of the park's north gatehouse.

7.0   An unmarked trail goes left; stay straight (south).

9.5   Make a switchback descent to Big Clifty Creek.

9.9   Reach a marker for Trails 1, 2, and 8 over the creek; follow Trail 2.

10.0 Trail 2 joins Trails 1 and 3; turn right onto Trail 1.

10.5 Arrive back at the trailhead.

39 CHARLESTOWN STATE PARK

WHY GO?

A loop trail travels through dense floodplain forest along exposed rock outcroppings above Fourteenmile Creek.

THE RUNDOWN

Location: Southeast Indiana on the Ohio River
Distance: 2.2-mile loop
Elevation change: Several elevation changes but never more than about 100 feet from the trail's beginning elevation
Hiking time: About 1.5 hours
Difficulty: Moderate to strenuous
Jurisdiction: Indiana Department of Natural Resources, Division of State Parks

Fees and permits: Park entry fee, higher for out-of-state vehicles; season passes available
Maps: USGS Charlestown; Charlestown State Park brochure
Special attractions: Fourteenmile Creek, Rose Island
Camping: 132 modern electric campsites, 60 full-hookup sites
Trailhead facilities: Water pumps located near the picnic shelters

FINDING THE TRAILHEAD

From the Henryville exit on I-65, go east 9.5 miles on IN 160 to its intersection with IN 403. Turn right (southeast) and go 0.8 mile to IN 62. Turn left (northeast) and go 1.1 miles to the Charlestown State Park entrance on the right (south). From the park gatehouse go 0.1 mile to a T intersection. Turn left (northeast) and go 1.1 miles to the Trail 1 parking lot.

THE HIKE

Established in 1996, this park has begun to catch on in popularity with the recent addition of modern campgrounds (including full RV hookups at sixty sites) and an award-winning boat ramp that provides access to the Ohio River.

The 5,100-acre park was carved from the larger Indiana Army Ammunition Plant (15,000 acres) that operated here from 1940 until closing in 1995. The area was farmed extensively prior to ownership by the US Army, which reforested the hills and valleys during its occupancy.

The beginning leg cuts at a northeast angle, then curves through the woods before descending toward Fourteenmile Creek. Depending on water levels in the creek, you are apt to catch sight of it before the trail takes a slow turn to the right (south). The creek winds through an unglaciated valley to the Ohio River. Locks and dams that control the Ohio River affect Fourteenmile Creek, giving it the appearance of a narrow lake rather than a flowing stream.

Once the turn is made at 0.9 mile, it is easy to see why the trail builders came this direction. The trail climbs along a narrower path, crosses a footbridge, and meanders through the high ground past moss-covered rock abutments. As you work your way up and down the east-facing slope of Fourteenmile Creek's valley, you'll pass several rock slabs that have sheared off the cliff and tumbled toward the creek. This can be the trickiest part of the trail during wet weather, which can transform the rich soil into slippery muck.

The trail curves southwest away from the creek, crossing another creek via a footbridge near the 1.5-mile mark amid a cedar thicket. Follow the trail as it swings back to the southeast below the ridgetop to a point overlooking Fourteenmile Creek. Here the trail curves back to the northwest on a 100-foot uphill climb over the next 0.25 mile.

The trail levels off at the 1.8-mile mark as it connects with the old service road. Look for the scattered concrete pilings that are remnants of the US Army era. It is a little more than 0.25 mile along a level grade to the Trail 1 parking lot.

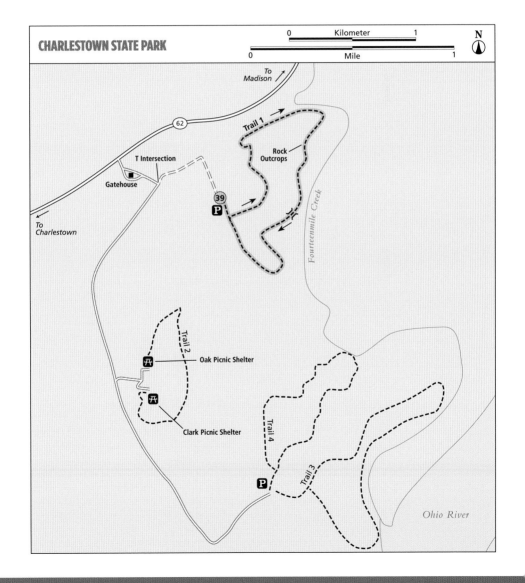

MILES AND DIRECTIONS

0.0 Begin at the trailhead and go northeast.

0.5 Make a right turn.

1.3 Pass rock outcrops.

1.5 Cross a footbridge over the creek.

1.8 Reconnect to the service road; go straight.

2.2 Arrive back at the trailhead.

OPTIONS

There are six other trails in the park. The most noteworthy is Trail 3, which features a steep 250-foot descent on a gravel service road to Fourteenmile Creek. The road leads to the Portersville Bridge which provides access to Trail 7—a 0.9-mile loop trail on Rose Island, where an amusement park and small zoo operated until a flood destroyed it in 1937. A small waterfall, rock outcroppings, and views of Fourteenmile Creek highlight the middle section of this trail before concluding with a gradual ascent to the parking lot.

40 ADVENTURE HIKING TRAIL

WHY GO?
A long-distance loop trail traverses forested river bluffs, ravines, sinkholes, and caves.

THE RUNDOWN

Location: Harrison-Crawford State Forest and O'Bannon Woods State Park, southeast Indiana between Corydon and Leavenworth

Distance: 23.8-mile loop (27.0 miles if starting and ending at Rock Creek trailhead)

Elevation change: 8 elevation increases of more than 200 feet, including 2 of 300 feet or more

Hiking time: 2–3 days

Difficulty: Strenuous

Jurisdiction: Indiana Department of Natural Resources, Division of Forestry and Division of State Parks

Fees and permits: Park entry fee at O'Bannon Woods State Park, higher for out-of-state vehicles; season passes available; no charge for parking at 3 trailheads in Harrison-Crawford State Forest

Maps: USGS Leavenworth and Corydon West; Adventure Hiking Trail map, available at state park or state forest office

Special attractions: Bluffs overlooking Ohio River, Blue River, and Indian Creek

Camping: O'Bannon Woods State Park—263 modern electric and 86 equestrian campsites. Backpackers can camp along the trail, which has 5 overnight shelters that are first come, first served.

Trailhead facilities: The Adventure Hiking Trail can be accessed at several spots, but the preferred starting location is the Pioneer Cabin Picnic Shelter near the south end of the park. Water is available in the O'Bannon Woods campgrounds and at other locations. It can be scarce along the trail though. Hikers often cache water where the trail crosses public roads prior to starting their hike but are expected to remove water containers after finishing the hike.

FINDING THE TRAILHEAD
From the intersection of IN 135 and IN 62 in Corydon, go west 7 miles on IN 62 to IN 462 and turn left (south). Immediately cross a bridge over the Blue River and continue for almost 6 miles through the state forest and the entrance to O'Bannon Woods State Park to reach the Pioneer Cabin Picnic Shelter. Some hikers will choose another trailhead (such as Rock Creek, just past the Blue River bridge) to avoid the park's entrance fee, but Pioneer Cabin Picnic Shelter is the recommended starting place for the Adventure Hiking Trail.

THE HIKE
There may not be a trail in Indiana that has undergone more changes and reroutes than the Adventure Hiking Trail. Hikers wanting to take it on need to be aware of its ruggedness and the fact that the bulk of the trail is in Harrison-Crawford State Forest, where

ongoing timber management can temporarily close or reroute significant sections of the trail.

A recent change moved the trail away from an old iron bridge that crosses the Blue River on the west side of the state park. The bridge once connected hikers to a longer version of the AHT, but the bridge fell into disrepair and provided a reason to close off an older north section of the trail.

Call the state forest office at (812) 738-7694 for trail updates. Hikers planning overnight stays should register their intent at the park's gatehouse or office.

The AHT can get the best of some hikers, who end up bailing somewhere along the route. For that reason, numbered (three-digit) signs are posted on the trail to assist safety personnel in locating anyone needing rescue.

Still, the AHT is a worthy entry that befits its name: adventure. Designated as a National Recreation Trail, the 23.8-mile loop offers a backpacking experience that takes a couple of days to complete, even for the most ambitious hikers.

Although most of the trail is on state forest land, recreational management duties belong to O'Bannon Woods State Park. The AHT also features several overnight shelter

A trail marker for the Adventure Hiking Trail

houses along the way. Primitive camping along the trail is an option as long as camp is made on public land, is at least 1 mile from all roads and recreation areas, and cannot be seen from the trail.

The AHT traverses terrain consisting of narrow ridgetops alternating with deep ravines, coupled with breathtaking views from bluffs 300 to 400 feet above the Ohio River and two of its tributaries—Blue River and Indian Creek.

With twelve climbs between 150 and 300 feet, the AHT typically takes two to three days to complete. It is marked with posts painted green and white and with numbers and letters designating specific locations along the trail. The trail is definitely rugged. Once poorly marked and confusing to follow, the AHT has benefited from trail maintenance in recent years. Traffic is usually highest around the Pioneer Picnic Shelter and the O'Bannon Woods campground, but overall the AHT gets a modest amount of use.

There are multiple trailhead options for the AHT, including three outside of the park property for those wanting to avoid the gate entrance fee. Others prefer the added security of parking vehicles inside the park.

The trail description begins at the Pioneer Cabin Picnic Shelter near the south end of the state park. From the picnic area, head left (northwest), and cross the park road to begin the first challenge—a 250-foot climb through the Mouth of Blue River Nature Preserve, a 470-acre parcel noteworthy for its combination of knobby hills, ravines, and bluffs. Atop the first climb, turn right (northeast) and follow the saddles that connect it to two more knobs.

At 2.5 miles the trail turns northwest as you near the O'Bannon Woods campgrounds and makes about a 270-foot descent over the next 1.9 miles before crossing a fire lane. On older maps, this is where the AHT crossed the Blue River on an old iron bridge.

From here, hike 1.7 miles along the edge of Blue River until climbing back uphill to a ridgeline that leads to the Hog Barn primitive shelter.

Leave the Hog Barn Shelter and continue northeast through Fox Hollow, a valley that once was home to several farms.

At 7.7 miles into the trail, the AHT reaches the Rendezvous Point near Greenbrier Knob Nature Preserve, one of three state-dedicated nature preserves inside the state forest. Hikers used to be able to turn off here and walk another 8.0 miles to Wyandotte Caves north of IN 62, but the current 1.7-mile spur leads only to Rock Creek trailhead, referenced previously as the starting point some use to hike the AHT.

Stay right (southeast) at Rendezvous Point and follow a ridgeline that rises gradually over the next 1.5 miles to a small gravel parking lot at IN 462 (9.2 miles). Cross the highway and resume the trail as it dips and rises as much as 250 feet over the next 2.0 miles to reach a crossing at Old Forest Road.

A small parking lot here is a popular place for stashing water.

The next stretch is almost a straight shot south, beginning with a steep descent before climbing to an extended section along a ridgetop leading to Indian Creek Shelter (14.2 miles). A sheer bluff overlooking Indian Creek 300 feet below is a good place to see turkey vultures and hawks as they soar near the cliff.

From there the trail descends gradually before skirting the high side of a ravine and passing several sinkholes. From a high knob descend a wide ravine on a southwest course and cross a creek before embarking on a climb of nearly 300 feet to the Old Homestead Shelter. It is located on a broad plateau at 18.5 miles and is built on the foundation of an 1860s-era log cabin belonging to the Deschamp family, who lived there until the early

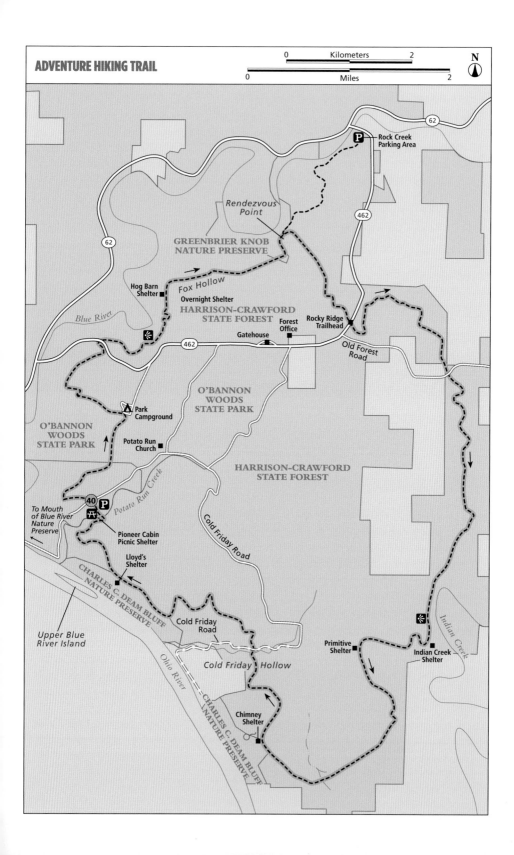

ADVENTURE HIKING TRAIL

Kilometers
0   2
Miles
0   2

N

Rock Creek
Parking Area

62

462

*Rendezvous
Point*

GREENBRIER KNOB
NATURE PRESERVE

62

Fox Hollow

Hog Barn
Shelter

Overnight Shelter

HARRISON-CRAWFORD
STATE FOREST

Forest
Office

Rocky Ridge
Trailhead

Blue River

462

Gatehouse

*Old Forest
Road*

O'BANNON
WOODS
STATE PARK

Park
Campground

O'BANNON
WOODS
STATE PARK

Potato Run
Church

HARRISON-CRAWFORD
STATE FOREST

Potato Run Creek

40

*To Mouth
of Blue River
Nature
Preserve*

Pioneer Cabin
Picnic Shelter

Cold Friday Road

Lloyd's
Shelter

CHARLES C. DEAM BLUFF
NATURE PRESERVE

Cold Friday
Road

Primitive
Shelter

Indian Creek

Indian Creek
Shelter

*Upper Blue
River Island*

Ohio River

Cold Friday Hollow

Chimney
Shelter

CHARLES C. DEAM BLUFF
NATURE PRESERVE

1900s. The original chimney is still standing, so the site may be listed on some maps as the Chimney Shelter. The spot is also referred to as French Hill and is on the edge of one of two sections of the Charles C. Deam Bluff Nature Preserve.

Go north from here for almost 0.5 mile before veering northwest to descend a broad ridge point into Cold Friday Hollow. Cross a creek and old Cold Friday Road (at 19.9 miles) in the hollow to reach a demanding stretch of the trail—three ridge and two ravine crossings in the span of just over 1.5 miles. The last climb curls southwest around a ridge point and into the second section of the Charles C. Deam Bluff Nature Preserve for arguably the most scenic stretch of the AHT along a steep bluff overlooking the Ohio River.

Lloyd's Shelter, aka the Ohio River Shelter on some maps, is located here at 22.4 miles. It is the last of the trail shelters and is considered the best since it is totally enclosed, with a wooden floor, windows, a door, and a roof.

Be sure to take in the scenic view of the Ohio River 400 feet below and perhaps see bald eagles that frequent the area, especially in spring.

Continue from the Ohio River/Lloyd's Shelter for another 1.4 miles to return to the Pioneer Cabin Picnic Shelter trailhead.

MILES AND DIRECTIONS

- **0.0** Begin at the Pioneer Cabin Picnic Shelter and head northwest across the main park road.
- **2.2** Approach the O'Bannon Woods State Park campground.
- **4.4** Cross fire lane.
- **5.8** Arrive at the Hog Barn primitive shelter.
- **7.7** Reach the Rendezvous Point and turn right (southeast). Going left will lead 1.7 miles to the Rock Creek trailhead.
- **9.2** Reach a small parking lot; cross over IN 462.
- **11.2** Uphill climb to Old Forest Road; cross the road.
- **14.2** Reach Indian Creek Shelter.
- **18.5** Reach the Chimney overnight shelter.
- **19.9** Cross Cold Friday Road.
- **22.4** Reach the Ohio River/Lloyd's Shelter.
- **23.8** Arrive back at the trailhead at the Pioneer Cabin Picnic Shelter.

41 KNOB LAKE TRAIL

WHY GO?

This loop hike, with a linear spur near the midpoint, includes climbs up some of the highest hills in the Jackson-Washington State Forest.

THE RUNDOWN

Location: East of Brownstown, south-central Indiana
Distance: 4.3-mile loop with spur
Elevation change: Difference of 345 feet between the trail's low and high spots
Hiking time: About 3 hours
Difficulty: Strenuous
Jurisdiction: Indiana Department of Natural Resources, Division of Forestry

Maps: USGS Tampico, Vallonia, and Seymour; Jackson-Washington State Forest brochure
Fees and permits: No fees or permits required
Special attractions: High Point Knob, Old Tower Site, Pinnacle Peak
Camping: Knob Lake Campground—54 non-electric campsites
Trailhead facilities: Pit toilets and drinking water available in the Knob Lake Campground

FINDING THE TRAILHEAD

 From its intersection with US 50 in Brownstown, go 2 miles east on IN 250 to the Knob Lake turnoff. Turn left (northeast) off IN 250 and follow the paved road. Pass the forest office and Knob Lake and continue past the Museum Shelter House (sitting on a hill above the lake) to a parking lot below the Civilian Conservation Corps (CCC) playground and Oven Shelter. Park in the lot and walk up the stone steps to the Oven Shelter. Walk to the south end of the playground to begin the trail.

THE HIKE

This hike combines portions of three trails and begins at a rather casual pace. But the last 3.0 miles are as challenging as it gets, with a string of high, round hills—or knobs—connected like a backbone. The Trail 1 portion gets more traffic than Trails 2 and 3, largely because of the attraction of Pinnacle Peak. All trails are well marked, well maintained, and easy to follow.

Begin at the CCC Shelter picnic area built by the Civilian Conservation Corps and placed on the National Register of Historic Places in 1997. Go to the southeast corner of the picnic area and continue along a wide gravel path until you reach the first trail marker. Cross a stone bridge at the north end of Knob Lake and turn right (east) at the Trail 3 marker. The trail curves to the right (southwest) and begins to climb nearly 100 feet to a ridge that runs southwest, gradually descending to a youth camp area.

At the camp take a left (east) turn onto the gravel road and follow it around to a service area at 1.0 mile before turning left at a Trail 2 marker. This is a transition point from the end of Trail 3 and the south terminus of Trail 2. Walk a short distance to the first Trail 2 marker and head northeast up a ravine along a meandering stream. Crisscross from one side of the stream to the other several times before turning away from the stream at 1.5 miles to begin the toughest part of the hike.

What starts as a gradual climb turns into a demanding scramble that rises more than 250 feet over the next 0.5 mile to a knob that is not the highest on the hike but is a pretty good warm-up. Over the next 1.0 mile, hike a series of six knobs, the second one, appropriately named High Point, at 2.5 miles. It is followed by the Old Tower Site at 2.7 miles, which is marked by the concrete footings of an old fire tower that was torn down years ago.

Turn right (north) from the Old Tower Site and proceed north, now on Trail 1, passing two points that intersect another trail (Trail 10). After the second intersection, skirt the east side of a knob and walk along a ledge that leads to Pinnacle Peak, an exposed face of loose rock that provides a spectacular scenic view to the south and east. From Pinnacle Peak (3.3 miles) backtrack to Old Tower Site and turn right (southwest) to stay on Trail 1, descending a steep grade that eventually levels off before returning to the CCC picnic area.

Trees frame High Point, the highest of several knob-like hills to be climbed on the rugged Knob Lake Trail.

MILES AND DIRECTIONS

0.0 Begin at the trailhead at the south end of the playground; turn right.

0.7 Pass the youth camp; turn left onto a gravel road.

1.0 Reach the service area.

1.5 Leave the stream and begin to climb.

2.5 Reach High Point Knob.

2.7 Arrive at the Old Tower Site; turn right toward Pinnacle Peak.

3.3 Reach Pinnacle Peak; backtrack to Old Tower Site and turn right (southwest).

4.3 Arrive back at the trailhead.

OPTIONS

Additional trails, including interpretive trails, are available in the area.

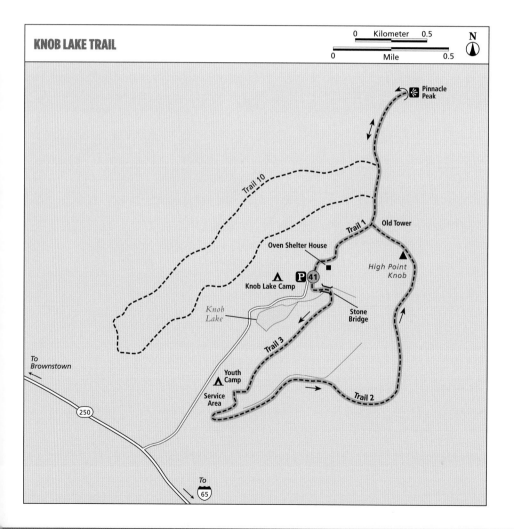

HILL COUNTRY

Time has not stood still in the picturesque Hill Country of south-central Indiana, but in many ways the region and its residents have not completely outgrown the pioneer lifestyle. Instead, they have capitalized on it.

The sleepy Brown County town of Nashville has been a tourist mecca since the 1930s because of its craft shops and artist galleries. An estimated 4 million visitors wander its streets each year in search of antiques, collectables, or something that simply looks old or handmade.

The area's greatest ambassadors were artist T. C. Steele and a cartoon character—Abe Martin.

Steele was an Impressionist painter of the early 1900s known for his Indiana landscapes.

Abe Martin was the creation of Indianapolis newspaperman and humorist Kin Hubbard who spun folksy wisdom about life in fictional "Bloom Center" and its odd assortment of residents. "It ain't a bad plan to keep still occasionally, even when you know what you're talking about," is one of the 16,000 sayings attributed to the fictional Abe. Hubbard's work went into syndication in 1910 and appeared in more than 200 newspapers. The lodge at nearby Brown County State Park is named for the popular cartoon character.

The park is the crown jewel of the state system. At approximately 16,000 acres, it is Indiana's largest state park and annually draws 1.2 to 1.9 million visitors, many who come to enjoy the autumn colors of the hardwood forest. The park and the neighboring town of Nashville are often favorably compared to Great Smoky Mountains National Park and Gatlinburg, Tennessee. Authentic log cabin homes are a common sight, and colorful place names are plentiful—Graveyard Hollow, Deadman Hollow, Gnaw Bone, Weed Patch Hill, Hesitation Point, Scarce O'Fat Ridge, and Greasy Creek, to name a few.

Spared from the forces of the last great glacier, the region is noted as much for its deep valleys and ravines as it is for rolling hills. Stripped of native timber more than a century ago, the land became an affordable dream for those hoping to carve out an existence on small farms. The thin, rocky soil, coupled with the highly erodible terrain, proved unsuitable for agriculture, however, and most of the pioneer farms failed during the Great Depression.

The state acquired approximately 40,000 acres of abandoned farmland in 1929 and established Brown County State Park and nearby Morgan-Monroe State Forest. Yellowwood State Forest was added to the picture in 1947 when federal land was deeded to the state.

The northern boundary of the Hoosier National Forest abuts the three state properties, creating a massive block of public land available for outdoor recreation opportunities. Farther south is Spring Mill State Park, noted for its karst cave topography. The area is riddled with sinkholes and caves.

Hikes in this section are presented in a clockwise sweep, heading north from Bloomington.

42 BEANBLOSSOM BOTTOMS NATURE PRESERVE

WHY GO?

An elevated boardwalk through floodplain forest, wet meadows, and wetlands.

THE RUNDOWN

Location: Near Ellettsville in south-central Indiana
Distance: 2.3-mile lollipop loop
Elevation change: 10 feet
Hiking time: About 1.5 hours
Difficulty: Easy
Jurisdiction: Sycamore Land Trust
Fees and permits: No fees or permits required

Maps: USGS Modesto
Special attraction: Designated state Important Bird Area by National Audubon Society
Camping: No camping permitted
Trailhead facilities: Parking lot only at trailhead; no restrooms or drinking water available

FINDING THE TRAILHEAD

From I-69 exit 120 near Bloomington, go west on IN 46 for 3 miles to North Union Valley Road in Ellettsville. Turn right (north) and go 2.5 miles to a T intersection with Monroe CR 250 West and turn right (east) on Delap Road. Stay on Delap Road for about 1 mile, keeping right at 2 Y intersections. At a 3rd Y, go left (northeast) on Woodall Road. Go 1.4 miles to a gravel parking lot on the right.

THE HIKE

Once ditched and drained for farming, the area containing Beanblossom Bottoms Nature Preserve and surrounding land is part of an extensive conservation effort that started small but continues to grow.

Barbara Restle got things going in 1993 when she donated 42 acres to Sycamore Land Trust for one of its earliest projects and another 78 acres to the US Fish & Wildlife Service for a satellite unit of Muscatatuck National Wildlife Refuge (66 miles to the east).

Beanblossom Bottoms was a mere 80 acres when it was dedicated as a state nature preserve in 1995. It now covers more than 700 acres and is part of the larger 1,500-acre Beanblossom Bottoms Bicentennial Conservation Area, one of five focus areas of the Bicentennial Nature Trust. The BNT provided $30 million for land conservation projects across the state in celebration of Indiana's 200th anniversary of statehood in 2016.

Anthony Robertson bought a cabin and 8 acres here in 1871 and cleared and drained 600 more acres for his farm. Roughly a century later farming had ended, and the fields began to naturally reshape as early successional forest. They also took on water when the ditches and nearby Beanblossom Creek flooded.

Blue flag iris at Beanblossom Bottoms Nature Preserve

That still happens today, although Sycamore Land Trust has made the nature preserve accessible most of the year with 2.5 miles of a crushed-stone entry path and elevated boardwalk. It's still advisable to bring waterproof boots during times when standing water can cover parts of the trail.

In addition to being a state-dedicated nature preserve, Beanblossom Bottoms has been recognized by the National Audubon Society as a state Important Bird Area and by the Society of Wetland Scientists as a wetland of distinction.

As reported in the Bloomington newspaper, a June 2022 bioblitz identified almost 300 plant species, fifty birds, and twenty amphibians and reptiles. A few noteworthy finds at the preserve have been the state-endangered Indiana bat and Kirtland's snake. Great blue herons and bald eagles are known to nest here.

The trail begins at a gravel parking lot that can accommodate eight vehicles.

Cross a 40-foot plastic boardwalk to a path of crushed stone and turn right (northeast). Continue on the crushed-stone path through floodplain forest for about a quarter mile to reach the start of the boardwalk.

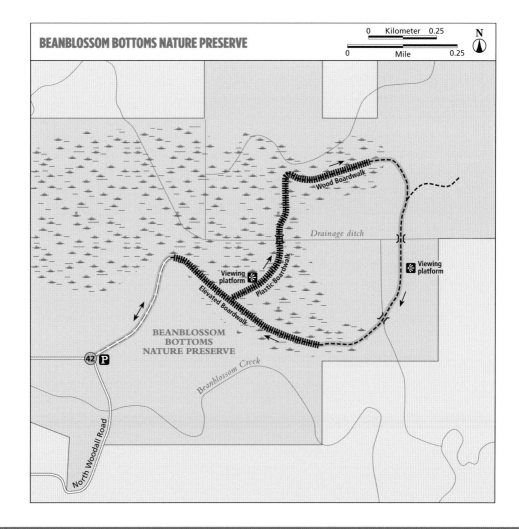

The boardwalk has two sections—plastic and wood. The newer plastic section is supported by metal pier posts and is used on about half the trail.

Turn right (northeast) off the gravel path onto the boardwalk and continue to a trail split at 0.5 mile. Go left (north) on the plastic boardwalk to an elevated observation deck at 0.6 mile that offers a decent view of the surrounding wetland. At 0.7 mile, cross a bridge over a drainage ditch.

The boardwalk switches from plastic to wood planks at 0.8 mile. It can be slippery when wet. The 10-foot-long planks are also bouncy in a few spots where the underlying soil has been washed away.

There's another noticeable change at 1 mile—the presence of larger trees. Swamp white oak, pin oak, red and silver maple, cottonwood, shagbark hickory, black gum, sycamore, and American hophornbeam are scattered about.

At 1.1 miles there's a spur trail to the left. Stay right on the wooden boardwalk for another 200 yards for the first of two footbridges over a drainage ditch. Just beyond the second footbridge is another observation deck on the left side of the trail.

Complete the boardwalk loop at 1.8 miles, turn left (southwest) on the plastic boardwalk and return to the crushed-stone path leading back to the parking lot.

MILES AND DIRECTIONS

0.0 Begin at the trailhead; cross a 40-foot boardwalk to crushed-stone path and turn right (northeast).

0.3 Reach the plastic boardwalk and turn right (southeast).

0.5 The boardwalk splits; go left (northeast).

0.6 Observation deck.

0.7 Footbridge over drainage ditch.

0.8 Spur trail to left; stay straight as boardwalk changes from plastic to wood planks.

1.1 Spur trail to left; go right (south) to continue on main trail.

1.2 Footbridge.

1.4 Footbridge.

1.6 Observation deck.

1.8 Return to trail juncture; turn left (northwest) on plastic boardwalk.

2.0 Return to the crushed-stone path; turn left (southwest).

2.3 Arrive back at the trailhead and parking lot.

43 LOW GAP TRAIL

WHY GO?

A loop trail covers steep forested ridges, ravines, creeks, and the Backcountry Area of Morgan-Monroe State Forest.

THE RUNDOWN

Location: Morgan-Monroe State Forest, midway between Bloomington and Martinsville, south-central Indiana

Distance: 10.0-mile loop

Elevation change: Several changes of 200 to 270 feet from ridgetops to ravines and back

Hiking time: About 7 hours or an overnight backpack

Difficulty: Strenuous

Jurisdiction: Indiana Department of Natural Resources, Division of Forestry

Fees and permits: No fees or permits required

Maps: USGS Hindustan; Morgan-Monroe State Forest pamphlet

Special attractions: Draper Cabin, rock cliffs in Sweedy Hollow

Camping: 35 non-electric campsites; additional sites located in the Scout Ridge youth tent area. The campgrounds are located on the main forest road north of the trailhead. Camping is also permitted in the Backcountry Area in the eastern section of Low Gap Trail. Campers must register at the forest office.

Trailhead facilities: Small gravel parking lot at the trailhead; water, restrooms, and picnic shelters available at several locations along the main forest road

FINDING THE TRAILHEAD

From I-69 south of Martinsville, take exit 134 onto Liberty Church Road. Turn right (southwest) on Old State Road 37 and go 4.0 miles to the Morgan-Monroe State Forest entrance. Turn left (southeast) onto Forest Road and go 4.5 miles to a parking area on the right (south) side of the main road just past North Bean Blossom Road. The trailhead is about 10 yards off the road.

THE HIKE

It is hard to imagine this area practically devoid of trees, but it was treeless after the original settlers cleared it in a vain attempt to establish farms. The rocky soil proved unsuitable for farming, and the land was abandoned. The state stepped in during the Great Depression to purchase 24,000 acres of the eroding hillsides and established Morgan–Monroe State Forest.

The intervening years have allowed the lush forest to be reestablished, including 2,700 acres designated as the Backcountry Area in 1981. Low Gap Trail passes through this area and is one of two 10-mile hikes in Morgan-Monroe State Forest. The trail is well marked with white blazes on trees. Although a good part of the trail follows abandoned roads and service roads, the rugged segments through Sweedy Hollow and along Gorley and Shipman Ridges can challenge the most avid hikers.

The trail begins at a small gravel parking lot just off the main forest road. (**Note:** This also is the north trailhead for the 42-mile-long Tecumseh Trail that goes south and off the property.)

Head west for 0.1 mile to connect with an old road and turn left (south), following the roadway and trail south along Tincher Ridge. At 1.0 mile turn left off the road and make the steep descent via a series of switchbacks over a fern-carpeted slope into Sweedy Hollow Nature Preserve. At the bottom of the ravine, follow the creek, which the trail crosses several times, for almost another mile before passing below stone cliffs that overhang the west side of the ravine. Continuing on the trail, make the steep climb out of Sweedy Hollow to reach the 2.0-mile mark on a ridgetop.

At 2.4 miles link up with Landram Ridge Road, a gravel service road. A sign marks the spot, pointing left (northwest) for the 3.0-mile Rock Shelter Loop and right (southeast) for the continuation of the Low Gap Trail. Go right, crossing the high end of a ravine while keeping to a southeast course. The service road soon breaks to the right (south), but the trail continues left (east) and downhill along a power line corridor.

Pass a pond after another 0.5 mile, and then leave the power line corridor to enter the woods. Continue downhill to the first crossover of Low Gap Road at 4.0 miles. A gravel

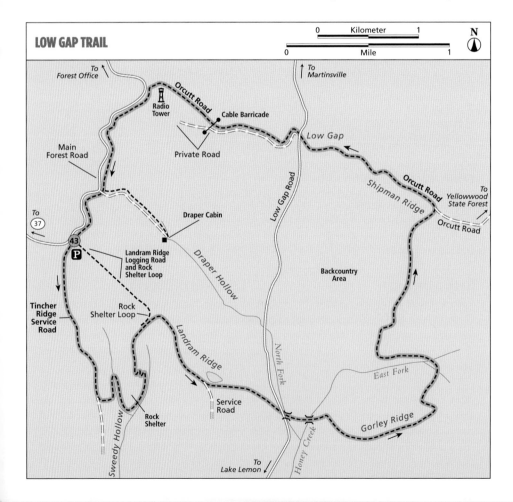

Rock overhangs are a rugged component of Sweedy Hollow
on the Low Gap Trail in Morgan-Monroe State Forest.

parking lot marks the entry to the Backcountry Area. Cross a pair of footbridges over the North Fork and East Fork of Honey Creek before making a steep uphill march to the top of Gorley Ridge, which is about the midway point of the hike. Part of the climb is over an old roadbed, but the trail eventually leaves the roadbed to drop into a ravine to the East Fork of Honey Creek. Cross the creek a couple of times before entering Low Gap Nature Preserve.

The last challenging portion of the trail begins with a climb to a narrow ridgetop that leads to Shipman Ridge and the linkup with Orcutt Road, a service road, at 6.8 miles. The Tecumseh Trail breaks off here, turning right (southeast).

Continue the Low Gap Trail by turning left (northwest) and following Orcutt Road as it winds gradually downhill to the second crossover of Low Gap Road.

Follow the service road past a radio tower and continue toward the main forest road.

Low Gap Trail turns left (west) off the service road about 50 yards before reaching the main forest road at 8.9 miles. Hike parallel to the main road, reaching a gravel road at the 9.8-mile mark. The gravel road leads south for 0.5 mile to the Draper Cabin, a rustic log home on the banks of the North Fork of Honey Creek. The cabin, which has wooden floors but no plumbing, can be rented for overnight stays between April and Thanksgiving and during winter, depending on weather conditions.

If you choose, visit the cabin, then backtrack uphill to the Low Gap Trail and turn left (south) to return to the hike. Follow a path parallel to the main forest road for less than 0.5 mile to reach the trailhead parking lot.

MILES AND DIRECTIONS

0.0 Begin at the trailhead southwest of the parking area.

0.1 Go left (south) on Tincher Ridge Service Road.

1.0 Go left (east) to Sweedy Hollow.

2.4 Link up with Landram Ridge Road; turn right (southeast).

2.8 At the trail junction, go right on the Landram Ridge logging road.

4.0 Cross over Low Gap Road to the parking lot and footbridge.

6.8 At the trail junction, turn left onto Orcutt Road.

7.8 Cross Low Gap Road and follow the gravel Orcutt Road uphill.

8.2 Go right on a logging road past the cable barricade.

8.7 Pass the radio tower on the left.

8.8 At the trail junction go left (west).

9.8 Take an optional spur trail (left) to Draper Cabin or go straight to complete the hike.

10.0 Arrive back at the trailhead parking lot.

44 THREE LAKES TRAIL

WHY GO?
This trail visits the steep, forested ridges, ravines, creeks, and lakes of Morgan-Monroe State Forest.

THE RUNDOWN

Location: Morgan-Monroe State Forest, midway between Bloomington and Martinsville, south-central Indiana

Distance: 10.0-mile loop

Elevation change: Five descents of 140 to 250 feet; four climbs of 140 to 200 feet

Hiking time: About 6 hours

Difficulty: Strenuous

Jurisdiction: Indiana Department of Natural Resources, Division of Forestry

Fees and permits: No fees or permits required

Maps: USGS Hindustan; Morgan-Monroe State Forest brochure

Special attractions: Lush woodland valleys, Bryant Creek Lake, creekbanks, a pioneer cemetery

Camping: 35 non-electric campsites; additional sites located in the Scout Ridge youth area. The campgrounds are located on the main forest road north of the trailhead.

Trailhead facilities: Small parking lot at the trailhead; water and restrooms located nearby at the Cherry Lake Picnic Shelter and at other locations in the state forest

FINDING THE TRAILHEAD
From I-69 south of Martinsville, take exit 134 onto Liberty Church Road. Turn right (southwest) on Old State Road 37 and go 4.0 miles to the Morgan-Monroe State Forest entrance. Turn left (southeast) onto Forest Road and go 4.8 miles to the first paved road. Turn left (north) and go 0.2 mile to a small paved parking lot on the right (northwest) overlooking Cherry Lake. The trail begins 0.1 mile farther down the road on the left (south) side at a metal gate blocking a forest service road.

THE HIKE
The name for this trail has been inaccurate for decades because it now only goes to two lakes—Bryant Creek and Cherry. The third lake on the original triangular-shaped trail, Beanblossom Lake, dried up after its dam failed in 1993. Regardless of its name, the Three Lakes Trail is every bit as demanding as the Low Gap Trail, the other long-distance hike in Morgan–Monroe State Forest.

Portions of the forest on this trail are part of the Hardwood Ecosystem Experiment, a hundred–year study led by Purdue University to evaluate how different timber harvest methods affect natural oak–hickory regeneration as well as select wildlife species. The project began in 2006 and has drawn participation from hundreds of undergraduate and graduate students from Purdue and other universities.

A sign explains the Hardwood Ecosystem Experiment.

The trail stretches along narrow ridgetops and through creek beds in deep ravines and requires a lot of up-and-down climbing. The seclusion of the hardwood forests, the abundance of wildflowers, and the opportunity to encounter wildlife make the Three Lakes Trail a quality hiking opportunity.

The trail is well marked with white blazes and brown plastic markers. Direction changes are clearly marked with double blazes. Most traffic revolves around the shelter houses at Cherry and Bryant Lakes.

Begin the hike on an old roadbed that starts downhill after about 100 yards and reaches the first of what will be several creek crossings over the next 10.0 miles. The creeks are small, however, and flow intermittently with seasonal rainfall, so they normally present little trouble.

Continue along the creek, breaking to the left (south) after about 0.75 mile to head up a ravine—again on an old roadbed. After leveling off, pass the Stepp Cemetery at 1.0 mile. Markers in the graveyard include at least three that memorialize Civil War veterans; another is for Isaac Hartsock, a private in the Virginia Militia during the War of 1812. An inscription on the headstone for Jay Alberto Coffa reads, "The quiet man who is dreaming a clear labyrinth."

Head southeast from the cemetery on the gravel road to reach the main forest road at 1.1 miles. Head left (east) from here along the main forest road for about 50 yards, then cross the road where the trail intersects a crushed-stone trail that parallels the main forest

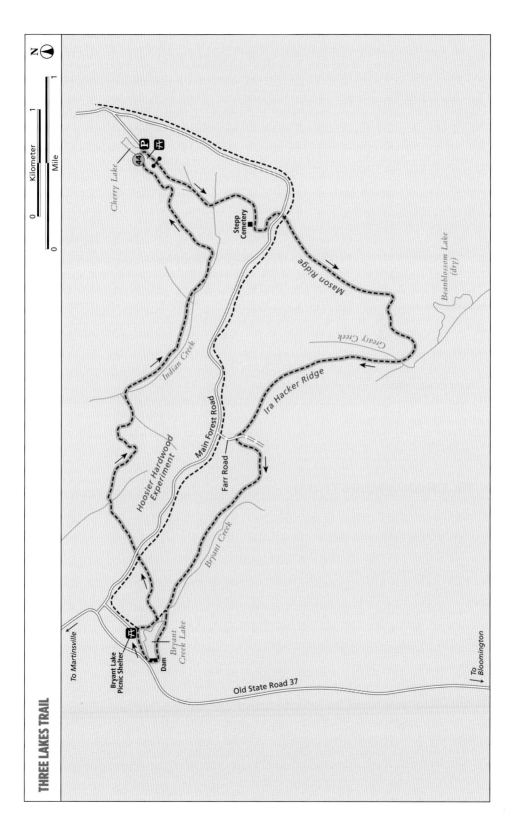

THREE LAKES TRAIL

road. Continue straight (southeast) over Mason Ridge toward Greasy Creek. You are about 0.25 mile north of the former Beanblossom Lake.

After crossing the creek, turn right (north) and begin a steep climb of 200 feet up Ira Hacker Ridge to follow a power line easement. When the power line takes a right (north) turn, the trail goes straight (northwest). At 3.5 miles the trail crosses Farr Road. Look for trail markers on the trees directly across from where the road bends. Weave through a stand of young trees before heading downhill to join Bryant Creek at 4.0 miles.

Follow the creek for almost 1.0 mile through heavy vegetation, climbing over a long, straight hump at one point before reaching a stand of pines near Bryant Creek Lake. At 5.0 miles reach and circle the lake in a clockwise direction, climbing wooden steps around the high south shoreline. Cross the dam at the west end of the lake and continue northeast toward a picnic shelter in the woods north of the lake.

Take a break at the shelter (gender-specific latrines are located there) or stop short of the shelter and continue the trail in a northeasterly direction.

From the shelter, the trail takes a quick drop into a ravine and skirts a ledge along the northern shoreline of Bryant Creek Lake. Head east over a broad ridge to reach the main road near the 6.5-mile mark. Cross the road and zigzag across an old roadbed to a double-blaze marker. Turn left and walk along a ridge before descending a switchback to cross a branch of Indian Creek. Head up the other side of the ravine and cross a ridgetop. Descend once more to Indian Creek and follow its banks for almost 1.0 mile, crossing several side creeks before turning left (northeast) at 8.5 miles and heading uphill on a steep ridge point.

Beyond the ridgetop, slip across a ravine to another ridgetop and follow a winding path through the woods to Indian Creek. Turn left (northeast) at the creek and follow it to the Cherry Lake Picnic Shelter at 9.6 miles. Go to the north side of the shelter and proceed in a clockwise direction across the dam at the lake to the trailhead parking lot.

MILES AND DIRECTIONS

0.0   Begin at the trailhead on an old roadbed.

1.0   Reach the Stepp Cemetery.

1.1   Turn left to the main road crossing.

2.3   Cross Greasy Creek.

3.5   Cross Farr Road.

4.0   Meet and follow Bryant Creek.

5.0   Reach Bryant Creek Lake; circle the lake clockwise.

6.5   Go straight at the main road crossing.

6.8   Cross Indian Creek.

8.5   Turn left (northeast) and go uphill.

9.6   Return to the Cherry Lake Picnic Shelter.

10.0   Arrive back at the trailhead.

45 SCARCE O'FAT TRAIL

WHY GO?

A loop trail travels along a ridgetop, through a deep ravine, and over a steep hill featuring a north-facing vista overlooking Yellowwood Lake.

THE RUNDOWN

Location: Yellowwood State Forest, between Bloomington and Nashville
Distance: 4.5-mile loop
Elevation change: About 220 feet from the trailhead to highest point, just north of Caldwell Hollow
Hiking time: About 3 hours
Difficulty: Strenuous
Jurisdiction: Indiana Department of Natural Resources, Division of Forestry
Fees and permits: No fees or permits required

Maps: USGS Belmont; Yellowwood State Forest brochure
Special attractions: Caldwell Hollow, High King Hill
Camping: 74 non-electric campsites and 11 equestrian campsites at Yellowwood State Forest
Trailhead facilities: Small parking lot but no water supply or restrooms; water and restrooms available at the forest office on Yellowwood Lake Road

FINDING THE TRAILHEAD

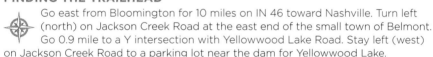

Go east from Bloomington for 10 miles on IN 46 toward Nashville. Turn left (north) on Jackson Creek Road at the east end of the small town of Belmont. Go 0.9 mile to a Y intersection with Yellowwood Lake Road. Stay left (west) on Jackson Creek Road to a parking lot near the dam for Yellowwood Lake.

THE HIKE

Scarce O'Fat Ridge is the name pioneer settlers gave to this site because of the difficulty they faced scratching out a meager living on the rocky ground. While Scarce O'Fat lends its name to the trail, the trail's best features are the segments through Caldwell Hollow and the finishing climb up and down High King Hill.

Although High King makes for a clever play on words (High King/hiking), it is so named because the hill is on property once owned by a man named King.

Also worth noting is the forest's name—Yellowwood. The yellowwood tree is a close cousin of the black locust and is common in the mid-South, but it is so rare this far north that it is on the Indiana list of endangered plant species. The forest covers 23,700 acres, of which only 200 are suitable yellowwood habitat.

What the first two-thirds of this trail lacks in scenic splendor, it more than makes up for in hiking ease. Also, the first section sets the stage for the solitude of Caldwell Hollow and the accomplishment of conquering High King Hill.

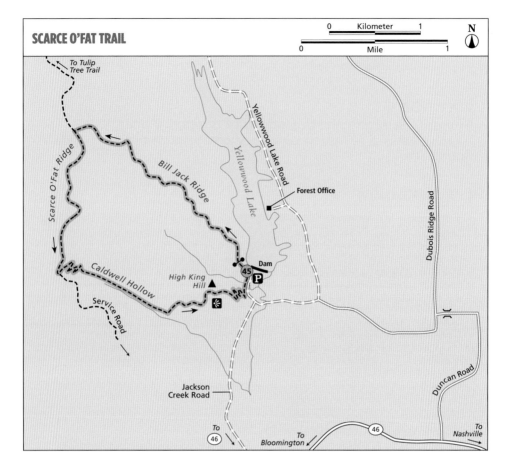

SCARCE O'FAT TRAIL

To Tulip Tree Trail

Scarce O'Fat Ridge

Bill Jack Ridge

Yellowwood Lake Road

Yellowwood Lake

Forest Office

Caldwell Hollow

High King Hill

Dam

45 P

Service Road

Dubois Ridge Road

Jackson Creek Road

Duncan Road

To 46

To Bloomington

To 46

To Nashville

Brown plastic posts and wooden signs mark the early segments of the trail. White blazes on trees and boot outlines on wood posts direct the way through Caldwell Hollow and over High King Hill.

The trail begins at the base of the Yellowwood Lake dam. From the small parking lot, it is easy to locate the marked trailhead at a gate that blocks a forest service road. It begins with a gradual climb of 140 feet to Bill Jack Ridge and winds through a forest of oak, beech, poplar, and shagbark hickory trees. If you schedule a hike for midsummer, you may find wild raspberries in plentiful supply along the edge of the road.

Once atop Bill Jack Ridge, the trail levels off for the next 2.0 miles. The trail is clearly marked along this portion with brown plastic signs. At 1.7 miles turn left (south) as the trail connects with Scarce O'Fat Ridge. The turnoff is marked by a wooden sign with two white blazes. Be alert for occasional spurs that veer to the right off the main service road; stay to the left (south). It is through this stretch that the trail reaches its highest point, but the elevation grade is so slight it is hard to notice.

At 2.8 miles another double-blaze marker and brown plastic markers indicate a left (east) turn into the forest. This begins the descent into Caldwell Hollow. The trail follows a switchback that drops almost 220 feet in elevation in the span of 0.5 mile. Trail markers through Caldwell Hollow consist of white blaze markings on trees and wood posts sporting the outline of a boot. Once at the bottom of the hollow, the trail crosses a creek bed several times as it meanders through a corridor of other ravines that converge with Caldwell Hollow.

At 3.8 miles turn left (northeast) and begin the climb up High King Hill. The steepest part is over the next 0.25 mile as the elevation changes almost 150 feet. The remaining climb is much more gradual.

Technically Scarce O'Fat Trail ends atop High King Hill, where it joins High King Trail for the final 0.25 mile. A series of switchbacks drops almost 200 feet to an intermittent streambed. Cross through the streambed to the road; turn left (north) and walk a few hundred feet back to the parking lot.

MILES AND DIRECTIONS

0.0 Begin at the trailhead at the gate.

1.7 Turn left (south) onto Scarce O'Fat Ridge.

2.8 Turn left (east) to enter Caldwell Hollow.

3.8 Turn left (northeast) to climb High King Hill.

4.3 Reach the High King Hill vista.

4.5 Arrive back at the trailhead.

46 BROWN COUNTY STATE PARK: TRAIL 8

WHY GO?
The trail loops through remote ravines of Brown County State Park.

THE RUNDOWN

Location: Outside Nashville, Brown County
Distance: 3.5-mile loop with spurs
Elevation change: More than 300 feet from Hesitation Point to the low end of Upper Schooner Creek Valley
Hiking time: About 2 hours
Difficulty: Moderate to strenuous
Jurisdiction: Indiana Department of Natural Resources, Division of State Parks
Fees and permits: Park entry fee, higher for out-of-state vehicles; season passes available

Maps: USGS Belmont and Nashville; Brown County State Park brochure
Special attractions: Hesitation Point vista, Upper Schooner Creek Valley
Camping: 377 modern electric and 31 non-electric campsites; 204 equestrian campground sites; rally and youth camping area
Trailhead facilities: Large parking area at the trailhead but no drinking water or restrooms; water available at other locations in the park, including the picnic area near Ogle Lake

FINDING THE TRAILHEAD

From Nashville go 2.5 miles south on IN 46 to Brown County State Park's west gatehouse and turn left (east). Continue 1.2 miles to the West Lookout Tower parking lot. The trail begins on the east side of the stockade-shaped lookout tower.

THE HIKE
Although Brown County is the largest state park in the Indiana system, it has a limited supply of trails designated just for hikers—eleven trails totaling just over 19 miles. Another 37 miles of relatively new mountain biking trails are open to hikers but be alert to the two-wheel traffic.

At 3.5 miles, Trail 8 is the longest hiking-only trail in the park.

Visited by thousands of people in the fall because of the brilliant displays as leaves change color, Brown County State Park is just as colorful in spring because of its abundance of wildflowers, including toothwort, Dutchman's breeches, Jack-in-the-pulpit, spring larkspur, bluets, large-flowered trillium, wood sorrel, celandine poppy, fire pink, and prairie trillium. The entire park suffered from severe grazing damage inflicted by an overpopulation of white-tailed deer until special hunts were implemented in the early 1990s. Deer culls have become routine here and at other state parks, resulting in remarkable recovery of native vegetation. The Upper Schooner Creek Valley is flush with wildflowers and ferns, representative of the richness of this park.

BROWN COUNTY STATE PARK: TRAIL 8

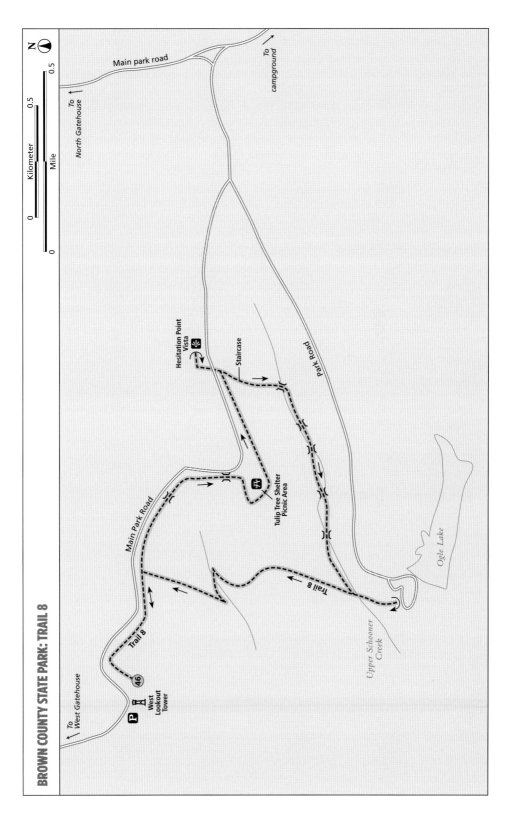

Boardwalks and staircases take some of the difficulty out of the portion of the trail between Hesitation Point and the ravine of Upper Schooner Creek. Although the trail is well maintained, it gets less traffic than other trails in the park. It is busiest near the West Lookout Tower and around Ogle Lake.

From the West Lookout Tower, head east as the trail skirts the main park road about 10 to 20 feet down the side of the ridge. At 0.4 mile the trail intersects the inbound leg of Trail 8, which joins from the right (south). Stay straight (east) and continue a course parallel to the main road for another 1.0 mile, passing over two footbridges and behind the Tulip Tree Shelter Picnic Area.

At 1.5 miles Trail 8 turns right (south); before you make this turn, go left (north) and cross the main road to Hesitation Point. Soak up the views from this north-facing vista and then backtrack to the south side of the park road. Follow Trail 8 south for a little less than 0.25 mile to a wooden staircase with about 150 steps leading down to Upper Schooner Creek (1.8 miles).

The Upper Schooner Creek Valley is long and narrow, with an extremely steep bluff all along the south side. The bluff to the right side of the creek starts out equally steep but begins to flatten over the next 0.5 mile. Cross five footbridges as the trail switches from one side of the creek to the other.

Walk under a canopy of mature trees and cross a lengthy boardwalk to the trail junction at 2.3 miles. Trail 8 turns north toward the West Lookout Tower. Instead go straight (south) to the parking lot west of Ogle Lake, one of two small lakes within the park boundaries.

Backtrack to the trail junction at 2.4 miles; turn left (north) and climb a ridge point before the trail makes a steep drop to the left (west) into another valley. Cross the creek at the bottom of the ravine and head uphill again to reach the trail junction with the outbound leg of Trail 8 at 3.1 miles. Turn left (west) and go 0.4 mile back to the lookout tower parking lot.

MILES AND DIRECTIONS

0.0 Begin at the trailhead at the east side of the tower.

0.4 At the Trail 8 junction go straight.

1.5 Reach the Hesitation Point overlook.

1.8 Enter the Upper Schooner Creek Valley.

2.3 At the trail junction go straight (south) to Ogle Lake.

2.4 Backtrack to the trail junction and turn left (north).

3.1 At the trail junction turn left (west) to return to the trailhead.

3.5 Arrive back at the trailhead.

47 TWIN CAVES/DONALDSON WOODS TRAIL

WHY GO?

A trail through a nature preserve features virgin timber and passes several caves and sinkholes.

THE RUNDOWN

Location: Spring Mill State Park, near Mitchell, Lawrence County
Distance: 2.5-mile loop
Elevation change: Minimal
Hiking time: About 1.5 hours
Difficulty: Moderate
Jurisdiction: Indiana Department of Natural Resources, Division of State Parks
Fees and permits: Park entry fee, higher for out-of-state vehicles; season passes available

Maps: USGS Mitchell; Spring Mill State Park brochure
Special attractions: Donaldson Woods Nature Preserve, Twin Caves, Bronson Cave
Camping: 46 full-hookup and 177 electric campsites
Trailhead facilities: Parking lot and a pit toilet at trailhead but no drinking water; water and restrooms located elsewhere in the park

FINDING THE TRAILHEAD

From its intersection with IN 37 on the southwest edge of Mitchell, go 3.3 miles east on IN 60 to Spring Mill State Park. Turn left (north) and go 0.4 mile to the gatehouse, then another 0.1 mile to a three-way intersection. Turn right (northeast) at the intersection; go 0.2 mile and turn right (southeast). Go another 0.1 mile and turn right (south). The road ends at the Twin Caves parking area. The trail begins from the west edge of the parking lot.

THE HIKE

Karst topography is the geological name given to an area of limestone bedrock featuring caves, sinkholes, and underground streams. The Mitchell Plain, which stretches from the Ohio River north to central Indiana, is one of the best karst examples in the world. The area in which Spring Mill State Park is located has one of the highest concentrations of sinkholes in the United States, with an average of one hundred per square mile. Just down the road near Orleans, an amazing 1,022 sinkholes were counted in 1 square mile.

The funnel-shaped sinkholes vary in size but play an integral role in the development of cave systems like the one at Spring Mill. Groundwater mixed with vegetation creates a weak acid that dissolves the limestone. Over time cracks become caves, and when caves collapse, they form exposed openings known as karst windows. Examples—Twin Caves and Bronson Cave—are found on the Twin Caves Trail (also known as Trail 3).

The trail can be hiked in either direction but is described here as a clockwise loop that begins at a stone archway on the west edge of the parking lot. The archway leads to Twin

Caves, where boat trips are offered April through October, depending on water levels in the cave. Backtrack from Twin Caves to the stone archway and turn left (north) to pick up Trail 3. Go 0.1 mile to a wooden viewing platform near the mouth of Bronson Cave.

Go west from the cave on a winding course through a forest dotted with sinkholes for 0.5 mile to cross the main park road. After crossing the road, begin heading north for another 0.5 mile to a paved road. Cross the road and follow a gravel trail along the rim above Donaldson Cave, which is connected to the other caves. Go past the overlook above Donaldson Cave and continue north, then south, crossing the first of two paved roads at 1.7 miles.

At 1.8 miles you cross the second road and reach the Donaldson Woods Nature Preserve. The 67-acre stand of virgin timber features several trees at least 300 years old, including one white oak protected by a split-rail fence near the south end of the preserve. The tree is believed to be between 400 and 500 years old. The preserve is named for George Donaldson, a wealthy Scotsman and nature lover who had a penchant for

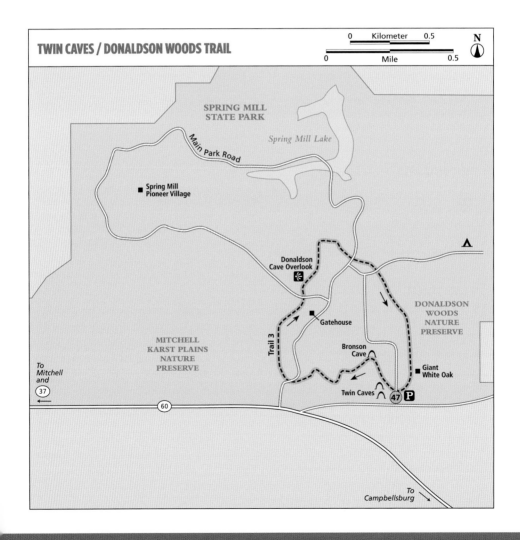

purchasing areas of unique beauty. Although he frequently hunted abroad, Donaldson zealously protected his property from disturbance of any kind.

Turn right (west) from the large oak tree to the Twin Caves parking lot.

MILES AND DIRECTIONS

0.0   Begin at the trailhead at the west end of the parking lot and go left.

0.1   Arrive at Twin Caves.

0.2   Come to Bronson Cave.

0.7   Cross the main park road.

1.2   Reach and cross a paved park road.

1.5   Arrive at trail junction on the left; go right (east).

1.7   Reach a paved park road; cross over.

1.8   Cross a paved park road.

1.9   Enter Donaldson Woods Nature Preserve.

2.5   Arrive back at the Twin Caves parking lot.

48 **VILLAGE TRAIL**

WHY GO?

The trail leads to a cave canyon, through a pioneer village, and to a pioneer cemetery.

THE RUNDOWN

Location: Spring Mill State Park, near Mitchell, Lawrence County
Distance: 2.0-mile loop, excluding optional tour of the village and cemetery
Elevation change: 150 feet
Hiking time: About 1.5 hours
Difficulty: Moderate to strenuous
Jurisdiction: Indiana Department of Natural Resources, Division of State Parks
Fees and permits: Park entry fee, higher for out-of-state vehicles; season passes available

Maps: USGS Mitchell; Spring Mill State Park brochure
Special attractions: Donaldson Cave, Spring Mill Pioneer Village, Hamer Pioneer Cemetery
Camping: 46 full-hookup and 177 electric campsites
Trailhead facilities: Parking for two dozen vehicles, picnic shelters, pit toilets, and a water supply at trailhead; water and restrooms located elsewhere in the park

FINDING THE TRAILHEAD

From its intersection with IN 37 on the southwest edge of Mitchell, go 3.3 miles east on IN 60 to Spring Mill State Park. Turn left (north) and go 0.4 mile to the gatehouse, then another 0.1 mile to a three-way intersection. Turn left (west) at the intersection and go 0.3 mile to the Donaldson Picnic Area parking lot on the right (northeast). The trail begins from the southeast edge of the parking lot.

THE HIKE

There are eight hiking trails in 1,672-acre Spring Mill State Park, including Trail 4. History is the overriding theme of this trail, beginning with its most dynamic natural feature—Donaldson Cave. Known as Shawnee Cave until George Donaldson purchased the area in 1865, the cave is part of a network that includes two other exposed caves in the park.

Professor Carl Eigenmann of nearby Indiana University began extensive studies of Donaldson Cave in the early 1900s and discovered northern blind cavefish, which have been placed on the state's endangered species list. The pinkish-white fish with no eyes has adapted to the dark cave, as have other critters—the blind cave crayfish, the cave salamander, assorted spiders, and of course bats.

Other highlights that can be added to this hike are Spring Mill Pioneer Village and Hamer Cave. Trail 4 no longer leads through the Pioneer Village, but the Stagecoach Trail provides access for a worthwhile visit. Pets are not allowed in the village.

The history of the village dates to the early 1800s, when Samuel Jackson Jr. capitalized on a spring-fed stream to build a small gristmill. A Canadian naval officer who served the United States in the War of 1812, Jackson sold the property in 1817 to two brothers—Thomas and Cuthbert Bullitt of Kentucky. The Bullitts built a three-story gristmill at the site, which is still in operation.

As a small village grew up around the prospering mill, ownership of the land changed hands several times. Hugh and Thomas Hamer purchased the mill and surrounding village in 1832, one year after its name was changed from Arcole Village to Spring Mill. The Hamer brothers had managed the mill for the previous owners for seven years. Under the brothers' ownership, the village thrived until the late 1850s. By 1898 it had been abandoned.

Envisioning a restored village as the centerpiece of a park, the State of Indiana began acquiring the land in the 1920s, and Spring Mill State Park was established in 1927. Besides the gristmill, which produces cornmeal for sale, there are nineteen other restored buildings in the village, including a post office, apothecary, blacksmith shop, tavern, distillery, and carpenter shop. Volunteers dressed in period clothing bring the village to life by performing routine daily chores.

The original mill at Spring Mill Pioneer Village was built in the early 1800s and is still in operation.

The clearly marked trail is well traveled, especially around Donaldson Cave and the pioneer village.

Begin the hike at the east end of the parking lot by descending an elaborate wooden staircase to the stream running from Donaldson Cave. Turn right (southeast) to reach the mouth of the cave at 0.2 mile. Access to the cave may be restricted to protect bat populations.

From the cave follow the left (west) side of the stream, crossing a long boardwalk before curling west to the Butternut Grove Picnic Shelter at 1.0 mile and a pair of limestone picnic areas built by the Civilian Conservation Corps (CCC) in the early 1930s.

Turn left (south) and follow a winding course that reaches the optional spur trail to the Pioneer Village at 1.3 miles.

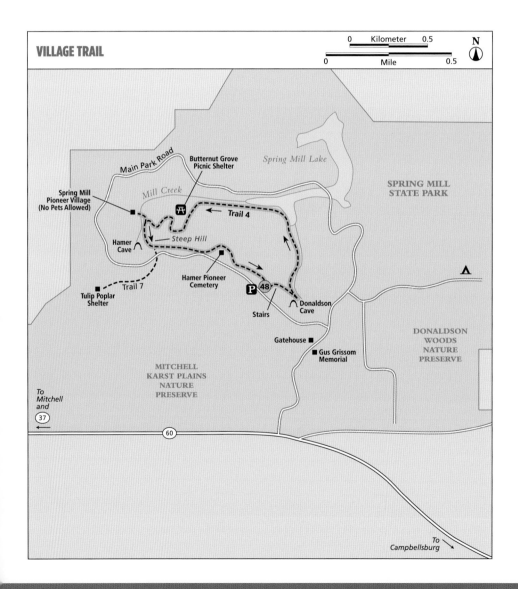

After exploring the village, backtrack to Trail 4 and turn right (south) to make a steep climb that will lead to Hamer Pioneer Cemetery at the 1.8-mile mark. The cemetery was established in 1832 and is typical of pioneer cemeteries—set on high ground to avoid flooding and as a way of putting the deceased closer to Heaven. Hugh Hamer, who established the cemetery, was buried here following his death from smallpox in 1872.

Continue east from the cemetery for 0.2 mile to the trailhead parking area.

Note: Another park feature is the Gus Grissom Memorial, a tribute to one of the original seven Mercury astronauts, who grew up in nearby Mitchell. The museum displays numerous artifacts, including his Molly Brown space capsule.

MILES AND DIRECTIONS

0.0 Begin at the trailhead at the southeast edge of the parking lot; descend the stairs and turn right (southeast).

0.2 Reach Donaldson Cave.

1.0 Arrive at Butternut Grove Picnic Shelter.

1.3 Reach spur to Spring Mill Pioneer Village.

1.8 Arrive at Hamer Pioneer Cemetery.

2.0 Arrive back at the Donaldson Picnic Area.

SOUTHWEST

The following hikes have been lumped into this region for lack of a better way to arrange them. They extend from Patoka Reservoir in south-central Indiana to Harmonie State Park on the Wabash River northwest of Evansville, and from Lincoln State Park near the Ohio River to McCormick's Creek State Park just west of Bloomington. They are listed in a clockwise sweep heading north from Evansville.

A few of the six trails—Patoka Lake and the two at McCormick's Creek, for instance—have interesting natural features. Others appear simply because they are nice hikes.

Patoka Lake is an 8,800-acre reservoir managed by the US Army Corps of Engineers. The Indiana Department of Natural Resources manages the 26,000-acre recreational area surrounding the lake.

McCormick's Creek, Indiana's first state park, features a beautiful waterfall and canyon. Stone was quarried from the park to help build the first state capitol. North of the canyon and creek is Wolf Cave, which is 57 yards from one end to the other. The cave opening ranges from more than 5 feet to a narrow 18 inches at the east end. An EF-3 tornado caused severe damage to the park in spring 2023, cutting through the campground and the center of Wolf Creek Nature Preserve at 150 mph. Some facilities and trails were temporarily closed during cleanup. Call the park office for updates at (812) 829-2235.

Harmonie and Lincoln State Parks have historical significance. Harmonie is located just south of New Harmony, the site of two utopian communities in the early 1800s. Lincoln State Park is situated near the pioneer farm where Abraham Lincoln spent his formative years, ages 7 to 21.

Shakamak State Park, south of Terre Haute, is a beehive on hot summer days as visitors take advantage of the popular park pool. The park and its three lakes are situated on abandoned coal mine property, which the citizens of Clay, Greene, and Sullivan Counties donated to the state in the late 1920s.

49 HARMONIE STATE PARK

WHY GO?
A combination of loop trails traverses ravines and forest.

THE RUNDOWN

Location: About 25 miles northwest of Evansville, southwest Indiana
Distance: 3.0-mile loop
Elevation change: About 70 feet
Hiking time: About 2 hours
Difficulty: Moderate
Jurisdiction: Indiana Department of Natural Resources, Division of State Parks
Fees and permits: Park entry fee, higher for out-of-state vehicles; season passes available

Maps: USGS Solitude; Harmonie State Park brochure
Special attractions: Stream crossings; ravines; large trees, including one of the largest pecan trees in Indiana
Camping: 200 modern electric campsites; youth tent area
Trailhead facilities: Picnic shelter and parking area but no drinking water at trailhead; water sources available at other park locations

FINDING THE TRAILHEAD
From New Harmony turn left (south) on IN 69 and go about 2.5 miles to IN 269. Turn right (west) and go 1 mile to the park gatehouse. From the gatehouse follow the main park road for about 4 miles; pass the pool and turn left (south) at the entrance to Sycamore Ridge Picnic Area. The trailhead begins about 15 yards off the main park road.

THE HIKE
Established in 1966, this park draws its name from the nearby town of New Harmony, the site of two failed experiments at developing a utopian community in the early 1800s. The first was a religious experiment led by Father George Rapp, a German immigrant, who sold the town in 1824 to Robert Owen, a Scottish industrialist. Owen sought to establish a community in which everyone shared the work and the profit. During Owen's short two-year leadership, New Harmony developed the first free public school and first kindergarten in America, providing equal education for boys and girls, and the first free public library. The town has been restored as a tourist attraction, but none of those elements are reflected in the park other than the name.

The hike is typical of Indiana state park hikes—an up-and-down venture over ridges and ravines with a couple of slow-moving streams.

Take the hike in a clockwise direction by picking up Trail 4 where it crosses the Sycamore Ridge Picnic Area access road (there is a trail marker). Turn left (west) from the access road. The trail parallels the main park road for less than 0.25 mile before swinging left (southwest) on a slight downward slope. At 0.25 mile it bends back to the right

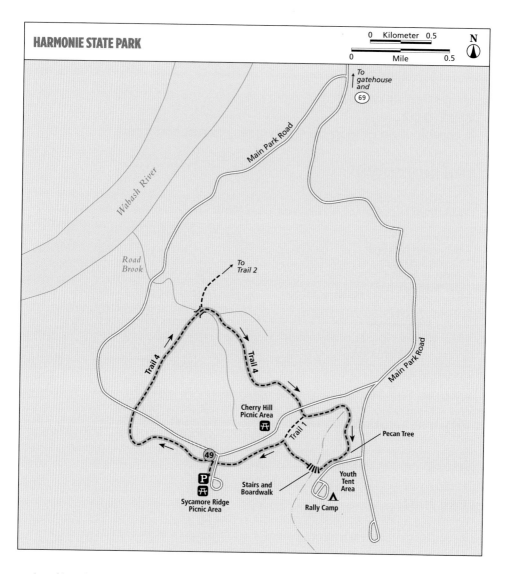

(north) and continues down and over an intermittent stream before rising on the other side to meet the main park road at the 0.4-mile mark.

Cross the main road and pick up the trail on the other side. Immediately you will begin a long but gradual descent into another ravine. Walk up the opposite side of the ravine and drop down once more to where two streams converge near a small bridge at 0.7 mile. Cross the bridge and turn right (southeast) to climb out of the ravine, reaching the 1.0-mile mark near the top of the hill that in spring blossoms with Dutchman's breeches, violets, and other wildflowers.

Continue east and southeast along a ridgetop before dropping down slightly and then up to reach the main road near the Cherry Hill Picnic Area. Cross the road at 1.5 miles and pick up Trail 1, turning left (northeast). Trail 1 parallels the south edge of the park road for 100 yards before bending right (south) at a trail marker and crossing the back end of a ravine. As the trail reaches the back of the youth tent area at 2.0 miles, pass beneath one of the largest pecan trees in Indiana. Cross through the open area and follow the paved road, passing a latrine before turning right (north) at a Trail 1 marker. Enter one final ravine. After walking up the other side, turn left (southwest) at a Trail 4 marker at 2.6 miles. Hike parallel to the main road for 0.4 mile west to the Sycamore Ridge access road and the trailhead.

MILES AND DIRECTIONS

0.0 Begin at the trailhead at the trail marker; go clockwise.

0.4 Cross the main park road.

0.7 Cross the bridge and turn right.

1.5 Cross the main park road and connect with Trail 1; turn left (northeast).

2.0 Reach the youth camp area.

2.6 Connect with Trail 4 and turn left.

3.0 Arrive back at the trailhead.

WHY GO?

This trail loops around Lake Shakamak, the smallest of three lakes in the park.

THE RUNDOWN

Location: South of Terre Haute, southwest-central Indiana
Distance: 3.5-mile loop
Elevation change: Minimal
Hiking time: About 2 hours
Difficulty: Moderate
Jurisdiction: Indiana Department of Natural Resources, Division of State Parks
Fees and permits: Park entry fee, higher for out-of-state vehicles; season passes available

Maps: USGS Jasonville; Shakamak State Park brochure
Special attractions: Backwater bays, boardwalks
Camping: 8 full-hookup, 124 electric, and 43 non-electric campsites; family or group cabins, including 2 ADA-accessible cabins
Trailhead facilities: Restrooms, nature center, swimming pool, and picnic area at trailhead

FINDING THE TRAILHEAD

Go 17 miles south on US 41 from Terre Haute to IN 48 and turn left (east). Go 9.5 miles to the park entrance on the west. After passing the gatehouse, turn right (west); stay right at the next fork, then go to the first intersection and turn left (west) to the nature center and swimming pool. The park's Trail 1 can be hiked in either direction by beginning at the parking lot. The best way is to begin at the nature center and head north of the parking lot alongside the swimming pool, hiking in a counterclockwise direction.

THE HIKE

Shakamak owes its name to the Kickapoo, a Native American tribe that lived in the area. The Kickapoo called the nearby Eel River *Shakamak*—meaning "river of long fish."

Shakamak was established as a state park in 1929, and much of its development was done during the 1930s by the Civilian Conservation Corps.

There are seven hiking trails in the park, totaling 13.3 miles. Trail 1 is the longest at 3.5 miles. It begins in a bustling area with a swimming pool, picnic area, and nature center, but it does not take long to escape the hubbub along the wooded lakeshore. For the most part, the trail is easy to follow because it hugs the lakeshore, although it is slightly confusing near the family cabin area. Trail use is modest, due in part to the popularity of the swimming pool.

From the north side of the nature center, facing the lake, walk down a set of stone steps and turn right to follow a path that skirts the shoreline for most of the hike. Footbridges, staircases, and boardwalks dominate the early portion of the hike, providing easy passage over areas prone to wetness or erosion.

At 0.3 mile you will reach a floating boardwalk at the back of a bay that forms the first of the lake's four fingers. After crossing the boardwalk, turn left (west) and continue along the shore to complete the first finger at 0.6 mile. It is another 0.7 mile over more boardwalks and footbridges around the second finger bay. At the back end of the second finger, Trail 2 cuts off to the right (north) and leads to the youth camp area. Instead stay left (west) and continue on Trail 1 to the third finger of Lake Shakamak.

The back end of the lake's third finger is somewhat swampy, but a boardwalk, which includes a small viewing deck, zigzags through it. Exit the boardwalk at 1.8 miles and turn left (south) along the shoreline to a point directly across the lake from the pool.

After bending to the right (northwest) around that point, begin hiking the final finger. The family cabins are on the opposite (southwest) shore of this bay. At the back end of

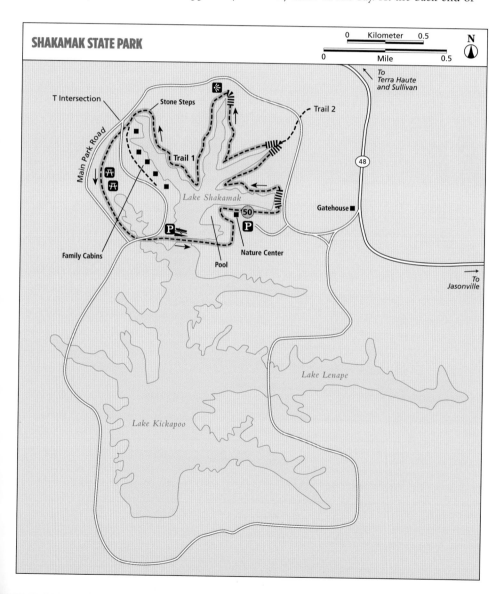

the bay, leave the lakeshore by hiking uphill via stone steps at 2.4 miles. Take a right (southwest) turn when the trail meets a T intersection; a left (south) turn goes to the family cabins. Walk through a stand of pine trees to the main park road at 2.7 miles.

The park road forks here; go directly across the left (east) fork and follow the trail through more pines and over small footbridges. Pass a pair of picnic shelters. At 3.0 miles reach a paved road that leads to the boat launch for Lake Shakamak. Turn left (east); pass the boat launch parking lot and pick up the paved pathway that leads over the earthen dam that separates Shakamak from the much larger Lake Kickapoo. After crossing the dam, turn left (north) to reach the parking area for the pool and picnic area.

MILES AND DIRECTIONS

- **0.0** Begin at the north side of the nature center and descend stone steps; turn right.
- **0.3** Cross a floating boardwalk and turn left to follow the lakeshore.
- **0.6** Complete the first finger bay.
- **1.8** Exit the boardwalk and turn left (south).
- **2.4** Climb stone steps near the family cabins.
- **2.7** Cross the main park road.
- **3.0** Reach the boat ramp road. Go left, cross the dam, and turn left (north) to return to the parking area.
- **3.5** Arrive back at the trailhead.

51 FALLS CANYON TRAIL

WHY GO?

A combination of park trails leads through McCormick's Creek Canyon from a canyon waterfall to the White River and back.

THE RUNDOWN

Location: McCormick's Creek State Park, west of Bloomington
Distance: 3.0-mile loop
Elevation change: About a 150-foot drop from the falls to the White River
Hiking time: About 1.5 hours
Difficulty: Strenuous
Jurisdiction: Indiana Department of Natural Resources, Division of State Parks
Fees and permits: Park entry fee, higher for out-of-state vehicles; season passes available
Maps: USGS Gosport; McCormick's Creek State Park brochure

Special attractions: McCormick's Creek Falls, the White River, old stone quarry
Camping: The campground is closed temporarily due to tornado damage. Call the park office at (812) 829-2235 for updates. Lodging available at family cabins and the park's full-service Canyon Inn.
Trailhead facilities: Ample parking at the trailhead for Trail 3; restrooms, water, and other facilities spread throughout the 1,961-acre park

FINDING THE TRAILHEAD

From its intersection with IN 37 near Bloomington, go 15 miles west on IN 46 to the McCormick's Creek State Park entrance. Turn right (north) to reach the gatehouse. From the gatehouse follow the main park road just over 0.25 mile to the Canyon Inn entrance (the second left turn). Turn left (north) and go to the main parking lot. Begin the hike on Trail 3 at the east side of the parking lot.

THE HIKE

The Canyon Inn, near the starting point of this hike, rests on the original foundation of a sanitarium that became a turning point in the history of the area. The sanitarium was built more than a century ago by a physician, Frederick Denkewalter, who believed the tranquil canyon and cliffs provided an ideal setting as a resting place for the wealthy. The parklike surroundings also became a popular picnic and hiking spot for area residents. After Denkewalter died in 1914, the state and Owen County purchased the land and established Indiana's first state park in 1916.

McCormick's Creek State Park has grown to more than five times its original size of 350 acres. Some sections of this loop are rough because the trail follows the rocky creek bed. Other sections are steep climbs into and out of the canyon on stone or wooden stairways. The area near White River may be impassable during high water.

The park sustained significant damage in March 2023 when a tornado swept through with winds approaching 150 mph that knocked down thousands of trees. Most affected

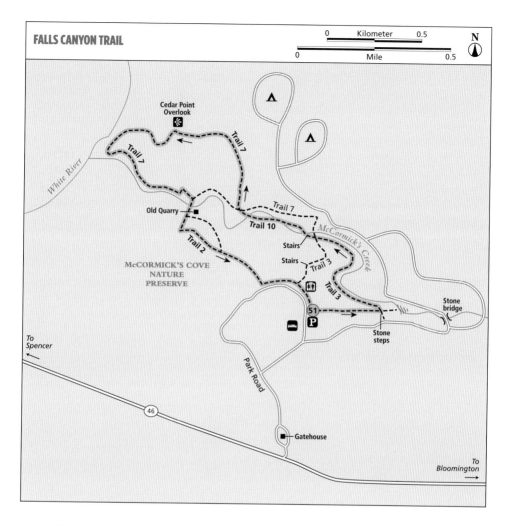

Cedar Point
Overlook

Trail 7

Trail 7

White River

Old Quarry

Trail 10

Trail 7

McCormick's Creek

Trail 2

Stairs

Stairs

Trail 3

McCORMICK'S COVE
NATURE
PRESERVE

Trail 3

Stone
bridge

51

P

Stone
steps

To
Spencer

Park Road

46

Gatehouse

To
Bloomington

was the campground, with dozens of sites destroyed. The campground is closed indefinitely for reconstruction, and some trails are temporarily closed for cleanup. The hike, as described, anticipates reopening of the closed trails.

The hike combines parts of Trails 3, 7, 2, and 10. Begin northeast of the inn near the center of the parking lot, where a gravel trail leads to a Trail 3 marker. Signs along Trail 3 warn of hazardous areas along the cliffs overlooking the canyon. A stone stairway leads down to the canyon floor and the falls at 0.3 mile. McCormick's Creek is named for John McCormick, the first settler in the area, who homesteaded nearly 100 acres along the creek and canyon. It is not a big creek—at times no more than 3 feet wide—which makes the high-walled canyon carved from the limestone bedrock even more impressive.

Turn left (northwest) at the creek and follow its rocky banks for about 0.5 mile before passing an elaborate wooden stairway (Trail 3) that leads up the left (south) side of the canyon and back to the stone restroom near the inn. Stay in the canyon and follow Trail 10. Cross over to the right (north) side of the creek; continue less than 0.25 mile to a bend in the creek and cross back over to the left (south) side. A connector trail joins from the left (south) at a steep wooden stairway at 1.0 mile. Cross once more to the right (north) side of the creek and turn right (north) to climb uphill on a different connector trail via another wooden stairway.

Cross over Trail 7 and continue north to the campground before curling left (west) along a gravel road that leads downhill to the White River. At 1.6 miles stop at the Cedar Point Overlook; a wooden shelter on a bluff to the right (north) of the road provides a nice spot from which to view the river. Before reaching the river, you will pass a water filtration plant that services the park.

Turn away from the river and head southeast to an elevated boardwalk. Once off the boardwalk, continue east along Trail 7 to intersect Trail 2 at 2.3 miles. Turn right (southeast) onto Trail 2, crossing the creek to an old limestone quarry at 2.4 miles. Blocks of stone are piled by the site, from which limestone was taken for use in construction of the statehouse in Indianapolis. This area is in the heart of McCormick's Cove Nature Preserve, one of two state-dedicated nature preserves in the park. The other is Wolf Cave Nature Preserve, home to the next hike.

Go left from the quarry and make a steep uphill climb out of the canyon on a course to the southeast. Continue uphill on Trail 2 to pass the trailside shelter house and Civilian Conservation Corps Recreation Hall and reach a paved road. Turn left (east) and follow the paved road about 0.25 mile back to the parking lot where Trail 3 began.

MILES AND DIRECTIONS

0.0   Begin at the trailhead at the Trail 3 marker, on the east side of the parking lot.

0.3   Reach the falls overlook and stone steps.

0.8   Arrive at the junction with a connector trail on the left.

1.0   Reach the junction with the second set of stairs, on the right.

1.6   Arrive at the Cedar Point Overlook.

2.3   At the junction of Trails 7 and 10, turn right (south) and cross the creek.

2.4   Reach the old quarry at the junction with Trail 2; go uphill on the quarry connector trail.

2.7   Reach the park road; turn left (east).

3.0   Arrive back at the trailhead.

52 WOLF CAVE TRAIL

WHY GO?
Travel through a state nature preserve to an open cave.

THE RUNDOWN

Location: McCormick's Creek State Park, west of Bloomington
Distance: 2.0-mile lollipop loop
Elevation change: Minimal
Hiking time: About 1 hour
Difficulty: Moderate
Jurisdiction: Indiana Department of Natural Resources, Division of State Parks
Fees and permits: Park entry fee, higher for out-of-state vehicles; season passes available
Maps: USGS Gosport; McCormick's Creek State Park brochure

Special attractions: Wolf Cave, Twin Bridges
Camping: A spring 2023 tornado ripped through McCormick's Creek State Park, temporarily closing the campground and some trails. Call the park office at (812) 829-2235 for updates. Lodging available at family cabins and the park's full-service Canyon Inn.
Trailhead facilities: Water available at several places in the park, including the stone restroom near the start of Trail 5

FINDING THE TRAILHEAD

From its intersection with IN 37 near Bloomington, go 15 miles west on IN 46 to the McCormick's Creek State Park entrance. Turn right (north) to reach the gatehouse. From the gatehouse follow the main park road past the Canyon Inn entrance (the second left turn). Continue in a counterclockwise drive that goes east, then west before reaching the Wolf Cave parking lot on the right (north) side of the road shortly before the park campground.

THE HIKE

Wolf Cave, the focal point of this trail, has a storied past. But which story is true? One legend tells of a young pioneer woman who was walking home after selling goods to flatboat operators at the nearby White River. Passing the cave, she encountered a pack of wolves. She was able to elude them by throwing off her gloves and bonnet as decoys. Another tale has her washing clothes at nearby Litten Branch when the wolves attacked. Less romantic is a third story, in which the last wolf in Owen County was killed near the cave in 1845.

The park sustained significant damage in March 2023 when a tornado swept through with winds approaching 150 mph that knocked down thousands of trees. Most affected were the campground and Wolf Cave Nature Preserve, where downed trees were stacked 6 feet high on the trail. While the campground is closed indefinitely for reconstruction, and some trails were affected, the hike, as described, anticipates reopening of the closed trails.

Regardless of how it got its name, Wolf Cave is an example of how caves are formed by groundwater erosion of the limestone bedrock prevalent in this park. The popularity of Wolf Cave, coupled with a new trailhead that eliminates crossing McCormick's Creek Canyon, makes this one of the busier trails in the park. Many visitors hike only to the cave and return the same way, skipping the eastern leg of the trail along Litten Branch. Those who do miss out on a pleasant stroll through the rest of Wolf Cave Nature Preserve.

To reach the cave, begin at the Trail 5 trailhead and walk north through a wooded area pockmarked with funnel-shaped sinkholes. At 0.3 mile, Trail 5 intersects Trail 8, a paved path from the campground (left) to the nature center and pool (right). Continue straight and enter Wolf Cave Nature Preserve at 0.4 mile and cross a footbridge over Litten Branch. Cross the creek a couple more times before reaching Wolf Cave.

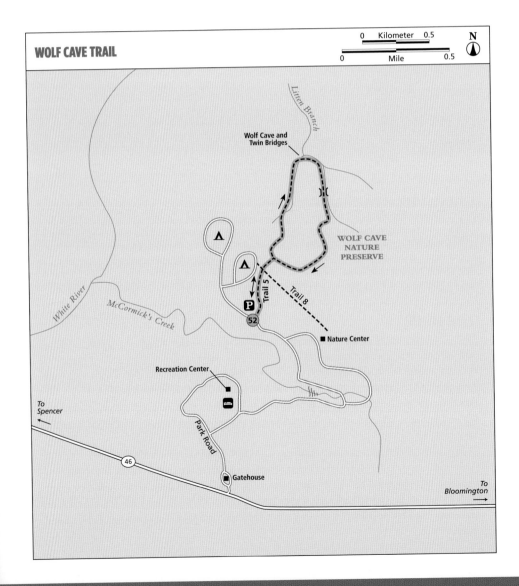

Follow the trail around the cave to Twin Bridges. Going through the cave may be prohibited to protect bats and their nesting habitat. Even if the cave is not marked as closed, the passageway is a challenge at 60 yards long with a narrow 18-inch opening at the far end. The cave is usually dry in summer but can be wet after extended periods of rain. Wear long pants and bring a flashlight. It is dark in the cave, plus the light helps in spotting critters, such as the cave salamander.

The cave opens at Twin Bridges, which was created when a roof section of Wolf Cave collapsed. Stay on Trail 5 and follow the east fork of Litten Branch south from Twin Bridges, crossing the creek once on a footbridge and then rock-hopping several more times over the next 0.5 mile. Near the 1.3-mile mark, the trail turns right (southwest) for a gradual uphill climb. Three benches are scattered along the trail, providing pleasant places to pause and enjoy the solitude of the surrounding forest. The beech tree is the dominant species in the preserve, but maple, sycamore, walnut, tulip poplar, and elm trees are also present. Oak trees—red, white, and chinquapin—prevail on the high ground, along with hickory trees.

At 1.7 miles cross Trail 8 again and continue on Trail 5 to the trailhead parking lot.

MILES AND DIRECTIONS

0.0 Begin at the Trail 5 trailhead.

0.3 Reach a junction with Trail 8; go straight.

0.4 Enter Wolf Cave Nature Preserve; go straight.

1.0 Reach Wolf Cave and Twin Bridges.

1.7 Reach the Trail 8 junction; stay straight on Trail 5 and return to the trailhead parking lot.

2.0 Arrive back at the trailhead.

53 PATOKA LAKE MAIN TRAIL

WHY GO?

This trail skirts the perimeter of a broad peninsula near the west end of Patoka Lake, the state's second-largest reservoir.

THE RUNDOWN

Location: Southern Indiana, about 18.5 miles south of French Lick
Distance: 6.5-mile loop
Elevation change: About 60 feet
Hiking time: About 3 to 4 hours
Difficulty: Strenuous
Jurisdiction: Indiana Department of Natural Resources, Division of State Parks
Special attractions: Totem Rock, Pilot Knob, other sandstone cliffs

Fees and permits: Park entry fee, higher for out-of-state vehicles; season passes available
Maps: USGS Cuzco and Birdseye; Patoka Lake hiking area brochure
Camping: Newton-Stewart State Recreation Area—445 electric and 81 non-electric campsites; 7 backpacking sites
Trailhead facilities: Large parking lot at the trailhead; restrooms and water available at the nature center; water also available at campgrounds

FINDING THE TRAILHEAD

From French Lick go 13.5 miles south on IN 145 to IN 164 and turn right (west). Go 1.3 miles to Dillard Road and turn right (north). Go just over 1 mile to the gatehouse, then another 1.7 miles before turning left (west) and going 1 more mile to the nature center parking lot. The trailhead is off the northeast corner of the building.

THE HIKE

Archaeological evidence indicates humans inhabited this area as long ago as 10,000 years. Stone tools, pottery shards, and flint points have been discovered here. Early white settlers found petroglyphs of three turtles carved into a rock and on nearby trees. No explanation was ever determined, but speculation was that the artwork represented some sort of totem or "family mark" to native peoples. Consequently, the site came to be known as Totem Rock. Although the carvings were destroyed more than a hundred years ago, the name stuck.

Totem Rock remains one of the highlights on this trail. The rock is in the beginning portion of the 6.5-mile loop that traces a clockwise path around the edge of Newton-Stewart State Recreation Area on the western end of Patoka Lake. The 8,800-acre reservoir was created by the US Army Corps of Engineers in the 1970s as a flood-control project for the Patoka River and more than a half-dozen smaller creeks and rivers.

The Main Trail is the centerpiece of a 15-mile trail complex on the 1,000-acre peninsula that makes up the Newton-Stewart area. Various shortcuts and spurs cross the trail,

A hiker passes beneath the shadows of Totem Rock at Patoka Lake Main Trail. The sandstone formation has long attracted people.

but the hike is simple to follow because of the prominent trail markings. Red circles are painted on trees and are visible from both directions. Each trail intersection is marked with lettered waypoint signs posted at intervals that vary in length from 0.25 to 1 mile. The first waypoint is M, and subsequent ones in order are A, B, C, D, E, K, and L.

Beginning on Trail 2, the outbound leg of the Main Trail along the western side of the peninsula presents the area's most rugged aspects—a continuous series of gullies and rolling ridges decorated by sandstone outcroppings. The first evidence of the sandstone formations comes just past the M waypoint. Go straight and make a short descent to a rocky bluff that offers a prelude to what lies ahead.

Totem Rock is the most impressive formation on the trail. Many hikers go no farther than this spot before backtracking to the nature center. Arrive at the large rock overhang

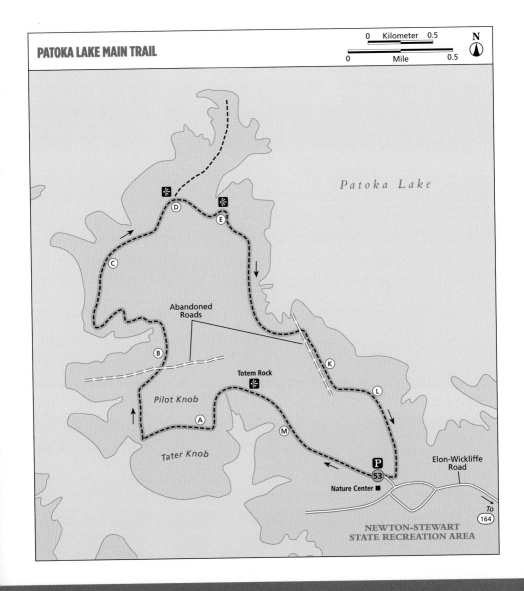

PATOKA LAKE MAIN TRAIL

at 1.4 miles. The rock served as a gathering place for settlers for many years, either for church services or picnics. Local residents also called it Saltpeter Cave.

Head downhill (south) away from Totem Rock, cross a creek, and head uphill to a meadow at Tater Knob. Cross the meadow on an uphill course to the northwest and reenter the woods before the 2.0-mile mark. Continue to pass through gullies and by rock ledges. At waypoint A, stay right (west) to circle around Pilot Knob to reach waypoint B near an abandoned road. Go straight to reach waypoint C.

Cross an abandoned road at about 3.7 miles and pass through a small meadow. The trail reaches waypoint D at 4.3 miles where a sign indicates that the lake is to the left (north); the Main Trail continues straight (east) and connects with Trail 3. Skirt the edge of two meadows, the second being the larger, as the trail crosses the north end of the peninsula then turns south at waypoint E and continues for the final 2.0 miles; L is the last waypoint before returning to the trailhead.

Almost half that distance is over a series of gullies that carry seasonal runoff. Beech trees dominate this area, but there is also a pine plantation along this side of the peninsula where bald eagles regularly nest in winter. A watchful hiker might be able to spot one.

MILES AND DIRECTIONS

0.0   Begin at the trailhead at the northeast corner of the nature center and go left.

1.0   Reach waypoint M and go straight.

1.4   Reach Totem Rock.

2.5   Arrive at Pilot Knob.

3.7   Waypoint C; cross an abandoned road.

4.3   Waypoint D; go right at the trail sign that reads "To Lake/Trail Continues."

4.5   Waypoint E; stay left.

6.5   Arrive back at the trailhead.

54 LINCOLN STATE PARK

WHY GO?

This hike combines several park trails over ground walked by Abraham Lincoln during his boyhood years.

THE RUNDOWN

Location: South of Dale, Spencer County
Distance: 5.2-mile double loop
Elevation change: Minimal
Hiking time: About 3 hours
Difficulty: Easy
Jurisdiction: Indiana Department of Natural Resources, Division of State Parks
Fees and permits: Park entry fee, higher for out-of-state vehicles; season passes available
Maps: USGS Chrisney and Santa Claus; Lincoln State Park brochure

Special attractions: Gravesite of Lincoln's only sister, Sarah; Sarah Lincoln's Woods Nature Preserve; Lincoln Lake; Lincoln Memorial Plaza
Camping: 150 modern electric and 89 non-electric campsites; youth tent area
Trailhead facilities: Parking lot, restrooms, and water supply at trailhead; water and restrooms available at other locations throughout the park

FINDING THE TRAILHEAD

From Dale drive 5 miles south on US 231 to IN 162 in Gentryville. Turn left (east) and go 1 mile to the Lincoln State Park entrance, which is across from the Lincoln Boyhood National Memorial on the left (north) side of the highway. Turn right (south) to the park gatehouse and go 0.1 mile to the Lincoln Memorial Plaza parking lot. Turn left (east) into the parking area. The trailhead is on the south side of the parking lot.

THE HIKE

Born in Kentucky and elected from Illinois as the nation's sixteenth president, Abraham Lincoln spent his boyhood days here in Indiana. Of his Indiana years, he is quoted as saying, "There I grew up."

The Lincolns moved from Kentucky to this area in 1816, the year Indiana became a state. Abraham was only 7 and his sister, Sarah, was 9. Thomas Lincoln, their father, settled on 160 acres of dense forest.

Young Abe helped his father clear the land for a frontier farm they worked for fourteen years before moving to Illinois. The actual farm site is across the highway from the state park at Lincoln Boyhood National Memorial, which is administered by the National Park Service. The gravesite of Lincoln's mother, Nancy Hanks Lincoln, is across the highway. She died in 1818 of "milk sickness," poisoning caused by consuming the milk or meat of cows that had eaten white snakeroot. The national memorial has a visitor center, a cabin site memorial, a living historical farm, and several short hiking trails.

The gravesite of Sarah Lincoln, sister of Abraham Lincoln. The cemetery and Little Pigeon Primitive Church are located in the park.

Although farming occupied much of young Abe's life, he no doubt explored some areas of the state park that bears his name. It is known that he frequented the Noah Gorden mill.

The following hike combines elements of Trails 1, 2, 3, and 5, which also have names— Lake Trail, John Carter Trail, Sarah Lincoln Grigsby Trail, and Mr. Lincoln's Neighborhood Walk, respectively.

From the Lincoln Memorial Plaza, hike north parallel to the main park road. Go about 0.1 mile before joining Trail 2; the John Carter Trail, named for a Lincoln family neighbor. Turn right (east) to enter a stand of pine trees. At 0.4 mile the trail angles to the northeast and makes the first of several crossings over Davis Enlow Ditch, a creek that trickles off to the northwest. There are several footbridges along the way.

Part of the trail is an old roadbed that runs parallel to railroad tracks within the park boundary. At 1.0 mile pass a couple abandoned coal strip mine pits, after which the trail turns to the west to go uphill slightly.

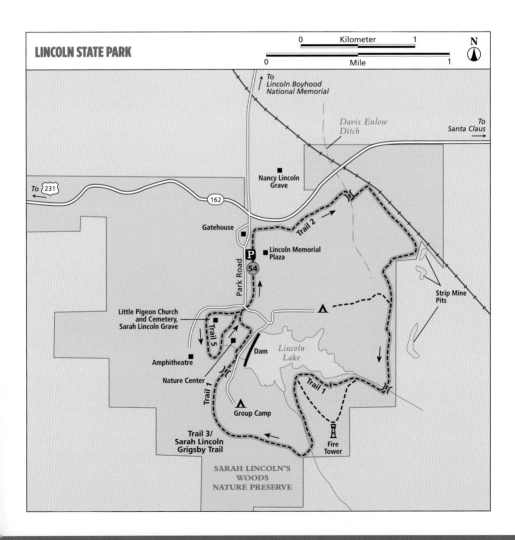

Turn south (left) at the hilltop, following the park's east boundary for more than 0.5 mile over a couple of ridges. At 1.5 miles an unmarked trail joins from the right. Keep going straight (south), crossing more footbridges before reaching a concrete bridge at 2.0 miles. Cross the bridge and walk parallel to the creek that feeds Lincoln Lake. Trail 2 ends at the lakeshore, where it links with Trail 1 (Lake Trail) at 2.2 miles.

Turn left (south) onto Trail 1, passing two spur trails that lead to a fire tower, and continue for about 0.5 mile to where Trail 1 joins Trail 3 (Sarah Lincoln Grigsby Trail). Turn left onto Trail 3, which leads through Sarah Lincoln's Woods Nature Preserve, a 95-acre area extending from the creek west over a ridgetop. The preserve has a variety of oak species—red, white, black, post, blackjack, and scarlet—plus many other common hardwoods like pignut hickory, sugar maple, white ash, and shagbark hickory.

Leave the west end of the preserve as the trail descends off the ridgetop to curl clockwise through a low spot. Cross a footbridge before exiting the woods just below the lake dam near the group camp area to reconnect with Trail 1 at 4.0 miles. Cross the dam on Trail 1 and a boat ramp for Lincoln Lake to intersect Trail 5 off the north corner of the dam.

Turn left (west) onto a gravel path that leads to the Little Pigeon Primitive Baptist Church, the church the Lincolns joined when Abe was 14. His sister is buried in the graveyard behind the church.

Continue west on the gravel road past the church and turn left (south) to pass the site of Noah Gorden's mill and home at 4.5 miles. Turn left (east) at the homesite and curl back through the woods to complete the loop just east of the church at 4.8 miles. Turn right (east) and cross the paved road; turn left (north) to cross the main park road and go up a set of stone steps. Follow Trail 2, which runs parallel to the main park road, to return to the Lincoln Memorial Plaza parking lot.

MILES AND DIRECTIONS

0.0 Begin at the trailhead on the south side of the parking lot.

0.1 Turn right (east) at the Trail 2 junction.

0.4 Cross Davis Enlow Ditch for the first time.

1.0 Pass abandoned coal mine pits.

1.5 Continue straight at an unmarked trail junction.

2.0 Cross a concrete bridge.

2.2 At the trail junction go right(west) on Trail 1 along lakeshore.

2.3 At the trail junction go straight (west).

2.6 At the trail junction go straight (south) to join Trail 3.

3.8 Reach the Lincoln Lake dam and reconnect with Trail 1; go left.

4.1 At the trail junction, go left (west) on Trail 5, a gravel road to Mr. Lincoln's Neighborhood Walk.

4.2 Arrive at the Little Pigeon Primitive Baptist Church and cemetery.

4.5 Pass the site of Noah Gorden's mill.

4.8 At the gravel road and Mr. Lincoln's Neighborhood Walk, turn right (east).

4.9 At the trail junction turn left (north).

5.2 Arrive back at the trailhead.

HOOSIER NATIONAL FOREST

From just south of Bloomington to Tell City on the Ohio River, the Hoosier National Forest forms a patchwork covering 204,000 acres. Despite its size, the Hoosier represents a mere 1 percent of the massive hardwood forest that blanketed Indiana before pioneer settlement.

Lumber was a major commodity by the late 1800s, and Indiana led the nation in timber production in 1899 by harvesting more than 1 billion board feet, mostly prime hardwoods like white oak, black walnut, and tulip poplar. It is estimated that an average 800 million board feet of timber were cut annually from 1869 to 1903. By comparison, less than half that amount is being harvested in Indiana today, but hardwood remains a vibrant commodity in an industry that has a $17 billion annual economic impact in the state.

In the 1800s, trees documented as being 6 to 12 feet in diameter were chopped down and sold off. Most of the virgin forest was gone in fifty years. In addition, wildlife species that once roamed Indiana were gone, including white-tailed deer and wild turkey.

The demolition of forestland happened everywhere across the state, but the consequences seemed most impactful in southern Indiana, where settlers learned a hard lesson. Land was cheap at $1 per acre, but the steep, rocky ground—devoid of trees and depleted of nutrients—was prone to erosion and unsuitable for agriculture.

Small farms were failing, and the Great Depression only made matters worse. As farms were abandoned, the tax-delinquent land created a mounting fiscal problem for state and local governments. In 1934 Governor Paul McNutt sought help from the USDA Forest Service, asking the agency to purchase land with the intent of establishing a national forest.

The first parcels were acquired in 1935, and in 1951 the Hoosier National Forest (HNF) was established. In the meantime, the Civilian Conservation Corps played a hand in reforestation efforts on the land. Although it does not match its pre-settlement glory, the forest has regrown and HNF has become the largest single landholding in the state. Within its scattered boundaries are some noteworthy sites.

The Charles C. Deam Wilderness, a 13,000-acre tract just south of Bloomington, is named for Indiana's first state forester. Granted federal wilderness protection by Congress in 1982, the Deam Wilderness borders Monroe Lake and contains forested ridgetops and ravines typical of southern Indiana. Inhabited by Native Americans nearly 12,000 years ago, the area's rugged terrain made it one of the last places in Indiana where European settlers attempted to put down roots. At one time eighty-one small farms and 57 miles of rural roads existed in what is now the Deam Wilderness; all that remains today are remnants of that bygone era.

Hemlock Cliffs is a box canyon carved out of sandstone by seasonal waterfalls. Eastern hemlock, an uncommon tree in Indiana, grows along the high cliffs of this canyon.

Pioneer Mothers Memorial Forest features an 88-acre stand of virgin timber that has been protected since 1816—the year Indiana became a state.

There are countless other treasures in the Hoosier National Forest, including an abundance of wildlife. The deer and turkeys that were once absent have been restored, making the Hoosier a popular area for hunters, who can also pursue squirrels and other game.

The forest service maintains a 260-mile trail system in the Hoosier National Forest, most of which are multiple-use trails for hikers, mountain bikers, and horseback riders. There are countless additional miles of abandoned trails, primitive roads, and forest service roads for the more adventurous explorer.

The trails in this chapter are presented south and southwest from Bloomington.

55 COPE HOLLOW LOOP

WHY GO?
This trail leads through the Charles C. Deam Wilderness of the Hoosier National Forest.

THE RUNDOWN

Location: South of Bloomington, south-central Indiana
Distance: 10.5-mile loop
Elevation change: Several drops and rises into and out of ravines along the way, steepest at 280 feet
Hiking time: About 6 hours
Difficulty: Moderate to strenuous
Jurisdiction: Hoosier National Forest, Brownstown Ranger District (Bedford)
Maps: USGS Elkinsville, Allens Creek, and Norman; Hoosier National Forest's Charles C. Deam Wilderness map (www.fs.usda.gov/hoosier)
Fees and permits: No fees or permits required for hiking; trail permit required for horse use; bicycles not permitted in Deam Wilderness

Special attractions: Todd Cemetery, Dennis Murphy Hollow
Camping: Walk-in camping is permitted anywhere in the wilderness area, except within 100 yards of Tower Ridge Road, and is restricted to designated sites when within 100 feet of ponds, lakes, trails, streams, and designated trailheads. Other wilderness rules on food and beverage containers also apply; group size is limited to 10 or fewer people. Equestrian sites available at nearby Blackwell Campground.
Trailhead facilities: 2 gravel parking lots on either side of Tower Ridge Road for about 16 vehicles; no restrooms or drinking water

FINDING THE TRAILHEAD
From the intersection of IN 46 and IN 446 on the east side of Bloomington, go about 12 miles south on IN 446 to Tower Ridge Road. Turn left (east) and go 5.5 miles to the Grubb Ridge parking area. The trail begins on the north edge of the small parking area. Additional parking is available on the south side of the road.

THE HIKE
The Hoosier National Forest boasts 260 miles of trails, of which less than 20 percent are dedicated solely for hikers. The Cope Hollow Loop is a multiuse venue, which means you may share it with horseback riders.

There is plenty to see on this hike, but it takes some effort to get to the highlights, like Todd Cemetery, Cope Hollow, and Dennis Murphy Hollow. Foot traffic is light, probably because horseback riders make heavy use of the trail. That makes for pretty rough trail conditions in certain spots. Be alert to abandoned trails that occasionally join the main trail. When uncertain, look for forest service trail markers—thin plastic markers about 3 feet tall.

Begin the hike at the Grubb Ridge trailhead by walking past the metal gate on the north side of the parking lot. This is the same starting point as the Peninsula Trail. At 0.1

mile turn left off the Peninsula/Grubb Ridge Trail to pick up the westbound leg of the Cope Hollow Trail. The trail does not wander far from the lightly traveled Tower Ridge Road over the next few miles. The trail does cross over the gravel road a couple of times.

At 0.6 mile the trail splits. The left (south) path is the inbound leg of the Cope Hollow Trail. Go right (west) and continue with Tower Ridge Road to the right (north) and the back end of Dennis Murphy Hollow to the left (south). Pass an abandoned trail that joins from the left (south). Cross over to the north side of Tower Ridge Road at 1.1 miles.

Pass through a stretch of clearings as the trail curves toward the southwest. A series of deep ravines drop off to the right (north) over the next 1.0 mile, but the trail keeps a relatively level course. The last of the ravines forms the east edge of Frog Pond Ridge, a 1.5-mile finger pointing almost directly north to Saddle Creek, which flows into Monroe Lake. Continue left (south), hugging Tower Ridge Road until coming to Todd Cemetery at the 3.0-mile mark. Pass along the west edge of the cemetery and make a fishhook turn to the northwest. Go another 0.5 mile to a trail split. Stay left, crossing Tower Ridge Road to the southwest at 3.5 miles.

Pass through a meadow and the edge of a ridge for approximately 1.0 mile. After descending the ridge, turn left (north) into Cope Hollow and cross Little Salt Creek at 4.7 miles.

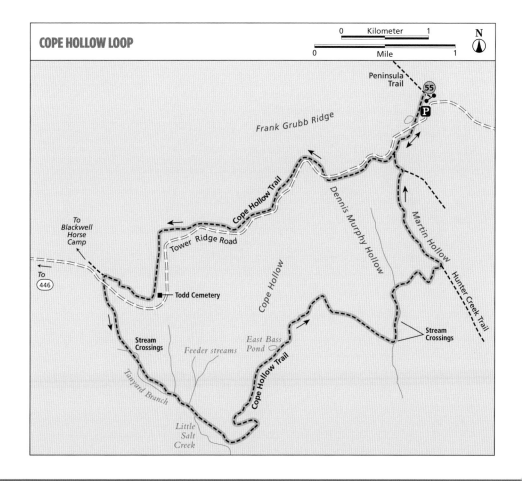

After crossing the creek, begin a sharp uphill climb of more than 100 feet to a ridge forming the eastern boundary of Cope Hollow. The next stretch of trail rises 100 feet over a span of about 1.25 miles, alternating between woods and meadows before reaching a wilderness campsite near East Bass Pond. From here, continue uphill to a ridgetop; turn right (southeast) then angle slightly left and drop into Dennis Murphy Hollow at 6.5 miles. After reaching the creek at the floor of the hollow at 7.1 miles, turn left (north). Follow the small stream through a fern-laden valley for 0.4 mile before turning right (northeast). Cross the creek and climb to a ridge that separates Dennis Murphy Hollow from Martin Hollow.

The ridge flattens out noticeably at the top as the trail passes through a couple of stands of pine trees before it intersects the Hunter Creek Trail at 7.8 miles. Turn left (northwest) at the intersection and drop just below the ridgetop to meander around a series of gullies that tumble into Martin Hollow. Move back up to the ridgetop and follow a northward course before reaching a trail intersection at 9.0 miles. Turn left (west), passing a small pond on the left before reconnecting with the outbound leg of the Cope Hollow Trail near Tower Ridge Road at 9.3 miles. Turn right (northeast) and follow the trail back to the Grubb Ridge trailhead.

MILES AND DIRECTIONS

0.0   Begin at the trailhead at the north edge of the parking area.

0.1   Turn left at the trail junction.

0.2   Cross to the south side of Tower Ridge Road.

0.6   At the trail intersection go right (west).

1.1   Cross to the north side of Tower Ridge Road.

3.0   Pass Todd Cemetery.

3.5   Cross to the south side of Tower Ridge Road.

4.7   Descend a ridge and turn left to reach Little Salt Creek at the opening to Cope Hollow.

4.8   Turn left (northeast), cross the creek, and climb uphill.

6.5   Descend to Dennis Murphy Hollow.

7.1   Reach the creek in the bottom of the hollow.

7.8   Arrive at the Hunter Creek Trail junction; bear left.

9.0   At the trail junction turn left (west).

9.3   Return to Tower Ridge Road and cross over to north side.

10.5   Arrive back at the trailhead.

56 PENINSULA TRAIL

WHY GO?

This hike through Charles C. Deam Wilderness leads to a peninsula jutting into Monroe Lake, the state's largest lake.

THE RUNDOWN

Location: Hoosier National Forest, 16 miles southeast of Bloomington, south-central Indiana
Distance: 10.5 miles out and back
Elevation change: 300 feet from trailhead to lakeshore
Hiking time: About 5 hours or overnight
Difficulty: Moderate
Jurisdiction: Hoosier National Forest, Brownstown Ranger District (Bedford)
Fees and permits: No fees or permits required for hiking; trail permits required for horse use; bicycles not permitted in Deam Wilderness
Maps: USGS Elkinsville; Hoosier National Forest map (www.fs.usda.gov/hoosier)

Special attractions: Peninsula campsite, Monroe Lake
Camping: 5 designated campsites near the end of the trail. Walk-in camping is permitted anywhere in the wilderness area, except within 100 yards of Tower Ridge Road, and is restricted to designated sites when within 100 feet of ponds, lakes, trails, streams, and designated trailheads. Other wilderness rules apply; group size is limited to 10 or fewer people. Equestrian sites available at nearby Blackwell Campground.
Trailhead facilities: 2 gravel parking lots on either side of Tower Ridge Road for about 16 vehicles; no restrooms or drinking water

FINDING THE TRAILHEAD

From the intersection of IN 46 and IN 446 on the east side of Bloomington, go about 12 miles south on IN 446 to Tower Ridge Road. Turn left (east) and go 5.5 miles to the Grubb Ridge parking area. The trail begins on the north edge of the small parking area. Additional parking is available on the south side of the road.

THE HIKE

This trail is a linear extension off another trail, the 12.3-mile Grubb Ridge Loop. The Peninsula Trail, which is shared with horseback riders, is a worthy stretch because of the destination—a backcountry campsite overlooking a sizable portion of Monroe Lake, the perfect setting from which to view spectacular sunsets. The area features two prominent ridges—Frank Grubb Ridge and John Grubb Ridge. The majority of the Peninsula Trail lies along the latter.

Established by Congress in 1982, the wilderness area covers nearly 13,000 acres. It is a well-used and well-marked area, largely because lengthy portions of the trail follow abandoned roadbeds.

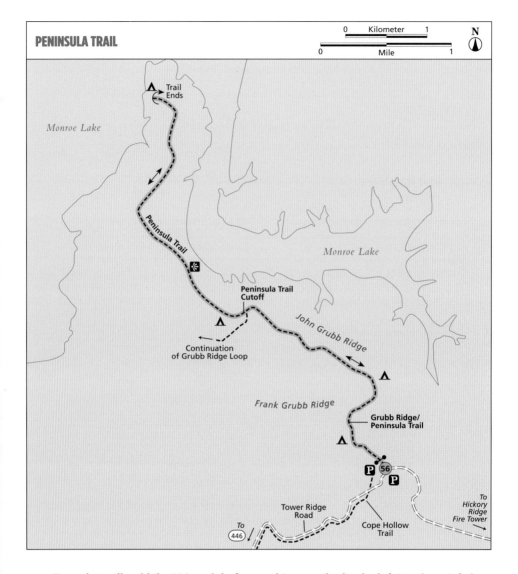

From the trailhead hike 100 yards before reaching a trail split; the left (southwest) fork begins the Cope Hollow Loop. The right (northeast) fork is the beginning of the Grubb Ridge Loop leading to the Peninsula Trail; take the right fork.

The trail, on an abandoned roadbed, curves through a forest of mixed hardwoods punctuated by occasional stands of pine trees. Backcountry campsites can be located along the trail. Eventually the route straightens out on a northwesterly course along John Grubb Ridge. The ridgetop provides a reasonably level path, with occasional uphill stretches, but most of the topographic changes occur on either side of the trail—gradual slopes to the left, sharper drops on the right toward Monroe Lake.

At 2.7 miles the trail splits. The Grubb Ridge Loop (Peninsula Trail cutoff) breaks to the left (southwest). Turn right (northwest) to continue toward the peninsula, passing through an area dotted with older hardwoods and little undergrowth. After 0.5 mile begin a descent of about 100 feet in elevation. Here, at 3.0 miles, the trail overlooks a steep drop-off to the lake nearly 200 feet to the right (northeast). The remainder of the hike is a gradual descent in which scenery alternates through pine and hardwood stands, forest openings, cedar thickets, and patches of scrub brush.

Near the end of the trail, look for signs of old farmsteads—fence posts, rusted barbwire strands, perhaps an old pot or two, or remnants of an abandoned vehicle. Walk right to reach the rocky shores of Monroe Lake, a 10,750-acre reservoir created when the US Army Corps of Engineers dammed Salt Creek and several smaller tributaries—Clear, Sugar, Allens, Moore, and Saddle. The east side of the peninsula borders the Middle Fork State Wildlife Refuge, a haven for waterfowl.

To complete the hike, retrace the outbound path to the Grubb Ridge parking area at 10.5 miles.

MILES AND DIRECTIONS

0.0 Begin at the trailhead at the north edge of the parking area. Walk 100 yards and bear right at the fork.

2.7 Go right (northeast) at the trail junction.

3.0 Reach the Monroe Lake overlook.

5.3 Arrive at the peninsula campsite, your turnaround point.

10.5 Arrive back at the trailhead.

57 SYCAMORE LOOP

WHY GO?

The trail leads along a creek and to ravine overlooks of the Charles C. Deam Wilderness.

THE RUNDOWN

Location: Southeast of Bloomington
Distance: 6.8-mile loop with spur
Elevation change: Gains and losses of 250 feet
Hiking time: About 3.5 hours or overnight
Difficulty: Moderate
Jurisdiction: Hoosier National Forest, Brownstown Ranger District (Bedford)
Fees and permits: No fees or permits required
Maps: USGS Elkinsville; Hoosier National Forest map (www.fs.usda .gov/hoosier)
Special attractions: Hiker-only trail, Sycamore Branch Valley, a pioneer cemetery, Hickory Ridge fire tower

Camping: There are 6 designated campsites on this trail. Walk-in camping is permitted anywhere in the wilderness area, except within 100 yards of Tower Ridge Road, and is restricted to designated sites when within 100 feet of ponds, lakes, trails, streams, and designated trailheads. Other wilderness rules apply; group size is limited to 10 or fewer people. Equestrian sites available at nearby Blackwell Campground.
Trailhead facilities: Gravel parking area; no restrooms or drinking water at trailhead

FINDING THE TRAILHEAD

From the intersection of IN 46 and IN 446 on the east side of Bloomington, go about 12 miles south on IN 446 to Tower Ridge Road. Turn left (east) and go 6 miles to the Hickory Ridge fire tower parking area. The trail begins on the north edge of the parking area on the other side of the gate.

THE HIKE

Of the handful of hiker-only trails in the Hoosier National Forest, this ranks near the top. Difficulty is moderate, and the chance for solitude is superb.

The trail gets its name from the Sycamore Branch of Salt Creek and about a third of the hike follows the meandering rocky stream on an easterly course through a thick stand of towering white pines. But it is the tall sycamores near the headwaters that make it obvious how settlers came to name the stream that trickles east and then northeast into the South Fork of Salt Creek, which feeds nearby Monroe Lake, the state's largest lake.

The secluded stretch is popular for overnight campers at marked and unmarked campsites. The beginning and ending legs of this trail receive the heaviest traffic because of campsite locations and the cemetery.

A sign for the Charles C. Deam Wilderness along the Sycamore Loop

Begin by hiking down the gravel road that leads to Terril Cemetery and will later serve as the inbound leg of this hike. At 0.25 mile turn right (east) off the roadway at a marked campsite and begin a gradual downhill walk along a ridgetop for another 0.25 mile. At the east tip of the ridge, the path becomes a little steeper and a series of switchbacks leads into a valley near the headwaters of Sycamore Branch.

As you cross the stream for the first time at the 1.0-mile mark, you may hear traffic along Tower Ridge Road on the high bluff to the right (south). Continue to hop back and forth across the stream several times over the next 1.0 mile while hiking through a valley dominated by white pines and tulip poplars.

At 2.4 miles take an abrupt left (northwest) turn to begin an uphill stretch of trail that is almost leisurely in that it takes a full mile to climb 250 feet from the valley floor to the top of Terril Ridge. Along the way the forest switches from the thickly clustered pine trees of the valley floor to a mixture of hardwoods—oak, hickory, beech—and occasional pine trees.

At 3.2 miles turn right (northeast) onto an old roadbed and head downhill for 0.1 mile, then back uphill to where the roadbed turns right (southeast) at 3.3 miles. Go straight (north) and continue uphill. At 3.5 miles turn left (west) and wind west and south along a ledge that overlooks the Jones Branch ravine on the right (northwest) side of the trail.

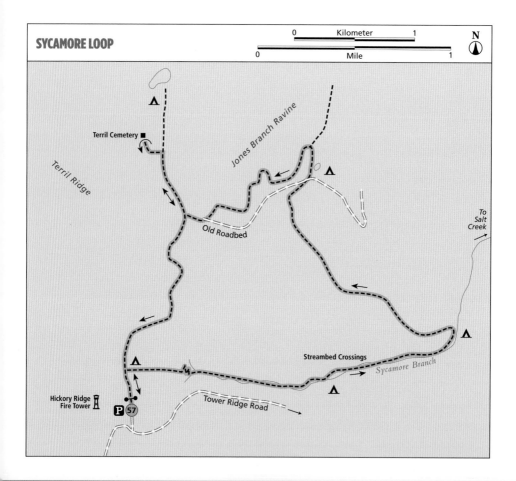

SYCAMORE LOOP

At 4.3 miles reconnect with the gravel road and turn right (north). At 4.7 miles turn left (west) toward the Terril Cemetery, which can be seen from the roadway, or continue straight (north) for 0.25 mile to a remote pond that offers camping possibilities.

Grave stones in the small cemetery mark the final resting place for members of the Terril, Axsom, and Grubb families, whose legacies survive as place names in the Deam Wilderness—Terril and Grubb Ridges and the Axsom Branch of Salt Creek. The fading headstones give a clue to the harsh times the families endured while attempting to scratch out a living during the late 1800s and early 1900s. With rare exception, dates indicate that few lived beyond sixty years. Hezekiah and Alice Axsom have five children under the age of 13 buried here, including four who died in one year—1931. The Whites lost a son who lived but two days.

Upon returning from the cemetery to the gravel road at 5.3 miles, turn right (south) and follow its winding path for about 1.5 miles back to the Hickory Ridge parking area at 6.8 miles. Before leaving, get an impressive view of the Hoosier National Forest and surrounding areas from the Hickory Ridge fire tower. It is the only remaining fire tower of eight that once were scattered around the Hoosier National Forest. Built by the Civilian Conservation Corps in 1939, this one was staffed for fire detection until the 1970s. It is 110 feet tall, with 133 metal steps up to the 7-foot-square cab.

MILES AND DIRECTIONS

0.0 Begin at the trailhead at the gate on the north edge of the parking area.

0.25 At the marked campsite, turn right (east) off the gravel road.

1.0 Cross Sycamore Branch.

2.4 Turn left (northwest) and leave the valley on the climb to Terril Ridge.

3.2 At the old roadbed turn right (northeast).

3.5 At the trail junction turn left (west).

4.3 At the gravel road turn right (north).

4.7 Take the left (west) turnoff to Terril Cemetery. (**Option:** Continue straight [north] for 0.25 mile for possible campsites.)

5.3 Return to the gravel road and turn right (south).

6.8 Arrive back at the trailhead.

58 PIONEER MOTHERS MEMORIAL FOREST

WHY GO?

This linear trail passes through an old-growth forest undisturbed since at least the early 1800s.

THE RUNDOWN

Location: Just outside Paoli, south-central Indiana

Distance: 1.4 miles out and back

Elevation change: 180 feet from the parking lot to the memorial wall

Hiking time: About 45 minutes

Difficulty: Easy

Jurisdiction: Hoosier National Forest, Tell City Ranger District

Fees and permits: No fees or permits required

Maps: USGS Paoli; Hoosier National Forest map (www.fs.usda.gov/hoosier)

Special attraction: Pioneer Mothers Memorial Wall

Camping: No camping permitted

Trailhead facilities: Parking lot; no restrooms or drinking water at trailhead

FINDING THE TRAILHEAD

From the Paoli town square go west on IN 56 for 1 block to the first stoplight. Turn left (south) onto IN 37 and go 2 miles to a parking area on the left (east) side of the highway. The trail begins at the north end of the parking lot.

THE HIKE

Joseph Cox was the original owner of this property, and it was his decision in the early 1800s that preserved the ancient trees gracing an 88-acre section of this 250-acre property.

Cox was not the first inhabitant, though. Archaeologists found evidence of a Native American village that dates to around 1380 AD.

Cox and his family managed to keep the woods untouched, despite numerous bids from timber companies. A community-wide effort to purchase the property from the Cox estate gained national exposure through the *Saturday Evening Post,* and the citizens were able to carry on Cox's pledge by raising the necessary $24,300. The USDA Forest Service acquired the property in 1944 and designated it as a "research natural area," which gave it federal protection while providing the forest service an area in which to study plant succession, tree growth, and forest conditions.

The Forest Service collaborates with Purdue University's forestry school to do periodic assessments of trees on the property. Although the trail remains open, you may notice some damaged trees from a 2023 tornado.

The trail is unmarked other than at the entrance, but it is easy to follow for the short distance to the memorial wall and back. The area is not heavily visited.

From the west-end parking lot, locate the trail near an information marker. Enter the woods and begin a gradual downhill walk through a cathedral of enormous hardwoods.

At 0.7 mile, reach the Pioneer Mothers Memorial Wall to the left of the trail. The wall was built in 1951. A picnic area that was near the wall years ago has been removed, and a paved road leading from the north trailhead off US 150 has been barricaded.

From the memorial wall, head uphill to the east-end trailhead before backtracking to the west-end parking lot.

MILES AND DIRECTIONS

0.0   Begin at the west-end trailhead at the north end of the parking lot.

0.7   Reach the Pioneer Mothers Memorial Wall. Retrace your steps to the trailhead.

1.4   Arrive back at the west-end trailhead.

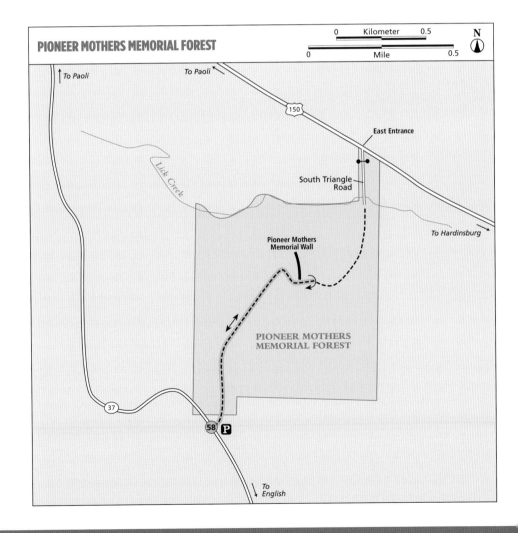

59 HEMLOCK CLIFFS NATIONAL SCENIC TRAIL

WHY GO?

This trail leads through a box canyon draped with hemlock and features seasonal waterfalls and high sandstone cliffs.

THE RUNDOWN

Location: 7 miles south of English, south-central Indiana
Distance: 1.4-mile loop
Elevation change: 70 to 80 feet
Hiking time: About 1 hour
Difficulty: Moderate
Jurisdiction: Hoosier National Forest, Tell City Ranger District
Maps: USGS Taswell; Hoosier National Forest map (www.fs.usda.gov/hoosier)

Fees and permits: No fees or permits required
Special attractions: Hiker-only trail, two waterfalls
Camping: No camping permitted
Trailhead facilities: Gravel parking lot; no restrooms or drinking water at trailhead

FINDING THE TRAILHEAD

From the intersection of IN 37 and I-64, go north 2.7 miles to Crawford CR 8 and turn left (west). Go 2.5 miles to an unmarked gravel road. Take the gravel road 1.7 miles west and then north to a marked entrance for Hemlock Cliffs National Scenic Trail. Turn right (north) at the sign and take the gravel road (FS 1134) to the loop at its end; park. The trailhead is east of the parking lot.

From the new IN 37, brown signs lead the way to the trailhead along county roads. Follow these signs to the trailhead.

THE HIKE

This trail has more dynamic scenery packed into its short distance than many longer hikes. There are two seasonal waterfalls, steep-walled box canyons, a meandering creek, and hemlock trees dotting the sandstone cliffs.

The trail's remote location serves as a limiting factor on the area. The box canyons were popular with rock climbers, but visitation started to decrease when the forest service imposed a ban on rock climbing in 1996.

The trailhead marker is easily visible east of the parking area. Follow the crushed-stone walkway downhill to the trailhead and turn right (south). At 0.2 mile the trail turns left (east) and descends through a gap in the ledge. Wiggle through the opening to the left and descend a set of natural-stone steps into the canyon. Its closed, bowl-shaped end to the right (south) is wet with a trickle of water even in the middle of summer.

The trail heads left (northeast) from the waterfall and crosses the small creek before reaching a Y intersection at the 0.6-mile mark. The right fork leads to another box canyon and small waterfall at 0.7 mile, which can be viewed from below or from a higher vantage point, depending on which side path is taken. Climbing or rappelling on the rock face of the box canyon and waterfall is prohibited by order of the forest service.

Return to the Y intersection and turn right to resume the hike. Sheer cliffs and gradual slopes shadow the passage as the trail crosses a meandering creek four or five times before heading out of the ravine at 1.1 miles on an uphill walk through woodlands. The trail gradually levels off before returning to the parking lot at 1.4 miles.

MILES AND DIRECTIONS

0.0 Begin at the trailhead at the east end of the parking lot; turn right (south).

0.2 Descend into the box canyon to the waterfall via a narrow gap in the cliff; go left.

0.6 Bear right at the Y intersection.

0.7 Reach the second waterfall. Return to the Y and turn right.

1.1 Go uphill to exit the ravine.

1.4 Arrive back at the trailhead.

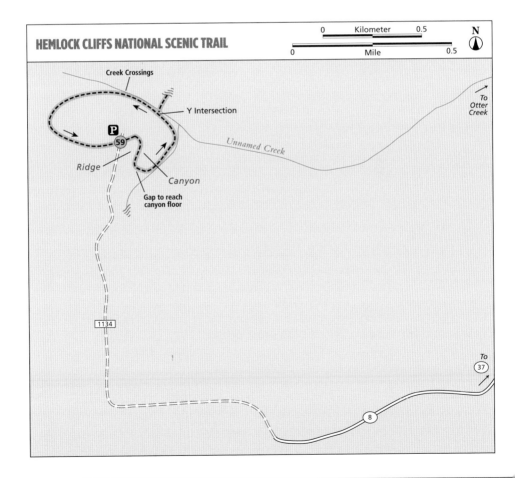

HEMLOCK CLIFFS NATIONAL SCENIC TRAIL

Creek Crossings

Y Intersection

To Otter Creek

Unnamed Creek

Ridge

Canyon

Gap to reach canyon floor

1134

To 37

8

60 **TWO LAKES LOOP**

WHY GO?

A double-loop trail circles Celina and Indian Lakes as part of the American Discovery Trail.

THE RUNDOWN

Location: Northeast of Tell City, southern Indiana
Distance: 15.3-mile loop
Elevation change: About 340 feet from high point to low point
Hiking time: Overnight
Difficulty: Moderate to strenuous
Jurisdiction: Hoosier National Forest, Tell City Ranger District
Maps: USGS Branchville and Bristow; Hoosier National Forest map (www.fs.usda.gov/hoosier)
Fees and permits: Parking fee Apr 15 through Oct 15

Special attractions: Hiker-only trail, sandstone bluffs along the northeast shore of both lakes, historic Rickenbaugh House, 2 stream crossings
Camping: 63 campsites at 2 adjacent locations near the east side of the property (rates vary per season and per site)
Trailhead facilities: Small gravel parking lot but no restrooms or drinking water at trailhead; drinking water, pit toilets, and seasonal shower facilities available in the campgrounds

FINDING THE TRAILHEAD

From Tell City go about 18 miles northeast on IN 37, passing IN 145 and IN 70 to the marked entrance to Indian-Celina Lakes of Hoosier National Forest. Turn left (west). From the gatehouse go about 2.5 miles to the trailhead parking lot on the left (south) side of the main road. It is the last of 6 parking lots on the main road leading to a boat ramp at Indian Lake.

THE HIKE

Restricted to hikers only, this trail is as easy to follow as those in state parks, but without the traffic. There are several stream crossings, including two over the Anderson River and Tige Creek that can be knee-deep or deeper. Take along a pair of thick-soled beach booties or water socks for these two short water crossings. Although there is an elevation difference of nearly 350 feet between the high and low points on the trail, there are few elevation changes of more than 100 feet at one time.

Begin at the designated parking lot between the two lakes. There are other entry points, but this trailhead provides the option of taking the entire hike (as presented here) or in two halves by using a connector trail that bisects the overall hike into almost equal parts that can each be handled without difficulty in a few hours.

From the parking lot go southwest on the connector trail, looking for markers that designate the path as part of the American Discovery Trail (ADT). Markers are varied on the trail—white paint blazes on trees, white plastic forest service tags, tin tags, ADT tags, and brown plastic forest service posts. Confused? All markers follow the same course. The only differences worth noting are the orange markings on the forest service brown posts that designate the connector trail.

The connector trail moves quickly into a stand of pine trees; look for a pond downhill to the left (east). After reaching the pond, join the main trail at a T intersection at 0.9 mile. A right (west) turn leads to Indian Lake; a left (east) turn goes to Celina Lake. Take the right option and head uphill toward a noticeable knob. Upon passing the knob, veer to the left (southwest) and continue toward another knob—the high spot of the Indian Lake loop at 775 feet elevation, or about 275 feet above the lake.

A saddle leads to another knob, but the trail bends before reaching the peak and takes a counterclockwise path around the knob while beginning a gradual descent toward Indian Lake. The north-facing slopes are a good location in spring to see toothwort, trillium, and dogtooth violet (trout lily). Round a stand of white pine trees and catch a glimpse of Indian Lake through the trees.

At 2.1 miles exit the woods to begin a stretch that goes over Indian Lake Dam. The dam forms 150-acre Indian Lake by controlling the flow from Anderson River and Tige Creek. At the west edge of the dam, turn right (north) and walk the west shore of Indian Lake, aptly named since it parallels an old Indian treaty boundary. The terrain is noticeably different here as the trail rolls over small ridges and through shallow gullies for about 1.0 mile. The landscape is punctuated by the presence of large rocky outcroppings above and to the left (west) of the trail.

After crossing a seasonal stream at 3.5 miles, begin climbing as the trail bends uphill toward the northwest and away from the lake. Reach a clearing near the top of the hill and connect with an abandoned roadway at a T intersection at 4.3 miles. Turn right (north) and follow the gravel road downhill to another T intersection, crossing a small concrete bridge over a stream. The gravel road turns left (northwest), but the trail turns right (southeast). Go 0.1 mile to cross another creek by hopscotching over the rocks. The trail is not well marked in this area, but the path can be located without much trouble on the other side of the creek.

Pass a stand of pine trees near the northeast corner of the lake—a stretch that can be muddy at times. In contrast are some beautiful sandstone cliffs about 50 yards inland from the lakeshore. At 5.6 miles, before you reach the northeast corner where Anderson River and Tige Creek flow into the lake, turn left (northwest) and head uphill. Daffodils bloom in abundance on this hillside in springtime. Near the top of the hill, pass through another pine plantation before sliding down off the ridge to Anderson River at 6.5 miles.

There is no bridge here, but the water is shallow enough under most circumstances to wade the 20-foot distance from bank to bank without getting wet above the calf. It is a good idea to remove your hiking boots before fording the river—no need to get them wet when you have another creek to cross and miles to go before completing the hike. The river bottom is gravel and rock, so take care to avoid cutting or injuring your feet if you did not bring the recommended beach booties or water socks.

Once on the other side, walk along a flat stretch that bends around the point of a ridge separating Anderson River from Tige Creek. After rounding the point, link up with Tige Creek and walk its bank for a less than 0.25 mile before having to cross the creek at 6.8 miles. Again, this may require removal of hiking boots, depending on the depth of the water. It is shallow enough at times to cross without having to change footwear.

After crossing the creek, enter a stand of tall pine trees. The pine stand is a suitable location for an off-trail campsite.

At the other end of the pines, turn right and head uphill for 0.75 mile to intersect the orange-marked connector trail at 7.6 miles. (**Option:** You can turn right here and take a 1.0-mile shortcut back to the trailhead parking lot.) For the described overnight hike, turn left (east) to add the remaining mileage around Celina Lake—a loop that begins by descending part of the way into a broad ravine and then climbing the other side to a pine plantation. A marked crossroad provides another chance to head back to the trailhead parking lot. Turn left instead to continue toward Celina Lake, heading northeast around the base of a knob that peaks at 815 feet in elevation.

The trail itself levels around 700 feet and then heads down to Winding Branch at 9.1 miles; this is the main tributary that feeds Celina Lake. Before you reach the creek, however, you will pick up an old roadbed and follow it on a southwest course to the main road. Turn left (southeast) at the road and walk about 100 yards before crossing the road at 9.2 miles to pick up another old roadbed. This goes south along Winding Branch for about 0.5 mile before the trail makes a sharp left (east) turn at 9.7 miles and heads uphill just as Celina Lake comes into view.

Go uphill away from the lake, passing the campgrounds and crossing the paved road leading to the Celina Lake boat ramp at 10.1 miles.

You can go straight (south) here but take the time to follow the short Celina Lake Interpretive Loop, which leads to the historic Rickenbaugh House. Jacob Rickenbaugh and his family settled here in the 1870s, largely because bark from the abundant oak trees provided tannin for his trade as a master hide tanner. He paid three Belgian stone masons $3 a day to build the sandstone block house, which took one year to complete. It served as the local post office and church meetinghouse until a church was constructed at Winding Branch, a small town now beneath the waters of Celina Lake.

When the 0.8-mile interpretive loop rejoins the main trail, turn right (south) and head downhill to cross a small stream. There is no need to change footwear here or at the final stream crossing. After crossing the second stream, go up over a ridge and drop into another ravine. Go up the other side of the ravine as the trail closes in on Celina Lake. Continue along the east shore of the lake with minor elevation changes, hiking in and out of a series of fingerlike coves that become increasingly larger, except for the last one. The first two coves require dropping down off the ridges to cross small streams before going back uphill.

After rounding the final, smaller cove, exit the woods at the southeast corner of the earthen dam at 13.5 miles. After crossing the dam, the trail turns slightly to the left (southwest) below a ridge and crosses one last stream. This one is filled with larger rocks and is easy to get over. Head uphill from the stream to where the trail turns right (north) along an abandoned road at 13.8 miles. Go about 300 yards before turning left (north) off the road. Go another 300 yards to intersect the orange-marked connector trail at 14.4 miles. Turn right (north); it is about 0.9 mile back to the main trailhead parking lot.

The cross-country American Discovery Trail winds its way through southern Indiana.

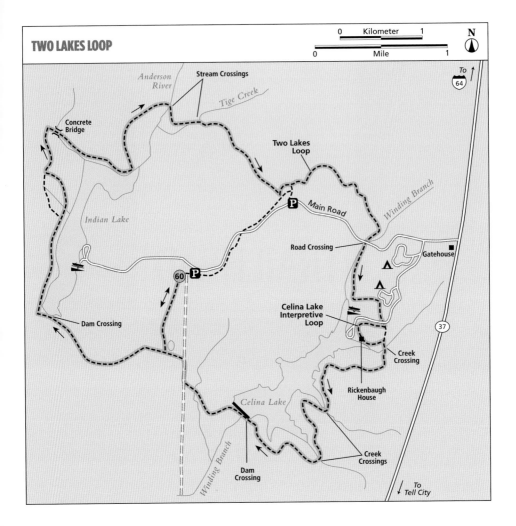

TWO LAKES LOOP

MILES AND DIRECTIONS

0.0 Begin at the designated main trailhead.

0.9 At the trail junction go right (west) to travel the loop in a clockwise direction.

2.1 Leave the woods to cross the Indian Lake dam.

3.5 Cross a seasonal stream.

4.3 Reach a trail junction at a logging road; turn right (north) onto the road.

5.0 At the trail junction turn right (southeast) onto the trail.

5.6 The trail changes direction; go left (north) and uphill.

6.5 Wade across Anderson River.

6.8 Ford Tige Creek.

7.6 At the trail junction go left (east) to continue Two Lakes Loop. (**Option:** Follow the orange-marked connector trail for 1.0 mile back to the trailhead.)

9.1 Reach Winding Branch and turn right (south).

9.2 Cross the main road; turn left (east) onto the gravel road and then turn right (south).

9.7 Turn left (east) and go uphill.

10.1 Cross the paved boat ramp road and turn right (west) onto the Celina Lake Interpretive Loop.

10.6 Visit the Jacob Rickenbaugh House (open seasonally).

11.1 The interpretive loop rejoins the main trail; turn right.

13.5 Reach the Celina Lake dam.

13.8 Turn right (north) onto the abandoned road.

14.4 Reach the trail junction; turn right (north) to return to the trailhead parking lot.

15.3 Arrive back at the parking lot.

61 TIPSAW LAKE TRAIL

WHY GO?
The trail loops around Tipsaw Lake.

THE RUNDOWN

Location: Northeast of Tell City, southern Indiana
Distance: 6.0-mile loop
Elevation change: About 80 feet
Hiking time: About 3 hours
Difficulty: Moderate
Jurisdiction: Hoosier National Forest, Tell City Ranger District
Fees and permits: Parking fee required for trailhead within Tipsaw Recreation Area; entry fee to access the campgrounds or boat ramp Apr 15 through Oct 15. A trail permit is required for mountain bikers age 17 and older.
Maps: USGS Bristow, Gatchel, and Branchville; Hoosier National Forest map (www.fs.usda.gov/hoosier)
Special attraction: Tipsaw Lake shoreline
Camping: 57 campsites; open mid-Apr to mid-Oct
Trailhead facilities: Parking lot and water fountain at the trailhead; restrooms available at the Tipsaw Lake Recreation Area campgrounds (gate fee)

FINDING THE TRAILHEAD

Go north from Tell City for 17 miles on IN 37 to the "Tipsaw Lake Recreation Area" sign. Turn left (west) and go 2 miles to the trailhead parking lot on the left (south) side of the road.

THE HIKE

Tipsaw Lake, formed primarily by Sulphur Fork Creek, Massey Creek, Snake Branch, and an unnamed stream, is one of four small reservoirs within this area of the Hoosier National Forest, all of which are circled by a trail. This may be the easiest of the four trails—a flat course except for a series of modest climbs at the outset that traverse the hillside between the boat ramp/picnic area and the campground. Otherwise this is hardly a challenge, but it is a pleasant hike.

Although the trail also is open to mountain bikes, it does not suffer from overuse. Hikers have the right-of-way over bikers. The trail is clearly marked with yellow diamond tags on trees, plus brown plastic marker posts. The yellow tags have black diamond directional arrows.

To begin, head southwest from the small trailhead parking lot on a crushed-stone pathway with stands of pine trees on one side and tulip poplars on the other. The trail continues a southwest course between the main road to the right (north) and Sulphur Fork Creek to the left (south). At 0.7 mile turn right (north) to cross the main road and hike up the wooded hillside, turning left (northwest) on a meandering stretch that works up and down the hill while crossing a footbridge and a couple of small streams.

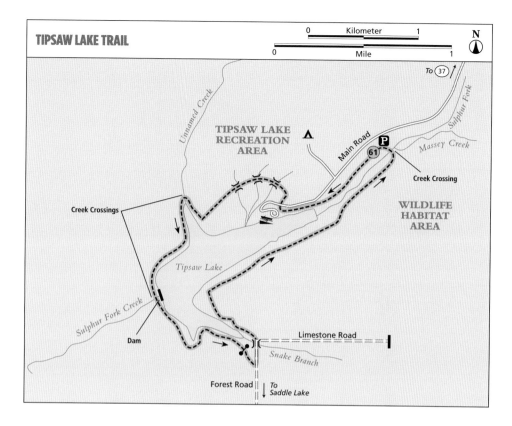

Return to the lake at 1.4 miles and hug the shoreline around a fingerlike bay pointing to the northwest. At the back end of the bay, cross an unnamed creek at 1.8 miles and continue south, then southwest, crossing several small seasonal creeks. Exit the woods at 2.0 miles to enter a shoreline meadow leading to the earthen dam at 2.4 miles. Hike across the dam to enter a stand of pine trees whose fallen needles help cushion the trail.

Cross a small creek at 3.0 miles. The trail then hugs the shoreline of another fingerlike bay, following an old roadbed for 0.5 mile. Pass a metal barricade at 3.5 miles; cross another small stream and briefly follow a gravel road that serves as a back entrance to the property. Turn left (north); cross Snake Branch at 3.6 miles.

The trail again follows the shoreline, first along the bay formed by Snake Branch and then turning northeast along the southeast shore of the main lake. Move up and down over small gullies and ridges for about 0.5 mile before coming to a large meadow that is managed as a wildlife clearing through a cooperative program of the US Forest Service and the Indiana Department of Natural Resources. The clearing is a good place to see deer or other woodland wildlife, so approach quietly.

At 5.9 miles the trail makes a hairpin turn to the left (northwest) and crosses Sulphur Fork Creek before returning to the trailhead parking lot.

MILES AND DIRECTIONS

0.0 Begin at the trailhead, southwest of the parking lot.

0.7 Turn right (north) and cross the main road.

1.4 Return to the lake and hug the shoreline.

1.8 Cross an unnamed creek.

2.0 Exit the woods and enter a shoreline meadow.

2.4 Cross the dam.

3.0 Cross a small creek.

3.5 Reach the metal barricade and gravel road; turn left (north).

3.6 Cross Snake Branch and stay straight on gravel road.

3.7 Reach intersection with Limestone Road; turn left (northwest).

3.9 Turn right (northeast).

4.4 Reach the wildlife clearing.

5.9 Cross Sulphur Fork Creek.

6.0 Arrive back at the trailhead.

62 SADDLE LAKE LOOP

WHY GO?

A short but scenic walk travels a hikers-only trail along the shores of Saddle Lake.

THE RUNDOWN

Location: North of Tell City
Distance: 2.2-mile loop
Elevation change: Minimal
Hiking time: About 1.25 hours
Difficulty: Moderate
Jurisdiction: Hoosier National Forest, Tell City Ranger District
Fees and permits: No fees or permits required except for overnight camping

Maps: USGS Gatchel; Hoosier National Forest map (www.fs.usda.gov/hoosier)
Special attraction: Lake views
Camping: 13 sites; fee per night/campsite
Trailhead facilities: Parking area, boat ramp, beach, and pit toilets at trailhead; no drinking water

FINDING THE TRAILHEAD

From Tell City go 10 miles northeast on IN 37 to the marked Gatchel exit. Turn left (northwest) and go 0.2 mile to a T intersection with Old IN 37. Turn right (northeast) and go 0.5 mile through Gatchel to a gravel entry road (FS 443) to Saddle Lake. Turn left (north) and go about 1 mile to a paved parking lot near the lake's boat ramp. Trail markers are located on the north side of the parking lot at the boat ramp.

THE HIKE

This trail can be hiked in either direction but is described here counterclockwise. The well-maintained trail appears to get little use.

Begin at the boat ramp and walk through a wooded area to a service road at 0.1 mile. Turn left (north) and head up a slight incline; enter the woods and continue along the southeastern lakeshore. Rocky outcrops punctuate the hillside to the right (east), and wildflowers dot the pathway in season.

Make the first creek crossing at 0.7 mile and enter a stand of large pine trees whose trunks are 2.5 feet in diameter. Make a slight climb out of the pines and back into hardwood forest to begin an up-and-down stretch over a series of moderate humps.

Cross a culvert at 1.0 mile and walk uphill again to a section of beech trees. Descend from this hump into a gully and the second creek crossing. Once more, go uphill and come close to a county road (Locust Road/Perry CR 18) before dropping back downhill to cross the lake's earthen dam at 1.4 miles. In spring and summer, wildflowers along the dam—bergamot, milkweed, butterfly weed, Queen Anne's lace, black-eyed Susan—attract an array of butterflies.

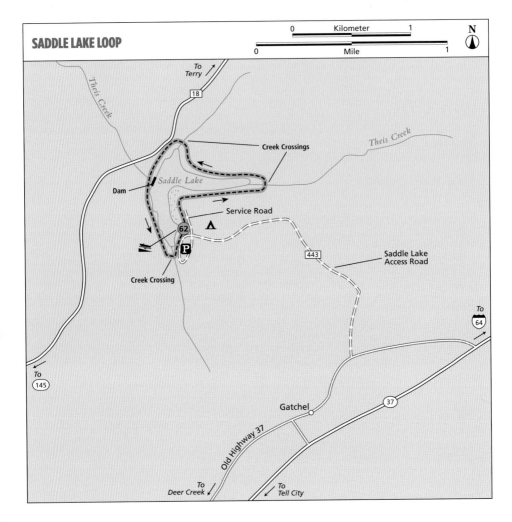

At the other end of the dam, follow a stretch of trail along the southwest shore of the lake that slips across two gullies. After the second gully, the trail is a straight shot on flat terrain about 30 feet above the lakeshore to another stand of pine trees. Drop off the flat at about 1.8 miles to make another creek crossover. The boat ramp is visible from here. Cross one last creek at 1.9 miles; go uphill and follow the gravel path back to the parking area.

MILES AND DIRECTIONS

0.0   Begin at the trailhead at the boat ramp.

0.1   Turn left (north) onto a service road.

0.7   Reach a creek crossing.

1.0   Cross a culvert.

1.4   Cross the Saddle Lake dam.

1.8 Make another creek crossing.

1.9 Make the last creek crossing.

2.2 Arrive back at the trailhead.

63 **MOGAN RIDGE EAST**

WHY GO?

The trail meanders through an abandoned farm field, over a narrow ridge, and across a shallow creek.

THE RUNDOWN

Location: Northeast of Tell City, near Derby
Distance: 6.4-mile loop, with new connector trail
Elevation change: 390 feet difference from Kuntz Ridge to Clover Lick Creek
Hiking time: About 3.5 hours
Difficulty: Strenuous
Jurisdiction: Hoosier National Forest, Tell City Ranger District

Fees and permits: No fees or permits required
Maps: USGS Derby; Hoosier National Forest map (www.fs.usda.gov/hoosier)
Special attractions: Kuntz Ridge, Clover Lick Creek
Camping: No camping permitted
Trailhead facilities: Parking area for about a half-dozen vehicles; no drinking water or restroom facilities

FINDING THE TRAILHEAD

Go 1 mile north on IN 66 from its intersection with IN 70 in Derby. Turn left (north) onto Perry CR 370/Utopia Road and pass the private boat ramp as you head uphill. The trailhead parking lot is on the right (east) side of the road, 0.7 mile from IN 66.

Alternate route: Because high water on the nearby Ohio River can flood access to the east trailhead, there is an alternate entry point. Go 2.9 miles west on IN 70 from the intersection with IN 66 in Derby to Perry CR 243/Ultimate Road. Turn right (north) and go 1.3 miles to a small gravel parking lot on the right (east) across from the Talley Cemetery. It is a 0.5-mile walk up the dirt road to a connector spur that joins the Mogan Ridge East and Mogan Ridge West Trails.

THE HIKE

It requires a little history lesson to understand how Mogan Ridge East got its name since no part of the trail is within a mile of Mogan Ridge. Once part of a larger multiuse trail, Mogan Ridge East has been set aside exclusively for hikers. Mogan Ridge West, which in part traverses Mogan Ridge, is an 11.0-mile trail that is open to hikers, bikers, and horseback riders. The two trails are connected by a 0.5-mile spur. Although only half as long, Mogan Ridge East is just as challenging as its counterpart.

The trail is marked with white diamonds and is easy to follow. Orange diamonds mark the new connector trail. Traffic typically is light.

Both the Mogan Ridge East and West Trails are part of the American Discovery Trail. Mogan Ridge East is a prime spot for wildflowers, especially in spring, when the path is festooned with splashes of sweet William, self-heal, daisy fleabane, wild geranium, Jacob's ladder, Virginia bluebell, and Virginia waterleaf.

To hike the Mogan Ridge East Trail from its east end, begin in the parking area off Utopia Road and cross the gravel road. Pass the metal gate and slip through a gap between a pair of knoblike hills. Go downhill to a trail junction at 0.4 mile. Turn left (southwest) and go through a meadow to the 0.6-mile mark, where the trail splits again. Turn left (south) and go uphill to the eastern tip of Kuntz Ridge.

At 1.8 miles swing clockwise around the base of a triangular-shaped ridgetop. Curl to the right (west) and pass a narrow backbone with sandstone cliffs dropping steeply off to the right (north) side of the trail. Continue along Kuntz Ridge, gradually turning northwest.

At 3.0 miles go downhill briefly before climbing again to a gravel road at 3.5 miles. This is the connector spur to Mogan Ridge West. Turn right (east) and continue along the Mogan Ridge East Trail as it follows the gravel road for about 0.5 mile. The surface of the road changes to dirt at a metal gate. Go straight (east), heading uphill briefly before descending to the edge of a meadow. Continue downhill, passing a stand of pine trees to a T intersection at 5.2 miles. Turn right (south) on a downhill course to Clover Lick Creek, which is at 6.0 miles.

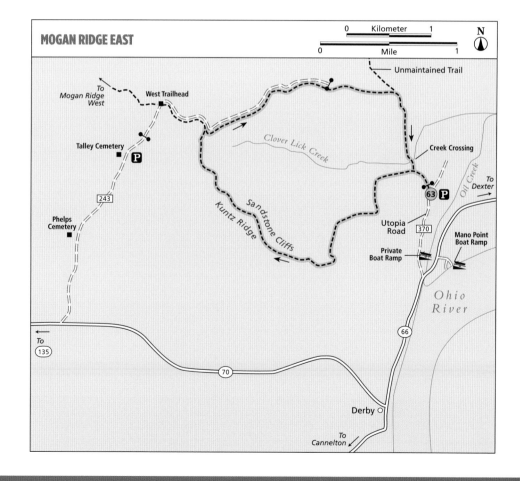

The rocky stream has an intermittent flow and is easy to cross most of the time. Go uphill for 0.1 mile from the creek to complete the loop at the trail junction at 6.1 miles. Turn left (southeast) and go 0.3 mile to return to the parking lot.

MILES AND DIRECTIONS

0.0   Begin at the trailhead past the metal gate.

0.3   Reach a trail junction and turn left (southwest).

0.6   The trail turns left (south).

1.8   Arrive at Kuntz Ridge and the sandstone cliffs.

3.5   Reach a trail junction and turn right (east). (**Note:** Left goes to Mogan Ridge West Trail.)

5.2   Turn right (south) at a T intersection.

6.0   Cross Clover Lick Creek.

6.1   Reach the trail junction and turn left (southeast) to return to the trailhead.

6.4   Arrive back at the trailhead.

64 GERMAN RIDGE LAKE TRAIL

WHY GO?

A short loop travels past sandstone cliffs overlooking the lake.

THE RUNDOWN

Location: East of Tell City, Perry County, southern Indiana
Distance: 1.0-mile loop
Elevation change: Minimal
Hiking time: About 45 minutes
Difficulty: Easy
Jurisdiction: Hoosier National Forest, Tell City Ranger District

Maps: USGS Rome; Hoosier National Forest map (www.fs.usda.gov/hoosier)
Fees and permits: No fees or permits required
Special attraction: Moss-covered sandstone cliffs
Camping: 20 primitive campsites
Trailhead facilities: Shelter house with pit toilets

FINDING THE TRAILHEAD

From Tell City go east on IN 66 through Cannelton to Rocky Point. Go 6.4 miles east on IN 66 from Rocky Point to Perry CR 3 and turn left (north). Go 0.75 mile to a gated entrance to German Ridge Recreation Area. After passing the gate, take the right fork to the picnic area. Locate the shelter house to the left (north) side of the parking lot. The trailhead is on the opposite (north) side of the shelter house.

THE HIKE

The German Ridge Recreation Area of the Hoosier National Forest is primarily devoted to horseback riding, but hikers get an exclusive look at a slice of it with this loop trail, described here in a clockwise direction. The trailhead behind the picnic shelter is marked with a brown plastic post and white diamonds. The trail is a wide path and easy to follow. German Ridge Recreation Area was developed in the 1930s by the Civilian Conservation Corps.

It doesn't take long to get to the focal point of this brief hike. After you cross a footbridge at 0.1 mile, the striking sandstone cliffs are almost immediately visible. Even on the hottest of summer days, the tree-shaded cliffs can be a cool setting. At 0.3 mile a feeder trail to the equestrian campground connects from the left (southeast). Be sure to take the path to the right (south) that leads in a clockwise direction. The cliffs rise on the left (south), while glimpses of the lake can be seen through the trees below and to the right (north). At 0.6 mile reach another feeder trail that connects to the equestrian campground to the south. Stay right (west and north) and walk downhill away from the cliffs to a T intersection near the lake's edge. Turn left and circle the lake to the beach near the parking lot and trailhead.

Exposed sandstone cliffs guard the trail at German Ridge.

Hoosier National Forest maps will show a 1.0-mile outer loop, but the Forest Service has imposed a closure of the section on the north side of the lake to protect forest resources.

MILES AND DIRECTIONS

0.0 Begin at the trailhead behind the picnic shelter.

0.1 Cross a footbridge.

0.3 Reach the sandstone cliffs.

0.6 At the trail junction stay right.

0.8 Come to a T intersection; turn left.

1.0 Arrive back at the trailhead.

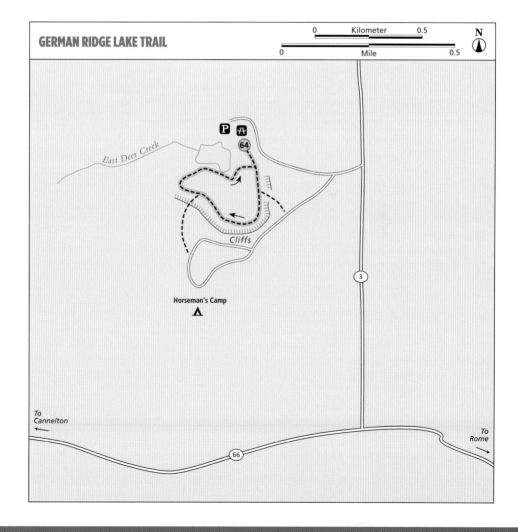

KNOBSTONE TRAIL

Hikers do not have to leave Indiana to get a taste of the Appalachian Trail.

A much shorter but more than adequate replica can be found in southeast Indiana along the state's most distinctive geographic feature—the Knobstone Escarpment. The escarpment appears like a fortress rising 300 to 400 feet above the Scottsburg lowlands to the east as it meanders for more than 100 miles from the Ohio River northwest toward Martinsville.

The Knobstone Trail (KT) follows the spiny ridges and deep ravines for 49 miles, beginning at Deam Lake State Recreation Area and ending at Delaney Park. It passes through 40,000 acres of public forestland. The area is richly diverse, with abundant fauna and flora.

The KT opened in 1980 and at the time measured only 32 miles. The Indiana Department of Natural Resources and hiking clubs like the Knobstone Hiking Trail Association are exploring ways to extend the trail farther. By the time it is finished, the KT may be triple its present length. It already is the longest hiking trail in the state.

Multiple trailhead locations along the way shorten the legs to between 6 and 12 miles, making it a popular trail not only for long-distance hikers but also for day hikers opting to tackle the KT in shorter pieces.

Backcountry camping is permitted along the KT as long as campsites are on public land and are at least 1.0 mile by trail away from all roads, recreation areas, and trailheads.

The KT is well marked with white blazes. Most locations where the various legs intersect are further marked with signs. All trailheads are marked with 4X4-inch KT posts on the access roads and large trailhead signs.

Water supplies along the trail are limited, so many hikers stash supplies at the trailheads. Many of the streams and creeks that the KT crosses are seasonal so do not count on them for water.

Most of the current KT passes through state forests, which are actively managed. When necessary, DNR Forestry reroutes sections of the trail for safety reasons during timber harvests.

For current trail conditions, go to www.in.gov/dnr/forestry/properties/knobstone-trail-conditions-reroutes-maps/.

Whether hiked in sections or its entirety, the KT has earned its nickname as "the little Appalachian Trail."

The KT is described here in linear sections on a northwest course from about 20 miles north of Louisville, Kentucky, toward Salem, Indiana.

65 DEAM LAKE TO JACKSON ROAD

WHY GO?

One of the shorter legs of the Knobstone Trail, this is a good warm-up for more challenging legs of the trail.

THE RUNDOWN

Location: Between Borden/New Providence and Sellersburg, Clark County

Distance: 6.5-mile shuttle

Elevation change: Two climbs of more than 150 feet

Hiking time: About 4 hours

Difficulty: Strenuous

Jurisdiction: Indiana Department of Natural Resources, Division of Forestry

Fees and permits: Gate fee required at Deam Lake State Recreation Area (when gatehouse is open); season passes available

Maps: USGS Henryville and Speed; Indiana Department of Natural Resources trail map of Clark State Forest and Deam Lake State Recreation Area

Special attractions: Bowery Creek, Bartle Knobs

Camping: Deam Lake State Recreation Area—108 modern electric campsites plus 96 sites in the equestrian campground; 12 cabins. Camping is permitted on public ground along the Knobstone if the campsite is at least 1 mile by trail from all roads, recreation areas, and trailheads and as long as the camp is not visible from the trail and all lakes. No camping allowed within 2 miles of the Deam Lake trailhead.

Trailhead facilities: The Deam Lake trailhead is located inside the Deam Lake State Recreation Area at the Buzzard Roost Shelter House. There is a large parking lot; access to a pit toilet and shelter house. Parking only at the Jackson Road trailhead.

FINDING THE TRAILHEAD

From the I-65 intersection with IN 60, head west on IN 60 through Hamburg for 8.5 miles to Deam Lake Road. Turn right (north) and go 1.2 miles to the Deam Lake State Recreation Area gatehouse. An entrance fee is charged when the gatehouse is staffed. Turn right (east) 50 yards past the gatehouse and follow the road to the trailhead parking lot.

THE HIKE

Deception is the best way to describe the opening leg of the Knobstone—it might not seem all that difficult at first. Once you hike a few miles in, however, you will know firsthand the kinds of challenges you will encounter along the remainder of the trail. Trail traffic may be high near the Deam Lake trailhead because of its proximity to the state recreation area.

The trail, marked by white blazes, starts at the Buzzard Roost Shelter House, continues past the site of the old Buzzard Roost School and through the forest to cross the top of

Deam Lake's dam. After crossing the dam, there's a gradual climb of about 120 feet over the next 1.0 mile.

From here the Knobstone is anything but easy. Over the next few miles you will experience the highs (hills labeled as various "knobs") and the lows (ravines labeled as "runs," "drains," or "branches"). The knobs represent the escarpment formation.

The first of these features is Bartle Knobs. From the creek to the highest knob, there is an elevation change of 400 feet, which is typical of what the remaining hike is like.

After peaking out at Bartle Knobs, slide down the back end of the Berry Run ravine and climb up once more to enter an area that was severely damaged by a tornado in March 2012. The F-4 tornado killed eleven people in nearby Henryville and flattened 1,300 acres of trees in a nearly 0.5-mile-wide swath of Clark State Forest.

From Bartle Knobs, the trail passes through Berry Run and Bartle Knob Run before nearing Round Knob, the 6.0-mile mark of the KT.

Turn left on a feeder trail to reach the Jackson Road trailhead.

The Deam Lake trailhead on the Knobstone Trail

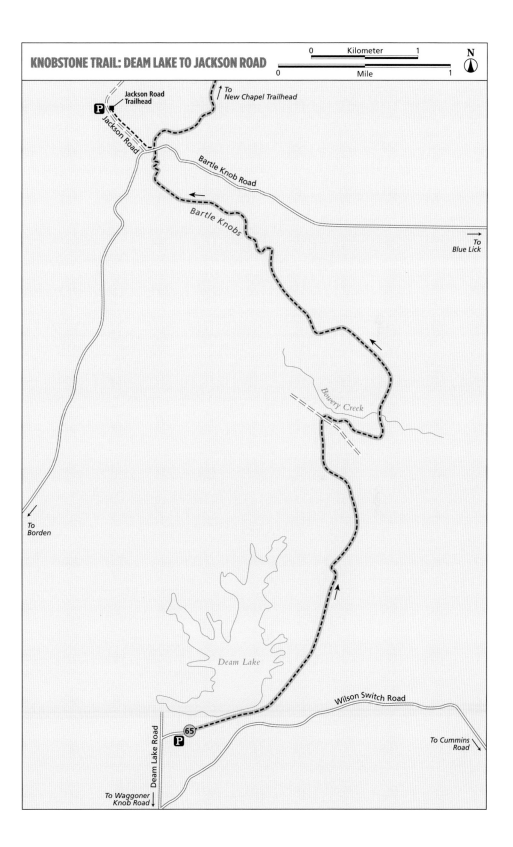

KNOBSTONE TRAIL: DEAM LAKE TO JACKSON ROAD

0   Kilometer   1

0   Mile   1

N

Jackson Road
Trailhead

To
New Chapel Trailhead

Jackson Road

Bartle Knob Road

Bartle Knobs

To
Blue Lick

Bowery Creek

To
Borden

Deam Lake

Wilson Switch Road

To Cummins
Road

65

Deam Lake Road

To Waggoner
Knob Road

MILES AND DIRECTIONS

0.0   Begin at the Deam Lake trailhead.

0.4   Cross the Deam Lake dam.

2.7   Cross Bowery Creek.

4.3   Hike over the Bartle Knobs.

5.5   Reach Bartle Knob Road; turn left (west) to the Jackson Road trailhead. (**Option:** Continue straight [north] to skirt another knob and connect with the strenuous spur to the Jackson Road trailhead.)

6.0   Reach spur trail to Jackson Road trailhead; turn left (west).

6.5   Arrive at Jackson Road trailhead parking lot

66 JACKSON ROAD TO NEW CHAPEL

WHY GO?

A demanding stretch of the Knobstone Trail travels along ridgetops and through ravines.

THE RUNDOWN

Location: Clark State Forest
Distance: 11.5-mile shuttle
Elevation change: Multiple climbs of more than 250 feet
Hiking time: About 8 hours or overnight
Difficulty: Strenuous
Jurisdiction: Indiana Department of Natural Resources, Division of Forestry
Fees and permits: No fees or permits required
Maps: USGS Henryville; Indiana Department of Natural Resources trail map of Clark State Forest and Deam Lake State Recreation Area

Special attractions: Round Knob, Virginia Pine–Chestnut Oak Nature Preserve
Camping: Deam Lake State Recreation Area—108 modern electric campsites plus 96 sites in the equestrian campground; 12 cabins. Camping is permitted on public ground along the Knobstone if the campsite is at least 1 mile by trail from all roads, recreation areas, and trailheads and camp is not visible from the trail and all lakes.
Trailhead facilities: Parking available at the Jackson Road and New Chapel trailheads; no restrooms or drinking water

FINDING THE TRAILHEAD

To reach the Jackson Road trailhead, leave the Deam Lake trailhead at the Buzzard Roost Shelter in Deam Lake State Recreation Area. Exit past the gatehouse, pass Miller Cemetery on the left, and turn left (east) onto Wilson Switch Road. Go about 2 miles to the intersection with Flower Gap Road. Turn right (south), staying on Wilson Switch Road for 0.2 mile to Cummins Road. Turn left (east) and go 1.3 miles to Crone Road. Turn left (northeast) and go 1.1 miles to Beyl Road. Turn left (northwest) and go 1 mile to the intersection with Percy King Road. Turn right (northeast) and continue on Beyl Road to Bartle Knob Road. Turn left (southwest) onto Bartle Knob Road, turning right (northwest) after about 0.5 mile, and continue another 3.4 miles to Hilltop Road, a paved road on the right. Turn right (northeast) and go to Jackson Road, a gravel road. Turn right to the trailhead parking lot.

To reach the Jackson Road trailhead from I-65, go northwest from exit 16 on Pixley Knob Road to Blue Lick. Turn left (southwest) onto Reed Road and go about 1.4 miles. Bartle Knob Road turns right (northwest). Go 3.4 miles to Hilltop Road and turn right to reach Jackson Road and the trailhead parking lot.

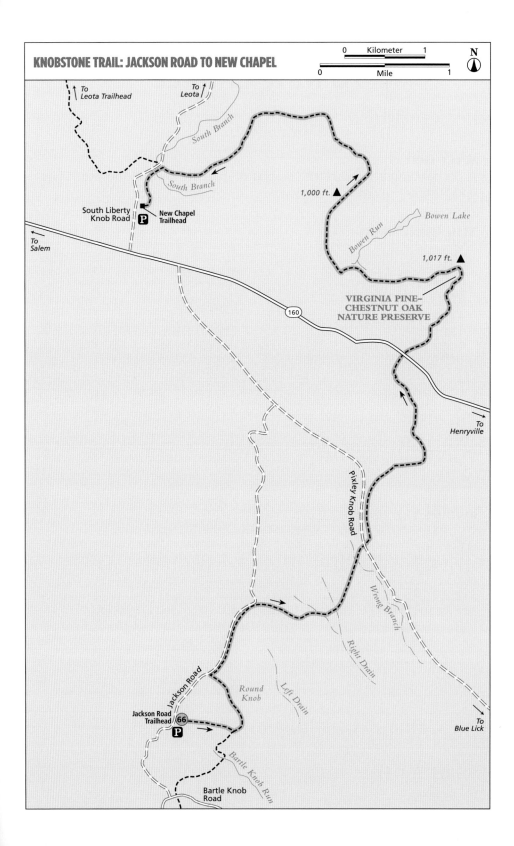

Kilometer

Mile

N

To Leota Trailhead

To Leota

South Branch

South Branch

1,000 ft. ▲

Bowen Lake

South Liberty Knob Road

New Chapel Trailhead

Bowen Run

To Salem

1,017 ft. ▲

VIRGINIA PINE– CHESTNUT OAK NATURE PRESERVE

160

To Henryville

Pixley Knob Road

Wrong Branch

Right Drain

Jackson Road

Round Knob

Left Drain

To Blue Lick

Jackson Road Trailhead

66

Bartle Knob Run

Bartle Knob Road

THE HIKE

This is the longest leg of the KT. From the Jackson Road trailhead go 0.5 mile to the main trail. Turn left and begin a gradual climb to Round Knob. The final 150-foot rise is covered in less than 0.25 mile.

This part of the trail passes through an area damaged by a tornado in 2012 that destroyed more than 1,300 acres of Clark State Forest's timberland. The trail was reopened after debris was cleared and offers the opportunity to observe the natural reforestation of this area over time.

Views from Round Knob are spectacular, especially to the southeast. On a clear day it is possible to see downtown Louisville, Kentucky, more than 20 miles away.

After leaving Round Knob, cross a saddleback that leads to Jackson Road. Turn right (northeast) and walk along the gravel road for nearly 1.0 mile before turning right (southeast) to hike through the Right Drain ravine. (Yes, there is a nearby ravine named Left Drain.) The trail soon crosses Wrong Branch, which later joins Right Branch. Cross Wrong Branch and Pixley Knob Road and turn left (north) to parallel the road a short distance while going up a narrow ridge point. You have made a 350-foot climb by the time you reach the top.

View from the Jackson Road trailhead

Go from one knob to another before a sharp downhill maneuver to cross IN 160 at 6.3 miles (11.8 miles total from Deam Lake trailhead). Cross the road and go uphill on an old logging road to the Virginia Pine–Chestnut Oak Nature Preserve. The 24-acre hilltop site is dominated by a native stand of Virginia pine, an uncommon tree in Indiana except in the Knobstone region. Chestnut oaks control the lower slopes. White oaks and scarlet oaks form a transitional zone between the Virginia pine and chestnut oaks.

After leaving the preserve, come to the highest point on the KT—a knob at 1,017 feet above sea level. Turn left (west) from here and follow a long, narrow ridge descending about 200 feet to Bowen Run, a feeder stream for Bowen Lake, a 7-acre impoundment about 0.5 mile to the northeast. Cross the creek a couple of times before heading uphill to another knob that is 1,000 feet above sea level. Swing northeast then northwest along a string of knobs before descending into a ravine and the South Branch of Big Ox Creek.

The New Chapel trailhead parking lot is about 0.25 mile southwest and uphill from the trail as it crosses South Liberty Knob Road, which also shows up on maps as CR 500 South.

MILES AND DIRECTIONS

0.0   Begin at the Jackson Road trailhead.

0.5   Reach main trail; turn left (north).

1.2   Reach Round Knob.

4.0   Cross Wrong Branch and Pixley Knob Road and turn left (north).

6.3   Cross IN 160.

7.3   Reach the Virginia Pine–Chestnut Oak Nature Preserve.

8.8   Arrive at Bowen Run.

11.5   Reach the New Chapel trailhead; go left (south) to the parking lot.

67 NEW CHAPEL TO LEOTA

WHY GO?

This part of the Knobstone Trail features long stretches along ridgetops with occasional drops into ravines, including scenic North Branch Valley.

THE RUNDOWN

Location: Clark State Forest, Scott County

Distance: 8.0-mile shuttle

Elevation change: Multiple changes of 250 feet or more

Hiking time: About 6 hours

Difficulty: Strenuous

Jurisdiction: Indiana Department of Natural Resources, Division of Forestry

Fees and permits: No fees or permits required

Maps: USGS Henryville, South Boston, and Little York; Indiana Department of Natural Resources Knobstone Trail brochure; Indiana DNR trail map of Clark State Forest and Deam Lake

Special attraction: North Branch Valley

Camping: Camping is permitted on public ground along the Knobstone if the campsite is at least 1 mile by trail from all roads, recreation areas, and trailheads and camp is not visible from the trail and all lakes.

Trailhead facilities: Parking available at the New Chapel and Leota trailheads; no restrooms or drinking water

FINDING THE TRAILHEAD

To reach the New Chapel trailhead from the Jackson Road trailhead, go left (east) from the Jackson Road intersection with Bartle Knob Road for 3.9 miles to Mayfield Road. Turn left (northeast) and go 1.3 miles to Blue Lick Road. Turn left (northwest), go 0.5 mile, and continue right (northeast) on Blue Lick Road. Go 1.5 miles to Beers Road. Turn left (northwest) and go 1.8 miles to a T intersection with IN 160. Turn left (west) and go 4.7 miles to Liberty Knob Road. Turn right (north) and go 0.4 mile to the New Chapel trailhead parking lot on the right (east) side of the road. To reach the New Chapel trailhead from I-65, go 5.7 miles west on IN 160 to Liberty Knob Road. Turn right (north) and go 0.4 mile to the trailhead parking lot on the right (east) side of the road.

THE HIKE

Unlike the earlier segments of the Knobstone Trail, where the highlights were knobs, the main attraction on this stretch is the North Branch Valley—a narrow, high-sided ravine rich with wildflowers, ferns, and some of the biggest trees on the KT. Traffic is generally not significant along the middle legs of the trail, but the area is open to hunting during regulated seasons.

The first half of the leg from New Chapel to Leota wanders along the edge of the forest and rolls along ridgetops, occasionally dipping across the back end of ravines. Near the 3.0-mile mark, drop into a ravine and cross the creek. Then climb the other side, cross

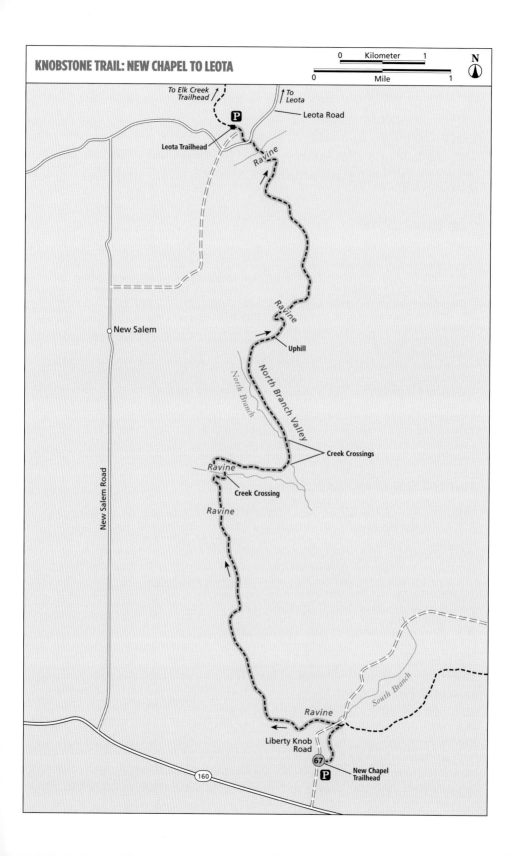

KNOBSTONE TRAIL: NEW CHAPEL TO LEOTA

To Elk Creek
Trailhead

To
Leota

P

Leota Road

Leota Trailhead

Ravine

Ravine

New Salem

Uphill

North Branch Valley

North Branch

Creek Crossings

Ravine

Creek Crossing

Ravine

New Salem Road

South Branch

Ravine

Liberty Knob
Road

160

67

P

New Chapel
Trailhead

0   Kilometer   1

0   Mile   1

N

over a narrow ridge, and make a steep descent into a side ravine of North Branch Valley. For those keeping track, this is about the 21.0-mile mark of the full KT.

Turn right (east) to round a point and then left (north) for a 1.0-mile walk through the lush ravine. Climb up the right (east) side of the ravine, cross the ridgetop, and descend into another ravine.

Go uphill again and follow the ridgeline north for 1.5 miles before turning northwest to traverse one last ravine. Cross the creek at the ravine bottom and head uphill to cross Leota Road. Continue up for 0.1 mile to the Leota trailhead parking lot. The parking area is along a utility corridor.

MILES AND DIRECTIONS

- **0.0** Begin at the New Chapel trailhead.
- **3.0** Drop into a ravine and cross a creek.
- **4.5** Reach the North Branch Valley.
- **7.9** Cross Leota Road.
- **8.0** Reach the Leota trailhead.

68 **LEOTA TO ELK CREEK**

WHY GO?

Three hills and several ravines lead to a scenic lake.

THE RUNDOWN

Location: Between Salem and Scottsburg
Distance: 7.0-mile shuttle
Elevation change: Climbs of 250 to 350 feet, descents of 150 to 250 feet
Hiking time: About 5 hours
Difficulty: Strenuous
Jurisdiction: Indiana Department of Natural Resources, Division of Forestry
Fees and permits: No fees or permits required
Maps: USGS Little York; Indiana Department of Natural Resources Knobstone Trail brochure; Indiana

DNR trail map of Clark State Forest and Deam Lake
Special attractions: Vic Swain Hill, Elk Creek Public Fishing Area
Camping: Camping is permitted on public ground along the Knobstone if the campsite is at least 1 mile by trail from all roads, recreation areas, and trailheads and camp is not visible from the trail and all lakes.
Trailhead facilities: Parking available at the Leota trailhead; parking and latrines available at the Elk Creek trailhead

FINDING THE TRAILHEAD

From the New Chapel trailhead parking lot, turn left (south) onto Liberty Knob Road and go 0.4 mile to IN 160. Turn right (west) and go 1.8 miles to New Salem Road. Turn right (north) and go 3.4 miles, passing through New Salem. At the 3.4-mile mark, turn right (east) onto Leota Road and go 1.7 miles to an unmarked gravel road on the left (north). Turn onto the gravel road and go 0.1 mile to the Leota trailhead entrance. Turn left (east) and go 0.1 mile to the parking lot and trailhead.

To reach the Leota trailhead from I-65, go approximately 7.5 miles west on IN 160 to New Salem Road. Turn right (north) and drive 3.4 miles to New Salem–Finley Knob Road. Turn right (east) and go 1.7 miles to an unmarked county road. Turn left (north) and proceed 0.1 mile to the trailhead parking lot.

THE HIKE

The trail from Leota to Elk Creek begins at an opening on the north side of the parking lot near a small pond. Descend from the Leota trailhead along a ridgeline that leads to Vic Swain Hill at 1.2 miles. The hill marks a departure from the mostly northward direction that the Knobstone Trail has followed until now. From here the trail heads west for the next 5.8 miles over a series of ridges and ravines.

After an especially steep climb near the 4.0-mile mark, spend the next 1.0 mile dropping into Monroe Hollow before going back uphill approximately 200 feet to another ridgetop.

KNOBSTONE TRAIL: LEOTA TO ELK CREEK

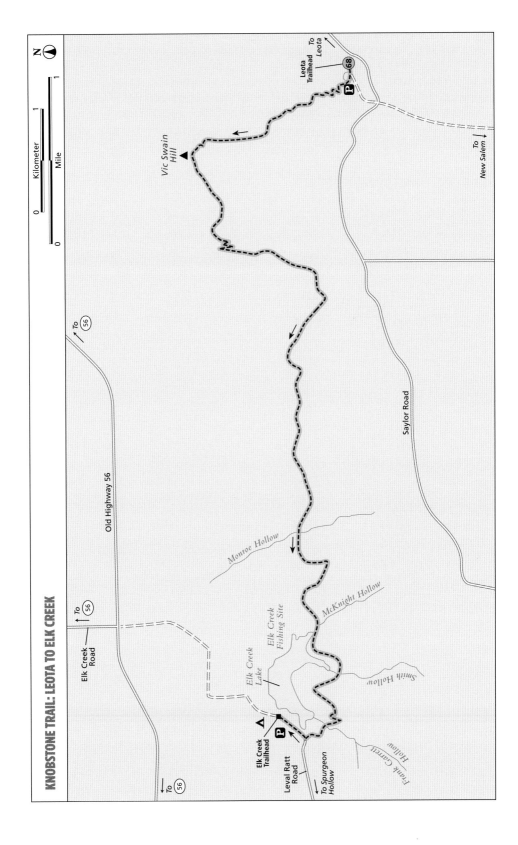

From there descend into McKnight Hollow and skirt the south edge of Elk Creek Lake. After crossing Smith Hollow, make a 300-foot climb to a knob overlooking the lake. Turn southeast to cross a saddle to another knob then go downhill into Frank Garrett Hollow. Near the west tip of Elk Lake, reach a trail junction. Go left (west) up Nowing Hollow to continue the KT or right (northeast) to reach the Elk Creek trailhead.

If you happened to pack fishing gear, 43-acre Elk Creek Lake has bluegill, sunfish, and largemouth bass.

MILES AND DIRECTIONS

0.0   Begin at the Leota trailhead.

1.2   Climb Vic Swain Hill.

4.7   Arrive at Monroe Hollow.

5.7   Cross McKnight Hollow.

6.2   Reach Smith Hollow.

6.7   Cross Frank Garrett Hollow.

6.9   Turn right (northeast) at the trail junction.

7.0   Reach the Elk Creek trailhead.

69 ELK CREEK TO OXLEY MEMORIAL

WHY GO?

This section of the Knobstone Trail covers 5.5 miles from Elk Creek Public Fishing Area across IN 56 to the Oxley Memorial Trailhead.

THE RUNDOWN

Location: Jackson-Washington State Forest, east of Salem
Distance: 5.5-mile shuttle
Elevation change: Multiple changes between 150 and 250 feet
Hiking time: About 4 hours
Difficulty: Strenuous
Jurisdiction: Indiana Department of Natural Resources, Division of Forestry
Fees and permits: No fees or permits required
Maps: USGS Little York; Indiana Department of Natural Resources Knobstone Trail brochure

Special attraction: Backcountry Area of Jackson-Washington State Forest
Camping: Camping is permitted on public ground along the Knobstone if the campsite is at least 1 mile by trail from all roads, recreation areas, and trailheads and camp is not visible from the trail and all lakes.
Trailhead facilities: Parking and latrines at the Elk Creek trailhead; parking only at Oxley Memorial trailhead

FINDING THE TRAILHEAD

To reach the Elk Creek trailhead from the Leota trailhead parking lot, turn left (south) and go 0.1 mile to the paved Leota Road. Turn left (east) onto Leota Road and go 1.1 miles to the first paved road (an unmarked county road) on the left. Turn left (north) and go 1.2 miles to a T intersection with Bloomington Trail Road. Turn left (northwest) onto Bloomington Trail Road and go 1.8 miles to IN 56. Turn left (west) and go 2.8 miles to the sign for Elk Creek Public Fishing Area. Turn left (south) and go 1.8 miles to the fishing area entrance. At the KT post turn left (west) to the Elk Creek trailhead.

To reach the Elk Creek trailhead from I-65, go 8.3 miles west from I-65 at Scottsburg on IN 56 to Elk Creek Road. Turn left (south) to reach the trailhead parking lot at Elk Creek Public Fishing Area.

THE HIKE

From one of the most remote stretches (Leota to Elk Creek), the Knobstone Trail switches to perhaps its least spectacular sections between Elk Creek and Oxley Memorial to the northwest, with a half-dozen road crossings, a power line corridor, and occasional logging operations interrupting the natural setting.

This part of the trail is not without challenges, however. There are several steep knobs to be climbed, although the severity of the elevation change is only 150 to 250 feet,

Signpost for the Knobstone Trail

unlike the 250- to 400-footers on the KT's southern sections. Traffic generally is not significant along the middle legs of the trail, but the area is open to hunting during regulated seasons.

Beginning at the Elk Creek campground, go south on the connecting trail to the main trail. Turn right (west) to walk through Nowing Hollow for about 0.5 mile before climbing a ridge. Make the first road crossing at Leval Ratt Road, beyond which the trail drops into a ravine and climbs on a northeast slant along a south-facing slope.

Atop the ridge, connect with a power line corridor for about 0.25 mile before dropping into a ravine. Climb the other side and cross Old SR 56. Cut across the back end of Shantaky Hollow and work uphill to a knob that at 974 feet above sea level is the high point of this KT section. Descend more than 200 feet to cross IN 56, then head back

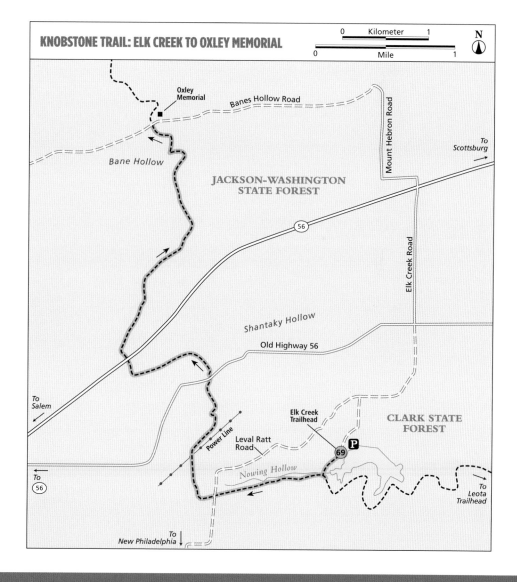

uphill to follow a ridgeline for about 1.0 mile as the KT enters the Jackson-Washington State Forest.

On a northward course over the next 2.0 miles, the KT crosses two roads and traverses several ravines, including Bane Hollow, to reach the John Stuart Oxley Memorial trailhead on Banes Hollow Road.

The memorial is in honor of an avid hiker and KT supporter, who died in 1998.

MILES AND DIRECTIONS

0.0 Begin at the Elk Creek trailhead; walk down connector and turn right (west) onto the KT.

1.1 Cross a gravel road.

1.6 Reach a power line corridor.

2.3 Cross Old SR 56.

3.2 Cross IN 56.

5.5 Reach Banes Hollow Road and the Oxley Memorial trailhead.

70 **OXLEY MEMORIAL TO DELANEY PARK**

WHY GO?

This section of the Knobstone Trail crosses ridgetops and ravines through the Jackson-Washington State Forest to Delaney Park.

THE RUNDOWN

Location: Jackson-Washington State Forest, east of Salem

Distance: 10.5-mile shuttle

Elevation change: Multiple changes between 150 and 250 feet

Hiking time: About 8 hours (shorter with optional routes)

Difficulty: Strenuous

Jurisdiction: Indiana Department of Natural Resources, Division of Forestry

Fees and permits: No fees or permits required

Maps: USGS Kossuth and Little York; Indiana Department of Natural Resources Knobstone Trail brochure

Special attraction: Backcountry Area of Jackson-Washington State Forest

Camping: Camping is permitted on public ground along the Knobstone if the campsite is at least 1 mile by trail from all roads, recreation areas, and trailheads and camp is not visible from the trail and all lakes.

Trailhead facilities: Parking at the Oxley Memorial trailhead.

Note: Delaney Park is managed by Washington County Parks Department and offers overnight camping, cabins, a restaurant, and a camp store.

FINDING THE TRAILHEAD

To reach the Oxley Memorial trailhead from the Elk Creek trailhead parking lot, return to IN 56 and cross to the north side of the highway. Turn left (west) at Mt. Hebron Road and then right (north) at a Y intersection onto Rutherford Hollow Road. Go about 0.5 mile to where the road curves left and intersects Banes Hollow Road. Turn left (west) and go 2 miles to the Oxley Memorial trailhead on the right.

To reach the Oxley Memorial trailhead from I-65, go 8.3 miles west on IN 56 in Scottsburg to Elk Creek Road. Turn right (north) and take the first left, Mt. Hebron Road; go to a Y intersection. Turn right (north) and drive 0.5 mile to Banes Hollow Road. Turn left and go 2 miles to the trailhead parking lot.

THE HIKE

Take your pick on what is a long windup to the Knobstone Trail with two options near the midpoint—a relatively easy hike through a valley or the more rugged hike from ridgetop to ridgetop. Both cut through the Backcountry Area of Jackson-Washington State Forest and are marked by DNR Division of Forestry blue blazes along with the white KT blazes.

KNOBSTONE TRAIL: OXLEY MEMORIAL TO DELANEY PARK

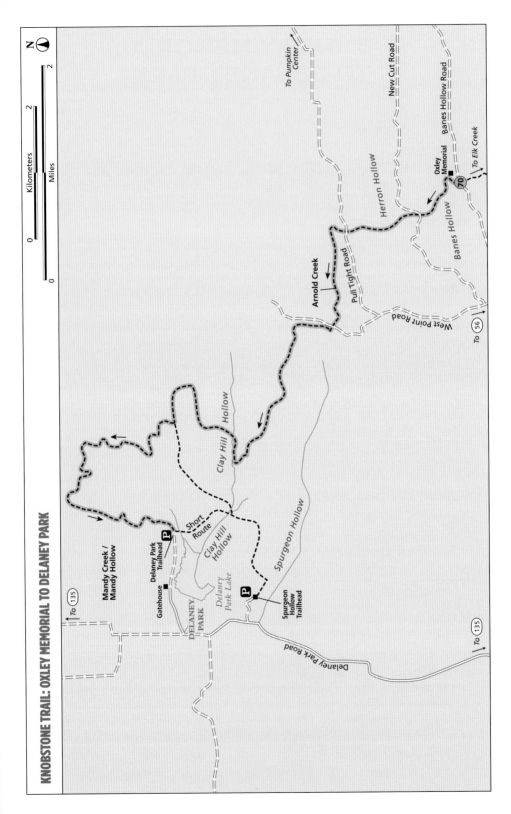

N

Kilometers
0   2   2

Miles
0   2

To Pumpkin Center

New Cut Road

Banes Hollow Road

Oxley Memorial

Herron Hollow

Banes Hollow

To Elk Creek

70

To 56

West Point Road

Pull Tight Road

Arnold Creek

Clay Hill Hollow

Spurgeon Hollow

Short Route

Clay Hill Hollow

Delaney Park Trailhead

P

Gatehouse

DELANEY PARK

Delaney Park Lake

Spurgeon Hollow Trailhead

P

Mandy Creek / Mandy Hollow

To 135

Delaney Park Road

To 135

You will have a few miles of hiking from the Oxley Memorial trailhead to make up your mind on the options.

From the trailhead go north and uphill to pass over a ridge that drops into Herron Hollow at the 1.0-mile mark. From Herron Hollow, go uphill for 0.5 mile and cross Pull Tight Road. Continue uphill another 0.25 mile and the KT turns left (west) at Arnold Creek. Hike up and down along a ridgeline to cross at West Point Road.

Just across the road, the KT splits at the 42.0-mile marker. Go left (west) for the shorter route to the Spurgeon Hollow trailhead or right (north) for the slightly longer (and hillier) option. The shorter option is fairly easy as it passes through Spurgeon Hollow, with more than half the distance squeezed within a steep-walled ravine.

The trail description that follows takes the longer, more rugged option that intersects twice with the Delaney Park loop and includes a backdoor route to the Spurgeon Hollow trailhead.

The longer option begins with an uphill climb that veers left after topping the hill then goes along a ridgeline before descending into Clay Hill Hollow. Turn right (east) at the bottom of the ravine and cross the creek to start a nearly 300-foot climb on a steep grade. Follow the trail along the ridge for about 1.5 miles to a fork just past the 45.0-mile marker.

Turn right to take a 3.5-mile romp through a few more ridges and ravines. After traveling north through two ravines, turn left (west) for 1.0 mile, curling along the back end of a ravine. The trail bends sharply left (south) for the stretch run to Delaney Park. Descend one steep hill to a creek that runs through Mandy Hollow and then climb up and over a ridge to another creek.

At the second creek turn right (west) and go 0.25 mile to the Delaney Park trailhead.

Delaney Park is the north terminus of the Knobstone Trail—for now. Plans are being evaluated to extend the KT along the Knobstone Escarpment toward the Tecumseh Trail south of Martinsville.

MILES AND DIRECTIONS

0.0 Begin at the Oxley Memorial trailhead.

0.9 Reach and cross New Cut Road.

1.5 Cross Pull Tight Road.

1.8 Reach Arnold Creek; turn left (west).

2.2 Cross West Point Road.

3.8 Trail junction; go right (northeast) for the long link to Delaney Park.

7.0 Trail junction; go right. (**Option:** Left turn is the shorter route to Delaney Park plus link trail to the Spurgeon Hollow trailhead.)

9.7 Cross Mandy Creek.

10.5 Reach the Delaney Park trailhead.

OPTION

At the trail intersection near the 45.0-mile marker, the left split provides a shorter, 2.0-mile route to Delaney Park. After 1.0 mile, the trail splits again, with the right leg going to Delaney Park along the pine-forested eastern shore of Delaney Lake while the left leg leads 1.5 miles to Spurgeon Hollow trailhead.

APPENDIX A: SUGGESTED READING

Allen, Durward. *Our Wildlife Legacy* (New York: Funk and Wagnalls, 1962).

Baker, Ronald L., and Marvin Carmony. *Indiana Place Names* (Bloomington, IN: Indiana University Press, 1975).

Deam, Charles C., and Thomas E. Shaw. *Trees of Indiana* (Indianapolis: Indiana Department of Conservation, 1953).

Green, Kat, and Woodward, Kayla. *Best Easy Day Hikes Near Indianapolis* (Essex, CT: FalconGuides, 2021)

Homoya, Michael. *Wildflowers and Ferns of Indiana Forests* (Bloomington, IN: Indiana University Press, 2012).

Jackson, Marion T. *The Natural Heritage of Indiana* (Bloomington, IN: Indiana University Press, 1997).

Jackson, Marion T. *101 Trees of Indiana* (Bloomington, IN: Indiana University Press, 2004).

Jordan, Christopher, and Ron Leonetti, photographers. *The Nature Conservancy's Guide to Indiana Preserves* (Bloomington, IN: Indiana University Press/Quarry Books, 2006).

Lindsey, Alton A., Damian Schmelz, and Stanley Nichols. *Natural Features of Indiana* (Indianapolis: Indiana Academy of Science, 1966).

Runkel, Sylvan T., and Alvin F. Bull. *Wildflowers of Indiana Woodlands* (Ames, IA: Iowa State University Press, 1994).

Seng, Phil T., and David J. Case. *Indiana Wildlife Viewing Guide* (Helena, MT: Falcon Publishing, Inc., 1992).

Strange, Nathan. *The Complete Guide to Indiana State Parks* (Beverly, MA: Quarry Books, 2018).

Thomas, Phyllis. *Indiana: Off the Beaten Path,* ninth edition (Guilford, CT: Globe Pequot Press, 2007).

Werner, Nick. *Best Hikes Near Indianapolis* (Essex, CT: FalconGuides, 2012)

Yatskievych, Kay. *Field Guide to Indiana Wildflowers* (Bloomington, IN: Indiana University Press, 2000)

APPENDIX B:
ADDITIONAL RESOURCES

FEDERAL AGENCIES

Big Oaks National Wildlife Refuge
1661 W. JPG Niblo Rd.
Madison 47250
(812) 273-0783
www.fws.gov/refuge/bigoaks
E-mail: bigoaks@fws.gov

Indiana Dunes National Park
1215 N. IN 49
Porter 46304
(219) 926-2255
www.nps.gov/indu/

Muscatatuck National Wildlife Refuge
12985 E. US 50
Seymour 47274
(812) 522-4352
www.fws.gov/refuge/muscatatuck/
E-mail: Muscatatuck@fws.gov

Patoka River National Wildlife Refuge
510 1/2 W. Morton St.
Oakland City 47660
(812) 749-3199
www.fws.gov/refuge/patoka_river/
E-mail: patokariver@fws.gov

US Fish & Wildlife Service
**Bloomington Ecological Services
Field Office**
620 S. Walker St.
Bloomington 47403-2121
(812) 334-4261
www.fws.gov/Midwest/Bloomington
E-mail: MidwestNews@fws.gov

**Northern Ecological Services
Field Office**
1574 N. 300 E.
Chesterton 46304-5716
(219) 983-9753
E-mail: MidwestNews@fws.gov

Hoosier National Forest
Supervisor's Office
811 Constitution Ave.
Bedford 47421
(812) 275-5987; TTY: (812) 279-3423
www.fs.usda.gov/hoosier
E-mail: r9_hoosier_website@fs.fed.us

Tell City Ranger District
248 15th St.
Tell City 47586
(812) 547-7051; TDD: (812) 547-6144

STATE AGENCIES
Indiana Department of Natural Resources
Customer Service Center
402 W. Washington St., Rm. W160A
Indianapolis 46204
317-232-4200 or 877-463-6367
www.in/gov/dnr/contact-us/

Executive Office
402 W. Washington St., Rm. W256
Indianapolis 46204
(317) 232-4020
www.in.gov/dnr

Division of Fish & Wildlife
402 W. Washington St., Rm. W273
Indianapolis 46204
(317) 232-4080

Division of Forestry
402 W. Washington St., Rm. W296
Indianapolis 46204
(317) 232-4105

Division of Nature Preserves
402 W. Washington St., Rm. W267
Indianapolis 46204
(317) 232-4052

Division of State Parks
402 W. Washington St., Rm. W298
Indianapolis 46204
(317) 232-4124

LOCAL AGENCIES
Allen County Parks & Recreation Department
7324 Yohne Rd.
Fort Wayne 46809-9744
(219) 449-3180
www.allencountyparks.org

Tippecanoe County Parks & Recreation Department
4449 SR 43 N.
West Lafayette 47906-5753
(765) 463-2306
www.tippecanoe.in.gov/187/Parks
-Recreation-Department

CONSERVATION AND HIKING ORGANIZATIONS
ACRES Land Trust, Inc.
1802 Chapman Rd.
Huntertown 46748
(206) 637-2273
https://acreslandtrust.org
E-mail: acres@acreslandtrust.org

Central Indiana Wilderness Club
PO Box 50083
Indianapolis 46250
https://ciwclub.org
E-mail: ciwcinfo@gmail.com

Fort Wayne Trails, Inc.
Auer Center for Arts and Culture
300 E. Main St.
Fort Wayne 46802
(260) 969-0079
www.fwtrails.org
E-mail: info@fwtrails.org

Greenways Foundation
PO Box 80111
Indianapolis 46280
E-mail: info@greenwaysfoundation.org

Hoosier Hikers Council
PO Box 1327
Martinsville 46151
(855) 812-4453
www.hoosierhikerscouncil.org
E-mail: hoosierhikerscouncil@gmail.com

Indiana Trails
PO Box 1688
Indianapolis 46206
(317) 237-9348
www.indianatrails.com
E-mail: trails@indianatrails.com

Knobstone Hiking Trail Association
PO Box 1814
Martinsville 46151
www.knobstonehikingtrail.org
E-mail: khtassociation@gmail.com

Little River Wetlands Project
5000 Smith Rd.
Fort Wayne 46804
(260) 478-2515
www.lrwp.org
E-mail: info@lrwp.org

Merry Lea Environmental Learning Center
2388 S. 500 W.
Albion 46701
(260) 799-5869
www.goshen.edu/merrylea/
E-mail: merrylea@goshen.edu

The Nature Conservancy
Indiana Field Office
Efroymson Conservation Center
620 E. Ohio St.
Indianapolis 46202
(317) 951-8818
www.nature.org/indiana/

INDEX

ABOUT THE AUTHOR

Phil Bloom is a native Hoosier and lifelong resident of Indiana. He enjoyed two careers before retiring from both—thirty-three years as a newspaper reporter and editor (the last eighteen as an award-winning outdoors editor at the *Fort Wayne Journal Gazette*) and ten years as communications director for the Indiana Department of Natural Resources.

Bloom is an active member of the Outdoor Writers Association of America and served as the group's president in 2008 and 2018. He is an Eagle Scout and an Indiana Certified Master Naturalist. He lives in Fort Wayne and is a volunteer with the American Red Cross.

THE TEN ESSENTIALS OF HIKING

American Hiking Society

American Hiking Society recommends you pack the "Ten Essentials" every time you head out for a hike. Whether you plan to be gone for a couple of hours or several months, make sure to pack these items. Become familiar with these items and know how to use them. Learn more at **AmericanHiking.org/hiking-resources**

 1. **Appropriate Footwear**

 6. **Safety Items** (light, fire, and a whistle)

 2. **Navigation**

 7. **First Aid Kit**

 3. **Water** (and a way to purify it)

 8. **Knife or Multi-Tool**

 4. **Food**

 9. **Sun Protection**

 5. **Rain Gear & Dry-Fast Layers**

 10. **Shelter**